Souled Out

Souled Out

RECLAIMING FAITH AND POLITICS
AFTER THE RELIGIOUS RIGHT

E. J. Dionne Jr.

Princeton University Press   *Princeton & Oxford*

Copyright © 2008 by E. J. Dionne Jr.
Published by Princeton University Press, 41 William Street,
Princeton, New Jersey 08540
In the United Kingdom: Princeton University Press, 3 Market Place,
Woodstock, Oxfordshire OX20 1SY

Library of Congress Cataloging-in-Publication Data

Dionne, E. J.
Souled out : reclaiming faith and politics after the religious right / E. J. Dionne, Jr.
p.   cm.
Includes bibliographical references (p.   ) and index.
ISBN-13: 978-0-691-13458-1 (hardcover : alk. paper)
1. Christianity and politics—United States. 2. Religious right—United States.
3. Christian conservatism—United States. I. Title.
BR516.D56   2008
261.70973—dc22   2007045172

British Library Cataloging-in-Publication Data is available

This book has been composed in Adobe Garamond and Helvetica

Printed on acid-free paper. ∞

press.princeton.edu

Printed in the United States of America

10 9 8 7 6 5 4 3 2

For friends along the journey, with gratitude

Msgr. Phil Murnion (RIP)
Peter and Peggy Steinfels
Father J. Bryan Hehir
Harvey Cox
Helen Boyle
John Carr
John DiIulio
Father Thomas E. Morrissey
Msgr. Tom Duffy
Father Percival DaSilva
William Galston
Tom and Sheilah Mann

And for

the Sisters of St. Joseph in Fall River, Massachusetts, and the Benedictine Community at Portsmouth Abbey

Contents

Introduction Is God's Work Our Work?
Faith, Doubt, and Radical Amazement   1

1 Is Religion Conservative or Progressive? (Or Both?)   25

2 Why the Culture War Is the Wrong War:
Religion, Values, and American Politics   45

3 What Are the "Values" Issues?
Economics, Social Justice, and the Struggle over Morality   71

4 Selling Religion Short:
When Ideology Is Not Enough   92

5 John Paul, Benedict, and the Catholic Future   126

6 What Happened to the Seamless Garment?
The Agony of Liberal Catholicism   151

7 Solidarity, Liberty, and Religion's True Calling   183

Notes   205

Acknowledgments   227

Index   235

Souled Out

Introduction

Is God's Work Our Work?

FAITH, DOUBT, AND RADICAL AMAZEMENT

Consider a political story told long ago that reminds us that the words "Jesus" and "religious" were not always reflexively associated with the words "right" or "conservative." It is the story of Mrs. O'Reilly and her son who was dutifully taking her to the polls on Election Day. Mrs. O'Reilly always voted straight Democratic. Her son, a successful member of the upper middle class, had become an independent and voted for many Republicans.

As was their routine, the son asked the mother how she would vote, and, as always, she answered, "Straight Democratic." The exasperated son replied, "Mom, if Jesus came back to earth and ran as a Republican, you would vote against him." And she snapped back, "Aw, hush, why should He change His party after all these years?"

A great many Americans have come to believe that He has, in fact, changed his party after all these years. On significant parts of the right and left, there is a sense that religion always has been and always will be a conservative force. There are Republican candidates and political operatives who assume that religious people live on the political right, care primarily about issues such as gay marriage and abortion, and will forever be part of the GOP's political base. There are liberals—though fewer than conservatives think—who buy this Republican account and write off religious people as backward and reactionary busybodies obsessed with sex.

This book insists that religious faith should not be seen as leading ineluctably to conservative political convictions. In fact, religious people hold a wide array of political views. Religion is not the enemy of reason (or science), and people of faith are not blind automatons who never question themselves or their deepest beliefs. At the heart of my argument is the view that religious faith, far from being inevitably on the side of the status quo, should on principle hold this world to higher standards. Religious people should always be wary of the ways in which political power is wielded and skeptical of how economic privileges are distributed. They should also be mindful of how their own traditions have been used for narrow political purposes, and how some religious figures have manipulated faith to aggrandize their own power. The doctrine of original sin and the idea of a fallen side of human nature apply to people who are religious no less than to those who are not.

Throughout history, our great religious traditions—this is especially obvious in the Christian and Jewish scriptures—have preached a message of hope for more just and decent human arrangements. One of my favorite teachers, the theologian Harvey Cox, argued many years ago that "the theological enterprise seeks to grasp the problems man faces in this historic present in the light of the past and his future, that is, in light of faith and hope." Cox was right to call for a church "which speaks with pointed specificity to its age, which shapes its message and mission not for its own comfort but for the health and renewal of the world." Or, as the bishop who confirmed my son James put it in his sermon, Christianity is a faith of the living.

Marx saw religion as the "opium of the people." But that can be true only if religion is seen as utterly indifferent to what happens in this world—or if it becomes a kind of decent drapery, to use Edmund Burke's evocative term, to disguise or rationalize the authority of the already powerful. Such a faith would be incapable of challenging injustices and unconcerned about how God's children are treated by their governments, by their employers, by their societies. Such a faith would reflexively support the status quo by offering its blessing to whatever happened to be fashionable or to whomever happened to be in power. But that is not the faith of the scriptures. It is certainly not my faith.

The title of this book can be read in two ways. It speaks to our country's exhaustion with a religious style in politics that was excessively dogmatic, partisan, and ideological. It is a style reflecting a spirit far too certain of itself, and far too insistent on the depravity of its political adversaries. Linking religion too closely to the fortunes of one political party, or to one leader or group of leaders, is always a mistake. It encourages alienation from faith itself—where, after all, did Voltaire come from?—by turning a concern with the ultimate into a prop for temporal power. It distorts great traditions by requiring their exponents to bob and weave in order to accommodate the political needs of a given moment or the immediate requirements of a given politician. Thus do great traditions drain themselves of their critical capacity. I do not for a moment pretend that this tendency is unique to political conservatives. The Left is also quite capable of using, and distorting, religion for its own purposes. But for more than a quarter century, it is the political Right that has used, and I believe abused, religion. A great many people—including a great many religious people—have had enough.

They have had enough for the reason embodied in the other sense of the title: reducing religion to politics or to a narrow set of public issues amounts to a great sellout of our traditions. It is common to speak of religion as "selling out" to secularism, or to modernity, or to a fashionable relativism. But there is a more immediate danger, particularly in the United States, of religion selling out to political forces that use the votes of religious people for purposes having nothing to do with a religious agenda—and, often enough, for causes that may contradict the values such voters prize most. It is a great sellout of religion to insist that it has much to teach us about abortion or gay marriage but little useful to say about social justice, war and peace, the organization of our work lives, or our approach to providing for the old, the sick, and the desperate. Religion becomes *less* relevant to public life when its role is marginalized to a predetermined list of "values issues," when its voice is silenced or softened on the central problems facing our country and our government.

II

I write at a moment when the religious winds are changing. Over the last two decades, and especially the last several years, we have witnessed a great commotion over religion and politics. As I argue in chapter 1, the commotion reflects both a broad renegotiation of religion's role in our public life and a particular political moment when conservative forces set about, with considerable success, to organize religious traditionalists as a voting bloc on behalf of the Republican party.

Much of the public discourse thus saw religion as a right-wing force. This assumption shaped how religion was covered in the mass media. Once, the media paid much attention to a broad range of religious figures—from Reinhold Niebuhr, Paul Tillich, and Karl Barth to John Courtney Murray, Billy Graham, and Martin Luther King Jr. Beginning in the late 1970s, the focus of interest narrowed. To be sure, Pope John Paul II earned his share of coverage. But in the United States, the attention lavished on Pat Robertson, the late Jerry Falwell, and James Dobson suggested that to be religious was to cling to a rather restricted set of social and political views. The public voice of religion, as reflected in the supposedly liberal mass media, was deeply inflected with the accents of a largely southern, conservative evangelicalism.

The future of religious engagement with American public life will not be defined by the events of the recent past. In the new millennium, fresh religious voices are rising to challenge stereotypical views of religious faith. I refer here not only to Jim Wallis, Amy Sullivan, Bob Edgar, and others who have joined them in speaking eloquently on behalf of religious progressivism. There is also Rick Warren, a religious and political conservative who nonetheless insists that if Christians do not care about the poorest among them in the world, they are not being true to their faith. There is Rich Cizik, a loyal conservative and a top official of the National Association of Evangelicals, who insists that a concern for life entails an engagement with the stewardship of the Earth and the problem of global warming. There is Bono, who said he could be considered a man of the cloth only if the cloth might be considered leather. He, too, challenged Christians to stand up for the poor. And religious liberals who had spent much time reacting to the religious Right in the 1980s by arguing against religious engagement in politics found their voices as people of faith insisting on a different interpretation of their traditions, and the scriptures.

The era of the religious Right is over. Its collapse is part of a larger decline of a style of ideological conservatism that reached high points in 1980 and 1994 but suffered a series of decisive—and I believe fatal—setbacks during George W. Bush's second term. The end of the religious Right does not signal a decline in evangelical Christianity. On the contrary, it is a sign of a new reformation among Christians—Warren and Cizik are representative figures—who are disentangling their great movement from a political machine. This historic change will require liberals and conservatives alike to abandon their sometimes narrow views of who evangelicals are and what they believe.

From the 1960s forward, the term "spiritual suburbanization" was used with some disdain by social critics, left and right, to refer to a kind of leveling down of spiritual demands, spiritual discipline, and spiritual authority. Yet the suburbanization of the United States has created its own spiritual style, much as the urbanization celebrated by Harvey Cox in his influential 1965 book *The Secular City* created distinctive approaches to spirituality. Much of what is interpreted in contemporary American Christianity as specifically Republican in politics and right-leaning in ideology owes far more to traditions associated with the most conservative parts of the rural white South—whose residents began finding a home in the GOP during the 1964 election—than to the growing, dynamic parts of the evangelical movement found in the new, often nondenominational, megachurches and in other suburban and exurban congregations.

Many members of these churches are, to be sure, moderately conservative in their inclinations, and most of them voted for George W. Bush in the 2004 election. But their approach to worship, faith, church membership—and their attitudes toward those who do not share their own commitments—reflect a contemporary and decidedly middle-of-the-road style associated with suburban and exurban life. On the whole, as Alan Wolfe demonstrated in books that shrewdly challenged conventional understandings, *One Nation, After All* and *Moral Freedom*, it is a style that resists being "judgmental," that emphasizes personal choice—"the idea of people having the freedom to choose their own way of believing," as Wolfe puts it—and insists that "any form of higher authority has to tailor its commandments to the needs of real people." The best word for this style was discovered by David Brooks, who speaks in his best-selling *Bobos in Paradise* of a yearning for "flexidoxy." He defines this wonderful word as "the hybrid mixture of freedom and flexibility on the one hand and the longing for rigor and orthodoxy on the other."

Robert Wuthnow, one of the nation's premier sociologists of religion, offered data that supports Brooks's intuition. In *American Mythos*, Wuthnow, reporting on his 2003 Religion and Diversity Survey, notes that while 58 percent of Americans agreed that "Christianity is the best way to understand God," only 25 percent "said it was best for everybody." These are more the views of flexidox believers in moral freedom than of a nation of "theocrats" intent on imposing a particular form of belief on everyone.

In his earlier book *After Heaven: Spirituality in America since the 1950s*, Wuthnow spoke of a "subtle reordering" of "how Americans understand the sacred itself." Wuthnow saw "a new spirituality of seeking" replacing the "traditional spirituality of inhabiting sacred places." For seekers, Wuthnow argued, "the congregation is less aptly characterized as a safe haven" than as "a supplier of religious goods and services." One may react to these developments in various ways, but this approach to spirituality is anything but authoritarian.

The builders of the new megachurches, notably the most successful such as Rick Warren, are closely attuned to the demands of the new believers. In a 2005 conversation with a group of reporters organized by the Pew Forum on Religion and Public Life, Warren offered a fascinating look at how he built his Saddleback Valley Community Church in Orange County, California, from scratch to a membership of more than twenty thousand. He spoke of spending twelve weeks going door to door, telling those who answered that "I'm not here to sell you anything, I'm not here to convert you, I'm not here to witness to you. I just want to ask you three or four questions." Warren's approach and his questions are revealing, even ingenious:

> Question number one: "Are you an active member of a local church—of any kind of religion—synagogue, mosque, whatever?" If they said yes, I said, "Great, God bless you, keep going," and I politely excused myself and went to the next home. When I'd find somebody who'd say, "No, I don't go anywhere," I'd say, "Perfect; you're just the kind of guy I want to talk to. This is great, you don't go anywhere. So let me ask you a question. Why do you think most people don't attend church?" And I just wrote the answers down. I asked, "If you were looking for a church, what kind of things would you look for?" And I'd just list them. "What advice would you give to me as the pastor of a new church? How can I help you?" So they'd say, "I think churches exist for the community; not vice versa," and I'd write that down.
>
> Now the four biggest reasons in my area why people didn't go to church—here's what they were: Number one, they said, "Sermons are boring and they don't relate to my life." So I decided I had to say something on Sunday that would help people on Monday. Number two, they said, "Members are unfriendly to visitors; I feel like it's a clique." Number three, they said, "Most churches seem more interested

in your money than you as a person." And number four, they said, "We want quality children's programs for our children."

Now it's interesting to me that out of the four biggest reasons why people said they didn't go to church, none of them were theological. They were all sociological. And I had people say, "Oh, it's not that I don't like God. I like God; I just can't stand church." I go, okay; we'll build a whole new kind of church.

This is a very American story. It is, in many ways (though not exclusively), a suburban story. The core concerns of the unchurched whom Warren brought back to worship are basic: a desire for inspiring sermons, a friendly congregation, a pastor who did not seem greedy, and a healthy concern with the lives of their children. It is certainly not a story about right-wing politics, theocracy, Republican organizing, or extreme orthodoxy. It is impossible to understand the religious future without taking Warren's testimony seriously.

III

My hope is that this book might contribute to broadening the conversation about religion and politics. It is aimed at both the believer and the nonbeliever, and it is unapologetically an attempt to influence the political dialogue in the post-Bush era. It is intended to make the case that liberals dare not relegate people of faith to some outer darkness of supposed ignorance—even if liberals have every right to oppose ideologues on the right who invoke faith for narrow electoral purposes. Liberals should respect the religious convictions of those who take their faith seriously and engage them in a common struggle on behalf of a common good.

But a word of warning: many liberals discovered God in the exit polls after the 2004 election. God, of course, can be discovered anywhere. Yet it would be a terrible mistake if liberals and Democratic politicians began treating religious people as just one more interest group, tossing a few bits of scripture into their speeches or inventing religious pasts for themselves that do not exist. This book is a case for taking religion seriously, not for using it in a slapdash way to win an election or two.

It is also intended to make the case to religious people that faith calls us to social as well as individual responsibility, and that politics is not primarily a realm of cultural combat in which only abortion and gay marriage matter. All believers should be wary of reducing a religious tradition to the moral seriousness of a political direct mail piece.

It is also an argument with those one might call the neo-atheists. The new atheists—the best known are the writers Sam Harris, Richard Dawkins, and Christopher Hitchens—insist, as Harris puts it, that "certainty about the next life is simply incompatible with tolerance in this one." That's why they think a belief in salvation through faith in God, no matter the religious tradition, is dangerous to an open society.

The neo-atheists, like their predecessors from a century ago, are given to a sometimes charming ferociousness in their polemics against those they see as too weak-minded to give up faith in God. What makes them new is the moment in history in which they are rejoining the old arguments: an era of religiously motivated suicide bombers combined with far less virulent challenges from various forms of religious fundamentalism to science and religious pluralism.

As a general proposition, I welcome the neo-atheists' challenge. Theirs is an unsurprising response to what Ronald Aronson, writing in the *Nation* in 2007, called "the in-your-face religion that has come to mark our society." The popularity of the neo-atheists' books suggests that those who have pushed religion to the right have done more to arouse enmity toward religion than to win adherents to faith.

The most serious believers, understanding that they need to ask themselves searching questions, have always engaged in dialogue with atheists. The Catholic writer Michael Novak's 1965 book *Belief and Unbelief* is a classic in self-interrogation. "How does one know that one's belief is truly in God," he asks at one point, "not merely in some habitual emotion or pattern of response?"

In 2004 the *New Republic* offered a delightfully ironic cover line, "God Bless Atheism." Inspired by arguments over whether the words "under God" should remain in the Pledge of Allegiance, Leon Wieseltier, the magazine's literary editor, praised atheists for taking the question of God's existence so seriously that they forced believers to do the same.

If the basis for religion "is not an intellectually supportable belief in the existence of God," Wieseltier wrote, "then all the spiritual exaltation and all the political agitation in the world will avail it nothing against the skeptics and the doubters, and it really is just a beloved illusion." He went on: "There is no greater insult to religion than to expel strictness of thought from it." Wieseltier made clear by implication why it is easy for the nonbeliever to insist upon religious freedom and pluralism. Since the nonbeliever sees faith as an irrational "preference" among many other preferences, government has no business privileging one preference over another.

The believer's basis for supporting religious freedom will necessarily be more complicated because the believer, by definition, sees faith not as a "preference" but as truth. The believer can certainly support religious freedom on pragmatic grounds. History has shown that the alternative is chaos, persecution, war, and mass murder. But it is also possible for the believer to be intellectually rigorous and still acknowledge a debt to the Enlightenment, to the Age of Reason—and, yes, to atheists.

The Jesuit theologian David Hollenbach has offered a stronger basis for religious liberty than simple "tolerance." He urges us to seek and live in "intellectual solidarity." I hope this book is written in that spirit. "Tolerance," Hollenbach noted, is "a strategy of noninterference with the beliefs and lifestyles of those who are different or 'other.'" That is the classic Enlightenment view. Intellectual solidarity demands more. It "entails engagement with the other . . . in the hope that understanding might replace incomprehension and that perhaps even agreement could result." Those who subscribe to various faiths or to none agree to put their own understanding of things at risk, "to listen as well as to speak, to learn from what they hear, and, if necessary, to change as a result of what they have learned."

Those who believe they possess truth should not fear entering what Hollenbach calls "a community of freedom." Doing so is not a sign of intellectual fuzziness or a lack of faith. On the contrary, it means embracing the very "strictness of thought" that Wieseltier rightly demands of believers. It is only in dialogue with others that our faith is tested, our ideas made explicit, our errors corrected.

Yet this view raises a difficulty for the neo-atheists, who often seem as dogmatic as the dogmatists they condemn. They are especially frustrated with religious "moderates" who don't fit their stereotypes. In his bracing polemic, *The End of Faith*, Sam Harris is candid in asserting that "religious moderates are themselves the bearers of a terrible dogma: they imagine that the path to peace will be paved once each one of us has learned to respect the unjustified beliefs of others."

Harris goes on: "I hope to show that the very ideal of religious toler-ance—born of the notion that every human being should be free to believe whatever he wants about God—is one of the principal forces driving us toward the abyss. We have been slow to recognize the degree to which religious faith perpetuates man's inhumanity to man."

Arguments about faith do not, in the end, hang on whether religion is socially "useful" or instead promotes "inhumanity." But since the idea that religion is primarily destructive lies at the heart of the neo-atheist argu-ment, its critics have rightly insisted on detailing the sublime acts of hu-manity and generosity that religion has promoted through the centuries.

There are many paradoxes here, of course. It's true that religious Chris-tians were among those who persecuted Jews. It is also true that religious Christians—if far too few—were among those who rescued Jews from these most un-Christian acts. And it is a sad fact that secular forms of dogmatism have been at least as murderous as the religious kind.

Particularly bothersome is the suggestion that believers rarely question themselves while atheists ask all the hard questions. History, as Michael Novak argued in a 2007 critique of the neo-atheists, suggests the contrary. "Questions," he noted, "have been the heart and soul of Judaism and Christianity for millennia."

"Christianity is not about moral arrogance," Novak insisted. "It is about moral realism, and moral humility." Of course Christians in practice often fail to live up to this elevated definition of their creed. Believers are always wrong—and usually disappointed with the results—when they seek to impose their faith through force and the power of the state. But atheists are capable of their own forms of arrogance. Indeed, if arrogance is the only criterion, the contest could well come out a tie. This book might be seen as a brief against arrogance where questions of faith are concerned. Arrogance is truth's enemy because it closes us to self-criticism, self-correc-tion, and honest doubt.

My friend Korin Davis had it right when she said in a conversation one day that the neo-atheists are *an overreaction to an overreaction*. Religious conservatives had a legitimate grievance against their sense of exclusion from elite conversations and elite culture. But the religious Right over-reacted by creating a dogmatic and partisan ideological movement. Athe-ists and secularists have a legitimate grievance against this narrowly politi-cized form of religion, its resistance to critical inquiry about faith, and the efforts of some on the religious Right to revive the old and destructive wars between religion and science. But the new atheists have overreacted by insisting, wrongly, that religious faith is irrational and reactionary in all its forms and by denying the good works and the great intellectual achievements that our faith traditions have called forth.

IV

The decision to believe or not to believe is an individual choice. We are all shaped by the traditions in which we are nurtured and by whether we grow to accept, reject, or modify them. Because this is so, it is fair for a reader to ask about the stories that shaped the narrative I offer here.

My own account would certainly include Sister Genevieve, my sixth-grade teacher, who may have had more influence on my views of racial justice and civil rights than anyone else. A warm and lovely woman with a deep southern drawl, she was teaching us kids in Fall River, Massachusetts, with our sharp New England accents because, as I always understood the story, she had been kicked out of Louisiana in the 1950s for organizing an integrated First Communion ceremony. Sister Genevieve was no radical. She was simply Christian. She thought all kids were children of God. How could one possibly imagine that the reception of the Eucharist should be organized by race?

When I was in high school, I was taught by a remarkable group of Benedictine monks. The head of the monastery, Dom Aelred Graham, spent years in dialogue with Buddhist monks and wrote—long before it became a fashionable topic—a book called *Zen Catholicism*. He later wrote a fascinating spiritual autobiography, *The End of Religion*. Reading it, I was struck by how a person could be so open and intellectually serious and at the same time so humble and matter-of-fact about his own simultaneous commitment to orthodox Catholicism and to a life of spiritual questing.

At that Catholic high school—then the Portsmouth Priory, now the Portsmouth Abbey—I was drawn to the writings of Dr. King and wrote an essay on his collection of sermons, *Strength to Love*. I have absolutely no memory of what I said. I do remember that the book forced me to think anew about the social and personal obligations of being a Christian.

Religion and politics were matters of constant discussion in our Catholic home when I was growing up. My parents were the sort of Christians who believed they should behave toward others in the ways their faith prescribed. Their faith was warm, not cold, embracing, not excluding, open-minded, not narrow. My dad, a dentist, set up a free dental clinic for poor kids in our city. Like most in his profession at the time, he was strongly opposed to socialized medicine; unlike many, he predicted its day would come because members of the medical and dental fraternity he loved (it was mostly a fraternity then) would be insufficiently generous toward those in need. My mom spent much of her life as a teacher, in both public and Catholic schools, and as a librarian. One of her great passions was getting kids who didn't have very many books in their homes to learn to love reading. When she died in 1994, students she had taught more than sixty years earlier came to her funeral, as did countless others she had encountered more recently.

My late dad was a warmhearted man, conservative in his politics but liberal in spirit. One of his dear friends, Dr. Murray Goldin, was a member of the NAACP in our city, which had a small black population. I once asked my dad why his friend belonged to the civil rights group. My dad explained that Dr. Goldin was a Jew, and that Jews, like blacks, had experienced discrimination. His friend, he said, felt it was important to stand up for others who had faced bigotry. My father was a Goldwater supporter at the time, but he spoke admiringly of his friend's moral commitment. That made an impression on me, too.

So I never had those personal resentments about religion that so many others have described in recounting their confrontations with what they saw as the hypocrisy of their parents or their congregations. My parents' behavior—behavior is, for kids, more important than words—said that faith mattered and that it demanded of those who held it certain standards of generosity and decency. Because of them, I have always seen faith as more enriching and challenging than oppressive.

I offer these stories not because they are exceptional, but because I think they are rather typical. More than many believers usually want to admit, our attitude toward faith, as toward many other things in life, is in part a predisposition shaped by our own experiences. (The same, of course, is true for nonbelievers.) We are influenced by events that end up teaching us larger lessons than we realize we're receiving at the time. I am sure my father had no idea that his offhand comment about his friend would affect my views for life on the matters of racism and anti-Semitism. Sister Genevieve probably *did* intend to affect our views on race. The monks who taught me definitely *were* trying to shape my faith. But here again, their actions and attitudes were probably at least as powerful as their words. Later in life, I always rejected the counsel of those who insisted that believers were inevitably ignorant, blind, culturally backward, or intellectually unsophisticated. Here were some of the most intelligent and sophisticated people I would encounter who could speak of faith—and also of culture and politics—with clarity, erudition, even elegance. This did not mean that they were right. It certainly meant that they were not fools.

In college, I found myself writing paper after paper on subjects related to religion and politics: the interactions between the Russian Orthodox Church and Stalin's government during World War II; the remarkable points of similarity—despite fierce, even deadly, differences—between mystics and anarchists during the Spanish Civil War; the sharply opposing stances taken by Catholic diocesan newspapers toward Joe McCarthy in the 1950s; and the complicated workings of a coalition of convenience between Christian and left-wing pacifists and pro-Nazi, pro-fascist forces when each side opposed American entry into World War II for rather different reasons. (That paper may have been the beginning of my lifelong love for Reinhold Niebuhr, the great progressive theologian who broke with pacifism in the face of Hitler's threat to humanity.)

Readers of this book will be spared my thoughts on these subjects. I mention the papers to suggest that it seemed to me perfectly natural in the late 1960s and early 1970s, long before the rise of the religious Right, to take an interest in the relationship between religion and politics. This can serve as a reminder that religious politics and political theology are not new, and are not exclusively right-wing. Indeed, in those years, I came to admire such religiously engaged and politically sophisticated writers as Peter and Peggy Steinfels, Peter Berger, Garry Wills, Abraham Heschel, Robert Coles, and Andrew Greeley, and theologians including Reinhold and H. Richard Niebuhr, Richard Rubenstein, Johannes Metz, Jurgen Moltmann, and, of course, Harvey Cox. Their work, in turn, led to engagement with other thinkers and writers—readers will run across many of them in this book—including Lisa Sowle Cahill, Jonathan Sacks, Avery Dulles, Monika Hellwig, Eugene Kennedy, Glenn Tinder, Martin Marty, and Jean Bethke Elshtain. Later still, I discovered the largely hidden world (hidden, that is, from large parts of the intellectual mainstream) of the new evangelical scholarship through Mark Noll, Grant Wacker, George Marsden, and Nathan Hatch.

I was also deeply affected when I was young by the moral witness of
Dorothy Day and the Catholic Worker movement and of the Berrigan
brothers, even if I decided early on that I was neither a pacifist nor a radical
in the sense that they were radical. Other inspirations included Michael
Novak and Richard John Neuhaus. Now staunch Catholic conservatives,
Novak and Neuhaus were in those days committed to the Christian Left.
They helped persuade me toward the views that I now hold, which in
many, maybe most, areas are views both of them now reject. I remain
grateful for what they taught me.

None of these biographical reflections constitutes a defense of belief,
let alone a rationale for a particular creed. By acknowledging that all of us
are shaped by our experiences, I am conceding a key point to critics of
religious faith: that the typical believer rarely arrives at his or her faith
through a process involving reason alone. On the contrary, faith can be a
form of loyalty (to one's parents or tribe or ethnic group or community).
It can be an aesthetic judgment (that a rational, well-ordered universe is
simply more attractive than a chaotic mess with no purpose or harmony).
It can be a pragmatic choice (all things being equal, religious belief encourages better behavior, a greater regard for others, an aspiration to things
higher than the self). It can be a psychological comfort (for many, it's
easier to live in a world with a loving God at the center and with a promise
of eternal life). Just to annoy our religion teachers—but also because I
think he believed it at the time—a high school friend would regularly wear
a button to class that read: "A Benevolent God is the Greatest Creation of
Man." It's worth mentioning that this friend won the Christian Doctrine
prize year after year.

I would insist with Novak that believers usually get around to thinking
seriously about whether what they believe is *true*. Does God exist? How
do we *know*? What was the nature of the covenant between God and
Moses? What is the meaning of the Exodus? Who was Jesus? Who did
Jesus think he was? What is the meaning of the empty tomb at Easter?
What is one to make of the different forms of revelation—to Muhammad,
to the Buddha—and how they relate to each other? Can one be a believer
in religious openness without falling prey to an "everything is everything"
relativism? Do believers in specific creeds *really* believe each doctrinal point
that they might recite from memory every Sunday? Are they fooling themselves or others? Or do they make mental compromises? Or are they just

disguising doubt behind bold declarations that whatever they believe is really a mystery to be taken on faith?

I offer this list—I think it's fairly typical of questions believers ask themselves at one point or another, and sometimes all their lives—to be honest with readers and to underscore that few believers are blind automatons who never subject their beliefs to serious inquiry. Mother Teresa was not alone among believers in asking why she was not hearing from God.

One other autobiographical note is relevant here. In the mid-1980s the *New York Times* sent me to Rome, which gave me the opportunity to cover the Vatican and some of the most vigorous days of the papacy of John Paul II. So much of what I cared about as a student—the relationship between faith and social justice, the rise of the liberation theologians I read in Harvey Cox's classes, the challenge of the modern age to believers and of believers to the modern age—was suddenly relevant to my day-to-day work. My personal interest in figuring out the relationship of faith, politics, and society became, in those years, a matter of professional obligation, even urgency. Some of those journalistic passions are also reflected in these pages. In particular, I have chosen to share reporting and reflections on the papacies of John Paul II and Benedict XVI, partly because both have influenced the course of religious and political life far beyond the confines of the Roman Catholic Church, but also because the challenge of coming to terms with their ideas and commitments has been part of my own religious and political journeys.

My specific interest in religion *as a liberal* arose from a concern developed many years before the 2004 election that some of my fellow liberals harbored certain prejudices against people of faith. I say *some* because there are many on the left who never harbored such prejudices. But there definitely *was* a sense on parts of the liberal Left that the "yahoos" of "Jesusland" supported George W. Bush out of their fanaticism and ignorance—and the intellectual seeds of that view were planted many years ago. I believe devoutly, if I may use that term, that this attitude toward people of faith is destructive to liberalism not only at the ballot box but also intellectually and morally. One of liberalism's great achievements has been its resolute opposition to bigotry. Bigotry against people of faith is not only ugly; it is inconsistent with the liberal creed.

But people of faith should not be harboring bigotry against liberals, either. Listen to some right-wing preachers and you'd imagine—I exaggerate a little—that liberals are out to destroy the family, burn down the

churches, require unwed teenagers to have sex and then abort their children, and insist that the schools teach atheism or exotic forms of New Age
spirituality. It never crosses the minds of these right-wing religious critics
of liberalism that many of their own evangelical forebears were at the van-
guard of progressive social action. Evangelicals spearheaded the movement
against slavery and struggled on behalf of so many other progressive causes,
from bringing an end to child labor to reclaiming the slums. Dr. King's
arguments for civil rights were rooted in Jefferson's Declaration of Independence—and in the scriptures. Unless you are willing to delete Isaiah,
Micah, Amos, and the Sermon on the Mount from the Bible, you cannot
deny the religious roots of liberalism.

Thus began the road that led to this book. The notion that religion
should be disconnected from politics always seemed odd to me simply
because I couldn't understand how you could separate the two. If religion
mattered, and if the content of your faith was true, it had to affect all you
did. And if politics also mattered, the obligation of the believer was to sort
out how politics and faith related to each other. The task was especially
complicated for believers who saw religious and political liberty as gifts to
be treasured and preserved. That meant working out the relationship between one's own faith and politics in a way that respected the beliefs of
others—including those who rejected faith as an irrational illusion.

This was why the rise of religious conservatism in the 1970s and 1980s
was, for me, both entirely understandable and peculiar. I will always defend the right of religious conservatives to bring their faith to bear on
political questions. I have always done the same, so it would be hypocritical
of me to do otherwise. Christian faith, as I came to understand it, pushed
me toward liberalism. I thus have no grounds for challenging the right of
conservatives to root their own views in faith. "Faith," St. Paul wrote in
his letter to the Hebrews, "gives substance to our hopes." The root of
the word "faith," as Jaroslav Pelikan wrote, "carries the connotations of
trustworthiness, reliability and loyalty, still suggested in the English adjec-
tive 'faithful.'" Surely these are virtues that believers and unbelievers alike
would wish to see reflected more perfectly in our politics.

Yet this is also at the heart of my argument with the Christian Right.
It is impossible to see Jesus as a tool of the Establishment. It is difficult to
imagine this revolutionary figure arguing that cuts in inheritance and capital gains taxes should be the highest goals in politics. Far more persuasive,
to me at least, is the account of Christianity offered by the theology of

hope. Jurgen Moltmann, one of the theologians who pioneered this view, argued that Christianity teaches "the passion for the possible" and keeps at the forefront the idea of "breaking with the old and coming to terms with the new." If religion means anything, as Michael Walzer has written about the meaning of the Exodus story, it means that the door of hope always remains open.

V

This is not a creedal book. It is intended as a description of our current religious situation and makes a series of arguments about how best to deal with it. It's an American's dialogue with his fellow Americans over how we should think about religion's public role—and, in passing, an American's argument with a great many Europeans who believe, wrongly, that ours is a nation of religious fanaticism. It's a liberal's argument with his fellow liberals over the respect owed believers and the impossibility of separating religion from politics—even if the state itself must remain disentangled from religion for the sake of religious liberty. It's a believer's argument with other believers over what faith asks of us—and in particular, an argument against a style of religious conservatism that has become too ideological and too partisan. It is an empirical argument that the categories we use to describe religion in public life are far more relevant to the 1980s or 1990s than to the current moment. The new reformation that has begun will privilege religious moderation over religious conservatism and, perhaps more importantly, broaden the agenda that religious people bring to politics. It is a Roman Catholic's argument with some in his church who believe that certain "nonnegotiable" issues such as abortion, stem-cell research, and gay marriage must always be more important in politics than the Church's rich social teaching that privileges the poor, insists on economic justice, calls the death penalty into question, and puts a heavy moral burden on those who would advocate for war. It is, finally, a rationalist's argument with the insistence of certain strands of neo-atheism that belief cannot escape becoming dangerous, fanatical, and destructive.

Yet if I do not propose a creed, certain beliefs are at least implicit in the text: that we know God by faith and hope, and that keeping God transcendent and absolute helps ensure that we work tentatively and humbly in our human realm, always open to self-correction in the light of new experience. "If God is God," wrote the Christian writer Jacques Ellul, "he obviously cannot be totally known or circumscribed or put into a human formula. There is always something more to know and understand and receive." Accepting the "social context" of our modern (or, perhaps, postmodern) condition, as Peter Berger wrote in *A Far Glory*, means "acknowledging the fact that the certainties of a traditional, pre-modern or nonmodern society are not available to us." Modern pluralism, Berger argues, presents us with "a challenge to hold convictions without either dissolving them in utter relativity or encasing them in the false absolutes of fanaticism. It is a difficult challenge, but is not an impossible one." This means, Berger insists, that competing religious traditions honor each other by arguing with each other, accepting together what, for believers, is the hardest fact of all: "the burden of God's silence." A belief in God can be accompanied by all manner of foolishness, including foolishness of a very dangerous sort. But the advantage of what H. Richard Niebuhr has called "radical monotheism" is that a belief in one God as the ground of being promotes a sensible skepticism about everything else. "Radical monotheism," Niebuhr wrote, "dethrones all absolutes short of the principle of being itself." It is my view that, perhaps paradoxically, believers may be *less* credulous and naive than unbelievers when it comes to worldly institutions and systems of thought. That is certainly their mission.

VI

This book is organized with the aim of developing these arguments about religion's role in American public life while also offering an account of our current political moment. Readers who disagree with some of the views I advance will, I hope, still find the analytical and historical material helpful in defining the stakes in our coming dialogues and debates.

Chapter 1 makes the case that to a far greater degree than we realize, the history of American liberalism is bound up in the nation's religious history. Without religious inspiration and the organizational role of the churches, many of the greatest achievements of American progressivism would have been impossible.

Yet although I can be fairly characterized as a Christian liberal, it is not my view that religion in general (if there is such a thing) or my own tradition in particular must inevitably side with the political Left. On the contrary, I also argue in the first chapter that there are deep affinities between religion and conservatism. The religious imagination is not an ideological imagination. George F. Will has written that conservatism is "a complex constellation of ideas and dispositions," and that description applies as well to our religious traditions. At the outset, I try to make clear that I am not looking for religion to do the work of liberals in our politics. Rather, I believe that at its best, religion—in particular, the Christianity and Judaism with which I am most familiar—challenges all ideologies. I also argue that the current engagement between religion and public life reflects a new stage in our more than two-century-long dialogue about how best to preserve religious liberty. This is not a development to be feared, but an opportunity to be seized.

Chapter 2 discusses the injuries caused to our public life by culture-war politics—it is, I argue, the wrong war—and how the culture-war debate has affected our politics. It goes on to examine the importance of cultural, religious, and moral factors in the 2004 and 2006 elections. For those who love data, it is the most data-rich chapter in the book, and also the chapter that focuses most specifically on recent political campaigns. While I lay out the indisputable evidence of religious polarization, I challenge the view that religion and morality were decisive in the 2004 presidential contest.

Because the 2004 election played such a central role in sparking new debates about religion and politics (and important new forms of religious activism in the center, on the left, and inside the Democratic party), I look at the results in some detail, balancing the impact of religion against other forces at work in our politics, including those of race, class, and region. If religion's role in our politics should not be demeaned or ignored, it does religion no favors to exaggerate its influence or to see its hand at work when it is not. Finally, I argue that the 2006 election created a new religious landscape, and that this new array of forces is more relevant to our future than were past alignments. The results reflected the declining influence of the religious Right, which has gone from being a major force in a majority coalition to acting as an irritant within a minority coalition. The difficulties the religious Right experienced in uniting behind a candidate in the early stages of the campaign for the 2008 Republican presidential nomination were a sign of its organizational difficulties and a certain ambivalence toward the movement within Republican ranks. Even one of the cause's strongest potential champions, former governor Mike Huckabee of Arkansas, went out of his way to link his faith to concerns about poverty, education, and health care.

Chapters 3 and 4 argue specifically for a broadening of the religious agenda. Chapter 3 looks at the rich history of religious debate over economic justice and pays attention especially to arguments among Catholics—fueled by the American Catholic Bishops in the mid-1980s and the social encyclicals of popes John XXIII and John Paul II. I pay particular attention to (and offer a critique of) Michael Novak's economic thinking. While I disagree with Novak, he usefully offers one side of an argument Christians should be having with each other. In the course of the chapter, I also argue that George W. Bush and Hillary Clinton represent two distinct traditions of argument among Christians about the causes and cures of social ills. If the tradition that inspired Bush's view was dominant in the first years of the new millennium, the version of Christian social thought reflected by Clinton, Barack Obama, and other prominent progressives is now in the ascendancy.

Chapter 4 grapples with the politics of moral issues in the Bush years, and the specific role played by George W. Bush himself. Bush has been much criticized for his use of religion and for seeming to suggest, at times, that his presidency was in some sense the product of divine inspiration. I offer many specific criticisms of my own. But I also argue that in certain respects, Bush's presidency marks less of a break from the past on religious questions than many assume. That's especially true of Bush's rhetoric, which is more consistent with past presidential pronouncements on religion than either his critics or his friends might believe. The chapter reflects my own efforts to come to terms with precisely what it is Bush believes and how best to understand the role of religion in his political life. It then moves to specific controversies of the Bush era, including the political clash over the fate of Terri Schiavo. It offers suggestions aimed at encouraging less polarized and more productive approaches to three of the thorniest moral issues facing us today: abortion, the battle against teen pregnancy, and gay marriage. It concludes with a discussion of the new directions in evangelical life bravely pioneered by Cizik and others who are seeking a more productive and less divisive relationship between faith and public action.

Chapters 5 and 6 focus specifically on the Catholic Church, the largest single denomination in the United States—and one in which, as I've already confessed, I have a personal interest. Chapter 5 is devoted to the papacies of John Paul and Benedict. John Paul is a paradoxical figure who simultaneously confirmed many of the liberal achievements of Pope John XXIII *and* moved the church to the right, especially on internal questions such as the Vatican's authority, the all-male celibate priesthood, and liberation theology. Benedict, as Cardinal Ratzinger, the head of the Congregation for the Doctrine of the Faith, was a prime mover in the Vatican's shift rightward and yet is a complex and intellectually fascinating figure who cannot be written off as an ideologue.

Chapter 6 focuses specifically on the struggles inside the American Catholic Church and the critical electoral role Catholics play as swing voters. If the evolution of evangelical Christianity in a less ideological direction is destined to have a large impact on American political life, so also will the battle over the future of American Catholicism. And both will also affect mainline Protestant churches, who once provided the civic and moral glue that held American public life together—and continue to play a far more important public role than many appreciate.

A concluding chapter looks at where our public conversation on religion is going. In the coming years, I believe, Christianity's liberal commitments will be seen as more relevant than its conservative impulses. Reinhold Niebuhr's theology will be far more influential than Pat Robertson's. The economic requirements for a decent family life will trump rhetorical appeals to "family values." Evangelical Christians are increasingly restive and dissatisfied with narrowly ideological definitions of their public role. Republicans who preached about their traditionalist commitments have had to come to terms with the private behavior of their party's own public figures—Mark Foley, David Vitter, and Larry Craig among them. They are being called upon to square their moralism at election time (and during the controversy over Bill Clinton's scandals) with the private behavior of many in their own ranks. If religious commitments are only about private matters, then religion's public role will be judged primarily in relation to the personal lives of public figures. This is surely not what religious conservatives should want, and it is not what religious progressives believe. These are among the reasons why I am hopeful that the coming religious conversation will be more productive, less divisive, and more inclusive than it has been in the recent past.

Two notes to readers: First, some may be jarred by the fact that my second references to clerical figures usually do not include their formal titles. For example, in second references to Cardinal Joseph Ratzinger before he became Pope Benedict XVI, I refer to him simply as "Ratzinger." I do so, following the approach typically used by Italian writers about the Vatican, not out of disrespect, but because other forms of reference ("former Cardinal Ratzinger") seemed clumsy and seriously cluttered the text.

Second, while this book is the work of a Christian, the influence of Jews and Judaism on my thinking is obvious throughout. This is both a biographical matter (I grew up as a Catholic in a Jewish neighborhood and have been personally close to Jews and the Jewish tradition all my life) as well as a matter of spiritual and intellectual inclination. There are moments in the book when I discuss "religion" and other times when I speak specifically about Christianity and Judaism. I have tried to avoid the popular "Judeo-Christian" formulation—except in quotations of others who used the term. Of course I believe the two faiths share common roots, a fact reflected in their scriptures and in the person of Jesus Christ. But I find the phrase less respectful to both traditions than it is designed to be. That is especially true in relation to Judaism, since the formulation is often invoked by Christians as a euphemism when they are really referring to their own tradition.

The role of Muslims in American politics—visible in our elections since 2000—is destined to grow. I do not, however, pretend to deal with this role in any comprehensive way. That's especially true in the parts of the discussion that focus on a time before the Muslim community began to loom larger in the minds of political strategists and political scientists. (I also avoid the successor phrase to "the Judeo-Christian tradition" intended to cover Muslims, "the Abrahamic tradition," out of the same desire to respect each tradition's specificity.) The rise of new faith communities in the United States—not only Muslims but also Hindus, Sikhs, Baha'i, Buddhists, and many others—is obviously critical to the next chapter in our nation's religious story. The presence of these new neighbors and fellow citizens will only highlight the power of our tradition of religious openness and pluralism, and the importance of nurturing it.

VII

It's obvious by now that I believe a serious embrace of Christianity inevitably leads one into politics, since sin is social as well as individual. That is why my critique of the Christian Right is about the content of the movement's politics, not the fact that it is politically engaged. Yet Christianity, as Reinhold Niebuhr so powerfully taught us, enjoins the believer to beware of the fanatical potential of all religion when it enters the social domain, to know that "the worst corruption is a corrupt religion." We need "a sense of modesty about the virtue, wisdom and power available to us" and "a sense of contrition about the common human frailties and foibles which lie at the foundation of both the enemy's demonry and our vanities." Americans, Niebuhr argued, are never safe "against the temptation of claiming God too simply as the sanctifier of whatever we most fervently desire." In making arguments for what Christianity has to say about political questions, all of us who are Christians can fall prey to the temptation simply to ransack the scriptures or the tradition to justify conclusions we've already reached. "Most of us are not really approaching the subject in order to find out what Christianity says," C. S. Lewis wrote. "We are approaching it in the hope of finding support from Christianity for the views of our own party." The believer must always ask whether the voice he or she hears inside is really the voice of faith.

Certain political beliefs are implicit and sometimes explicit in these pages. Above all, I am impatient with the ways in which the political discourse of recent years has divided what are typically called "values" issues from economic issues, cultural questions from matters of social policy. These divisions are artificial and misleading—and not just because inequality and social injustice relate no less to our "values" than do our views on abortion and gay marriage. As I will be arguing in the book's early chapters, it is impossible to talk about parental responsibility, healthy family lives, reducing the number of abortions, and creating communities that nurture our moral sense without dealing with issues related to the structure of work, the distribution of wealth and income, and the promotion of genuinely equal opportunity.

This book draws upon many years of research, writing, and conversation about religious issues, and questions related to religion and politics. I try in the acknowledgments to discharge my many debts to the publications that allowed an early testing of some of these ideas, to the institutions that have supported my interest in this subject, and to dear friends, colleagues, and teachers who have helped me grapple with these issues. But precisely because this book is the product of a lifetime of reflections—imperfect, to be sure—it is, finally, a very personal book. Thus do I write a great deal about society, politics, and culture, but I also write about flesh-

and-blood human beings who, for me, embody the spirit that Abraham Heschel, the modern Jewish prophet, argued should characterize our approach to the world: a sense of "radical amazement."

"Wonder rather than doubt is the root of knowledge," Heschel insisted. "Doubts may be resolved, radical amazement can never be erased." The people who helped me keep the faith in the face of my own doubt and skepticism lived by the Heschel Imperative: to "keep our own amazement, our own eagerness alive." I hope, in a modest way at least, that this spirit is alive in these pages.

1. Is Religion Conservative or Progressive? (Or Both?)

Consider Democrat Tim Kaine's successful campaign for governor of Virginia in 2005. Kaine was not shy about speaking openly of his religious faith and his work as a Christian missionary in Latin America. He was actually a Catholic volunteer, but his political consultants miraculously replaced the word "Catholic" with the word "Christian" in the ads they ran on Christian radio stations heard mainly by evangelical Protestants.

And so when the time came for his Republican opponent Jerry Kilgore's entirely predictable attack on the Democrat's opposition to the death penalty, Kaine's consultants quickly went on the air with advertisements that said he would enforce the state's death penalty laws but, more interestingly, explained why he opposed capital punishment. "My faith teaches life is sacred," Kaine said. "I personally oppose the death penalty."

Now here's the interesting thing. The Kaine campaign had, through focus groups, carefully tested how various responses to various attacks would play with voters. David Eichenbaum, a Kaine adviser, explained that the groups were shown, as Eichenbaum put it, "the worst attacks against Tim that they would use to make him into a big bad liberal." The groups were then shown footage of Kaine "talking about the importance to him of his religious values and convictions." The result? "Almost to a person," Eichenbaum reported, "they would say that he must be a moderate or a conservative, and that he couldn't be a liberal."

That is: if Kaine was religious, *he could not possibly be a liberal.* Now there is a sobering finding for liberals, and especially for liberals with strong ties to faith.

Yet there was a time, not long ago, when conservatives were desperate to keep religion out of politics and saw their liberal enemies as politicizing God's message. "Preachers," one critic declared, "are not called upon to be politicians but to be soul-winners." As it happens, this is not a secular liberal denying faith's legitimate influence on politics. The words were

Jerry Falwell's, in 1965. His scorn was directed at the church-based civil rights movement in the South. Falwell knew that without the black church, there would have been no civil rights movement. It bothered conservatives such as Falwell that the civil rights preachers were so judgmental, so eager to associate their cause with God's. "If we are wrong, God Almighty is wrong!" a young preacher named Martin Luther King Jr. declared in December 1955 at the Holt Street Baptist Church in Montgomery, Alabama. "If we are wrong, Jesus of Nazareth was merely a utopian dreamer and never came down to earth!" It was not a view of the Savior congenial to southern segregationists.

The greatest victory of the religious Right was not its success in turning out the vote of religious conservatives. The Christian Right damaged liberalism most by calling forth a liberal reaction against religion's public role. Too many liberals have been complicit in the conservatives' redefinition of "moral values" as always involving sex, and "religious activism" as always referring to the work of Pat Robertson and his friends. Confronted with a new religious Right from the 1970s on, many liberals were tempted to be at least as critical of religion as they were of the Right.

Consider where the scriptures lead. The Christian Gospel certainly does not seem to endorse the status quo when we learn from it that "He has cast down the mighty from their thrones, and has lifted up the lowly. He has filled the hungry with good things, and the rich he has sent away empty!" Such are not the biblical quotations that typically appeared in Karl Rove's direct mail pieces.

Isaiah has spoken to reformers through the ages. It was appropriate that the publisher of a collection of letters from the antislavery agitator William Lloyd Garrison chose as its title *Let the Oppressed Go Free*, which reflects Garrison's debt to Isaiah. In his inaugural address, John F. Kennedy was drawn to the same passage when he spoke of the shared obligations of the United States and the Soviet Union, adversaries in the Cold War, to "undo the heavy burdens" on the poor and the oppressed.

Dr. King drew on Amos to declare that "we are not satisfied, and we will not be satisfied until justice rolls down like waters and righteousness like a mighty stream." Amos, by the way, is the increasingly hot book among Democratic speechwriters.

Jesus himself demands that we feed the hungry and clothe the naked and tells us we will be judged by how we treat "the least among us." No wonder the historian Michael Kazin has written that the American Left "has never advanced without a moral awakening entangled with notions about what the Lord would have us do."

Now liberals can be as guilty as conservatives of engaging in proof-texting, finding whatever passages in scripture best suit their purposes. It is increasingly popular among Democrats in Congress who oppose cuts in programs for the poor to cite scripture against conservative Republicans. Personally, I like the idea of challenging religious conservatives in this way, but there can be something terribly contrived and opportunistic about using scriptural passages as if they were phrases that had passed under the scrutiny of focus groups. And finding politically congenial passages from the Old Testament prophets and the sayings of Jesus of Nazareth can deflect attention from their core religious purposes. If a political message can be distilled from Jesus's preaching, as Tod Lindberg has argued, his message was ultimately about salvation and redemption, not politics.

Religious liberals should also acknowledge that conservatives have not invented the history of opposition between various forms of liberalism and religion. Eighteenth- and nineteenth-century liberal anticlericalism veered toward outright opposition to faith itself. This tendency is very much alive among the neo-atheists. Liberalism has always included a strong strain of secularism, a proper wariness about the abuses of religious authority, and a particular fear of the Catholic Church. "Rationalism" was seen as the enemy of "obscurantism," "reason" the antithesis of "faith." "Neither Pope nor King" was a popular liberal slogan. The separation of church and state was a noteworthy liberal victory for freedom of conscience—even if it is forgotten that disestablishment was a cause pursued with passion by devout believers loyal to denominations that found themselves in the minority in the United States and elsewhere. The neo-atheist writers have provided vigorous restatements of the old arguments against faith, God, and religion. They, like their religious foes, are operating within a tradition.

Nor can there be any doubt that established religious institutions, particularly the beleaguered mid-nineteenth-century papacy, saw liberalism as an enemy. In his superb essay on "the failed encounter" between the nineteenth-century Catholic Church and liberalism, Peter Steinfels reminds us of the ferocity of the antiliberal polemics that issued from some of the papacy's defenders. (Incidentally, in a useful note for our times, Steinfels points out that some of the fiercest attacks were not on atheists or secularists, but on liberal Catholics.) In 1866 Louis Veuillot published *L'Illusion liberale*, the Liberal Illusion, in which he attacked "godless, soulless anti-Christian liberalism" for relegating religion and morality to "the privacy of conscience." In order to defend Christian society, the state should do the bidding of the pope, Vieuillot insisted. "Force in the hands of the Church is the force of right," he wrote, "and we have no desire that right should remain without force."

Steinfels tells us about a pamphlet published in Spain in 1886 with the unequivocal title *El Liberalismo Es Pecado*, Liberalism Is Sin, written by Don Felix Sarda y Salvany. The essay was so ferocious that even the Vatican's Holy Office condemned it, while also rebuking its detractors. Liberalism, Don Felix declared, is "a greater sin than blasphemy, theft, adultery, homicide, or any other violation of the law of God." It is "the evil of all evils," "the offspring of Satan and the enemy of mankind." He condemned the "odious and repulsive attempt to unite Liberalism with Catholicism." The Catholic liberal, he said, is "both a traitor and a fool," a pagan at heart, a pawn of the devil, "less excusable than those Liberals who have never been within the pale of the Church." Was it sufficient for loyal Catholics simply to dodge the liberal's blows? "Not at all," he wrote, "the first thing necessary is to demolish the combatant himself." Imagine a figure who could make Dobson or Robertson, Limbaugh or O'Reilly, look like Paul Wellstone or Hubert Humphrey or even Sam Harris.

But one need not be an ultramontane extremist to see that liberalism and religion can make a bad fit, or that conservative sentiments and impulses can fit quite well with religious faith. In a classic critique of religious liberalism, H. Richard Niebuhr argued that liberal Protestantism seemed to posit that "a God without wrath brought men without sin into a Kingdom without judgment through the ministrations of a Christ without a Cross." Is it any wonder that many in search of a demanding faith turn toward conservative religion?

Consider what most religious believers and conservatives have in common. There is, first, that word "tradition." It is an essential word for most conservatives and for most believers. It is in the nature of liberals and the Left to revolt against tradition. In his 1953 book *The Conservative Mind*—a work central to the postwar conservative revival—Russell Kirk listed a series of "canons" of conservatism that were quite congenial to people of faith. They included a "belief in a transcendent order, or body of natural law, which rules society as well as conscience." He argued that "custom, convention and old prescription are checks upon man's anarchic impulse and upon the innovators' lust for power." And in a line that may well have had an impact on the Vatican, Kirk warned that "hasty innovation may be a devouring conflagration rather than a torch of progress." Large numbers of religious people instinctively believe many or most of these things.

If religious people believe in tradition, many also believe in authority, either of religious leaders or of scripture—or both. My sister, who is a captain in the navy reserves and has spent over a quarter century connected with the military, has said that the military may be disproportionately Catholic and southern because Catholics and southerners are able to deal instinctively with authority and hierarchy. Conservatives are, on the whole, the party of authority, and liberals are, with equal pride, anti-authoritarian. Liberalism arose in part as a revolt against the authority of the church, of scripture, of the divine right of kings. Liberals, again instinctively, worry that authority is often the enemy of reason, liberty, and self-direction.

Kirk also notes that conservatism has "an affection for the proliferating variety and mystery of human existence, as opposed to the narrowing uniformity, egalitarianism and utilitarian aims of most radical systems." His phrase teaches us a great deal about why conservatives, especially religious conservatives, disagree with liberals, especially secular liberals, on such matters as abortion and stem-cell research.

One sentence from a manifesto on cultural conservatism released in 1987 by the Free Congress Foundation captures the ways in which these strands of religious conviction and conservative sentiment came together in our politics. "Cultural conservatism," the manifesto declared, "is the belief that there is a necessary, unbreakable and causal relationship between western, Judeo-Christian values, definitions of right and wrong, ways of thinking and ways of living—the parameters of western cultures—and the secular success of western societies."

Nothing any liberal says will alter these fundamental affinities between religion and conservatism. And yet some of us insist that they are not the only affinities, that in American history, at least, there is a parallel tendency in which religion's reverence for tradition is challenged by (and sometimes leads to) religion's insistence upon justice and its rebukes to the status quo. Large parts of the tradition work *against* traditionalism. This is in keeping with Jaroslav Pelikan's insightful observation that where tradition is the *living* religion of the dead, traditionalism is the *dead* religion of the living.

II

There is another important fact about religion and liberalism in the United States: precisely because we Americans did not experience the religious wars as Europe did, American liberalism was always more tempered in its attitude toward faith than the European variety. It is why the rise of the neo-atheists comes as something of a surprise in the American context. By and large, religious Americans returned liberalism's favor, embracing the regime of liberty and pluralism. The conflict between liberalism and religion over the last three decades is thus a break from U.S. history, an anachronistic replay of Europe's nineteenth-century battles that Peter Steinfels described.

American liberalism cannot be understood apart from an understanding of its religious sources. No less a rationalist than John Dewey, nurtured in a New England Congregationalism from which he drifted, could call the great fundamentalist William Jennings Bryan "the backbone of philanthropic social interest, of social reform through political action, of pacifism, of popular education." Today, Bryan is best known for his passionate opposition to Darwin and evolution. But it was Bryan, says Michael Kazin, his definitive biographer, who "transformed his party from a bulwark of conservatism . . . into a bastion of anticorporate Progressivism." Bryan preached "a simple pragmatic Gospel: only mobilized citizens, imbued with Christian morality, could save the nation from 'predatory' interests and the individuals who did their bidding." Garry Wills has noted that Bryan could point with pride to the success of the many causes he had championed "in their embattled earlier stages." The catalogue is impressive: women's suffrage, the federal income tax, railroad regulation, currency reform, state initiative and referendum, a Department of Labor, campaign fund disclosure, and opposition to capital punishment.

Bryan's progressivism was not eccentric among believers. The Social Gospel arose in the early twentieth century from the reflections of religious social workers and activists confronting the contradiction between the promises of God's kingdom and the conditions in the slums. Advocates of the Social Gospel were among those who cheered Theodore Roosevelt in 1912 when he declared, "We stand at Armageddon and we battle for the Lord." The Lord, in this instance, was presumed to be on the side of TR's Progressive party.

The progressive spirit was alive within Catholicism no less than within Protestantism. The Catholic Bishops' 1919 Program of Social Reconstruction was a primary source of New Deal ideas—I explore this in more detail later—and laid the basis for the close cooperation between the Church and the trade-union movement in the 1930s and 1940s. The link between religion and social reform was not artificial; it was the natural outgrowth of religion's skepticism of materialism and its search for what was called in the civil rights years a "beloved community." The religiously inspired could not help but question the impact of industrialization on family life—and on the morals of those packed into impoverished urban neighborhoods. What's striking is that the American religious reformers did not, on the whole, lapse into nostalgia for rural life. They were occasionally utopian, but most were realistic and, as Bryan's record shows, creative in the reforms they proposed.

If religious reformers nurtured liberalism's communitarian wing, American liberalism also strengthened the advocates of toleration and pluralism within the religious community. The great reforms in the Catholic Church at the Second Vatican Council were championed by American bishops, inspired by John Courtney Murray. The American theologian helped overturn that earlier orthodoxy declaring liberalism "a sin." Murray deserves part of the credit for Pope John XXIII's achievement. American liberalism may thus have helped ease Europe's conflicts between believers and secularists. That makes all the more peculiar our recent turn toward European-style polarization between religion and liberal values.

Religious thinkers also transformed liberalism itself, and no one more so than Reinhold Niebuhr, who taught liberals about St. Augustine and original sin. Liberalism was easily attacked for a soupy optimism about human nature and for a self-righteous idealism that had little self-awareness. With the rise of the Nazis and the Stalinists in the 1930s, this optimism collapsed. Niebuhr imbued American liberalism with realism—about the world in general and human nature in particular. He thus rescued the liberal creed from sentimentalism. He was tough on liberals who thought they could stay out of the world's conflicts (which is why today's hawks love him), but also tough on liberals who would engage in crusades and disguise self-interest behind noble, utopian claims (which means that today's doves are coming to appreciate him as someone who would likely have warned against the hubris underlying our intervention in Iraq). Niebuhr provided liberals with a credo: "Man's capacity for justice makes democracy possible, but man's capacity for injustice makes democracy necessary." Hope for democracy is tempered by an awareness of sin that only reinforces the democratic imperative. No wonder a Harvard historian announced the creation of a notional organization called Atheists for Niebuhr. No wonder Abraham Joshua Heschel would write upon Niebuhr's death that "the world will be darker without you." Heschel was right in ways he might not have imagined.

It would be decidedly un-Niebuhrian to believe that the American love affair between religion and liberalism could continue uninterrupted by contention. It was, to begin with, a love affair between liberalism and *certain kinds* of religion. There was an Old Christian Right—its history is brilliantly documented by the historian Leo Ribuffo—that had nothing in common with liberalism and flirted with anti-Semitism and fascism. There were liberals and socialists who never lost their antipathy to religion as an opiate of the masses, and some, like the best-selling journalist of the 1940s and 1950s, Paul Blanshard, who never gave up their mistrust of the Roman Church. There were conservative Christians who, as Niebuhr wrote in 1960, held to "the old individualistic Calvinism, which assumed the private virtues of industry, honesty, and thrift made public policy in dealing with rising industry unnecessary." There were segregationists who believed that the separation of the races was ordained by God.

But there can be no denying that beginning in the 1960s, there was a new rupture between liberalism and those religious traditionalists who had once been allied to progressivism. That decade saw the rise of a new skepticism about social control and a new emphasis on personal autonomy in moral matters. Until then, most religious progressives believed that self-improvement and self-control were intimately linked to the cause of social reform itself. They were prepared to use the state to regulate not only rapacious capitalists, but also the behavior of individuals. Their great experiment in this regard was Prohibition, which failed, but the link it embodied between self-improvement and social improvement endured for decades, a point that will draw more attention in chapter 3.

Yet, since the 1960s, as Peter Steinfels has said, "American liberalism has shifted its passion from issues of economic deprivation and concentration of power to issues of gender, sexuality, and personal choice. . . . Once trade unionism, regulation of the market, and various welfare measures were the litmus tests of secular liberalism. Later, desegregation and racial justice were the litmus tests. Today the litmus test is abortion." And, one might add, stem-cell research, gay marriage, and Hollywood culture.

This rupture, and not simply shrewd organizing by Jerry Falwell, Ralph Reed, or Karl Rove, accounts for the rise of the religious Right. The liberalism of Niebuhr's day lived comfortably within an old-fashioned world evoked movingly by his daughter Elisabeth Sifton in her book *The Serenity Prayer*. Contemporary liberalism is understandably conflicted about that world, given the huge advances in freedom over the last forty years for women, homosexuals, and, of course, African Americans. Niebuhr, himself a strong civil rights advocate, helped pioneer many of these changes. But it is undeniable that the new moral issues split the very religious institutions that, in an earlier time, were largely sympathetic to liberalism's demands for social reform. One wonders: What would William Jennings Bryan do? Would he be furious at Karl Rove for hijacking evangelicals into the party that supports corporate power and wants to reverse the progressive tax code? Or would Bryan, reluctantly perhaps, join with Republican social conservatives to defend his values and his faith?

That question may seem beside the point to latter-day liberals. They would note, correctly, that many religious Americans are already allied with liberalism, or at least the Democratic party: a large majority of Jews, at least half of Roman Catholics, a growing number of mainline Protestants, most African American churchgoers, a significant minority of white evangelicals, and most followers of traditions other than Christianity and Judaism. As for right-wing Christians, they did not support liberal causes in Niebuhr's or Abraham Heschel's day either. And secular voters represent a slowly rising share of the electorate.

This is true, but it fails to address the tug of social conservatism on many Americans who are otherwise open to the very kind of liberalism that Bryan (or, for that matter, Niebuhr) represented. It fails to deal seriously with religious moderates whose social views are broadly tolerant but who share with conservatives an unease about the direction of the culture—people who may be sympathetic to gays and lesbians but have no use for trashy television. It fails to recognize that there is loss as well as gain when too sharp a line is drawn between those in politics who emphasize social change and those who emphasize self-improvement. You do not have to be a neoconservative to believe that the public interest does depend, at least in part, on private virtue, as James Q. Wilson argued long ago.

Many have longed for a new Reinhold Niebuhr to inspire a new generation of religious liberals. I have shared in that longing. But it is doubtful that even Niebuhr could be Niebuhr now. In any event, can you think of a talk show that would book him? But I would imagine that Niebuhr, with his gift for searching for the truth in his adversary's error and the error in his own truth, would insist that liberals abandon their prejudices about people of faith, even those who vote the wrong way. Liberals, after all, regularly call on others to abandon their own prejudices. One could imagine Niebuhr and religious progressives of his stripe calling upon liberals to challenge some aspects of the commercial culture. When TV networks and Hollywood exploit sex to make money, shouldn't liberals ask why the very free market so revered by the right wing promotes values that the very same right wing claims to despise? I could see Niebuhr asking why liberals are often tongue-tied in exposing this contradiction.

And even when they espouse choice on abortion, is it so difficult for liberals to describe the choice itself as, at best, tragic? Is it really hard to see abortion as a moral problem and to understand why many of liberalism's potential allies see it as a moral evil? At the very least, liberals should insist that the surest way to reduce the number of abortions is to improve social conditions, especially the circumstances of the poor. (As we will see in chapter 4, many liberals are coming to exactly this conclusion.) The vast majority of religious Americans, including many who call themselves conservative, still feel a calling to the poor, still understand that families have interests that the market does not defend, and still worry, as Bryan did, about concentrated power—economic as well as political. These, too, are moral issues.

III

The current moment is best understood as the third stage in our ongoing national debate over religious liberty.

The first and longest stage so far—it lasted from the founding of the Republic to well into the twentieth century—was the era of white Protestant hegemony. I use this phrase not in a pejorative sense, but simply as a description of reality. Protestantism did much to shape our national character, our nation's identity, and much of our public rhetoric, to the point where American Jews and Catholics and Muslims and Sikhs and atheists are more than a little bit Protestant. That's something my friends in the Vatican used to note with some frustration when I was covering Rome as a journalist in the mid-1980s. Our nation drew upon this shared Protestant spirit to connect people to one another and to the institutions of their common democracy. Lincoln's second inaugural address may have been one of the finest statements of this common identity—particularly powerful because it acknowledged the ironies of both the North and the South praying for victory to the same God in the midst of a great Civil War.

If not everyone shared in this Protestant identity in a theological sense, everyone more or less identified with the institutions it upheld. One of the great virtues of this American Protestantism is that it underwrote religious toleration and liberty. It is that commitment to religious liberty that allowed Catholics and Jews and then Muslims and many others to settle here and, ultimately, help unsettle Protestant dominance.

White Protestant hegemony in America—the first stage—began to erode with the Scopes trial and the end of Prohibition, arguably the last political project to unite mainline and fundamentalist Protestants. But the formal dominance of Protestantism was not repealed until the 1960s—with, it must be said, the strong support of many moderate and progressive Protestants themselves. Thus began the second stage.

The second stage involved a hard push for church-state separation, reflected in decisions by the Supreme Court under Chief Justice Earl Warren—notably the ruling banning prescribed prayer in the public schools. It was no accident that all this occurred as the country was coming to terms with its historic treatment of minorities.

This stage was marked by John F. Kennedy's election as president, which symbolized the full entry of Roman Catholics into the mainstream of American civic life. At the same time, the civil rights movement sought to right historic wrongs done to African Americans. Long-standing barriers to Jews, including the effective end of restrictive covenants, were swept away. It led to new movements to defend the rights of immigrants from Latin America, Asia, and the Caribbean. Their numbers became even larger after the liberalization of immigration laws in 1965. In all their racial diversity, these groups brought with them religious diversity as well. All this brought the pervasively white and Protestant ethos in government-financed institutions and society into question.

The third stage of the debate, which we are still going through now, reflects a concern—and it's a concern that goes beyond the religious Right—that the push to reduce Protestant Christianity's role has had the effect of marginalizing faith's public role altogether. Had the public square become not simply neutral, not simply more open, but actually hostile to religion? Had our nation, as Stephen Carter asked in *The Culture of Disbelief*, replaced old prejudices (of race and religion) with a new prejudice against belief itself?

The new activism of stage three, which took root slowly in the 1960s and burst out into the open in the early 1980s, came from a sense that religious voices had been marginalized for far too long in the dominant cultural and political discourse. Many white evangelical Christians in particular felt they had been treated as ignorant hicks by a variety of elites, including journalists, intellectuals, and the producers of the programs that appeared on the televisions in their homes. They reacted against the Supreme Court for its ruling on abortion in *Roe v. Wade* and the ban on prescribed public school prayers—which tended to be Protestant in inspiration, one reason why the Court saw them as discriminatory against religious minorities, including Catholics and Jews.

Central to the polemics of the 1980s, after the rise of the Moral Majority, was the insistence that in a democratic republic, religious citizens had as much of a right to political influence and respectful attention as those who held secular views. "The religious person is entitled, if not to prevail, at least to be heard," wrote Terry Eastland, later the publisher of the *Weekly Standard*, in an influential 1981 essay, "In Defense of Religious America." Eastland argued that the "religious person can expect to be allowed a voice in matters of public policy. He can expect that his religion will not disqualify him from speaking on political matters, and that if he offers a religious or ethical justification for his position on a public issue, it will not *ipso facto* be considered out of the bounds of public discourse." Richard John Neuhaus published *The Naked Public Square* in 1984, warning that marginalizing religion had deleterious effects on public life and that new religious voices would have to be accommodated:

> If the myths of secularism are collapsing, and if there is a resurgence of publicly potent religion, we need to look for quite unprecedented ways of relating politics and religion. Our question can certainly not be the old one of whether religion and politics should be mixed. They

inescapably do mix, like it or not. The question is whether we can devise forms for that interaction which can revive rather than destroy the liberal democracy that is required by a society that would be pluralistic and free.

At the moment Eastland and Neuhaus were offering their arguments, such defenses of religion's public role were frequently seen as an apologia for religious conservatism. Religious conservatives undeniably played a key role in this challenge by pushing for a restoration of the consensus on values they saw as existing before the revolts of the 1960s. But this misses the fact that many religious Americans *who were not conservative* also objected to what they saw as an ingrained bias in mainstream media, academia, and politics against the efforts of people of faith to influence politics for religious reasons.

It's worth noting that most of the religious conservatives who mobilized politically during this third stage have repeatedly insisted that their goal is not the creation of a Christian nation—even though some in their ranks talked that way—but to preserve their own culture and faith commitments. The Christian conservatives cast themselves as a beleaguered minority suffering under the oppression of Washington and Hollywood. This talk bears out what Nathan Glazer has written in another context, that "we're all multiculturalists now." Religious conservatives saw themselves demanding recognition as African Americans and Latinos had done beginning in the 1960s. Ralph Reed, the Christian conservative leader, was careful in his choice of words in describing his movement's goals. He said the Christian Right sought "a place at the table." He did not propose to take ownership of the table, or to drive others away from the table. You might argue that the use of the phrase "a place at the table" by a leader of the religious conservative movement represents the true triumph of religious pluralism—even if many on the religious right seemed to want far more than Reed claimed they did.

IV

The clearest symbol of the difference between the second and third stages is the sharp contrast between the way John F. Kennedy treated his faith as a public issue in the 1960 presidential campaign and how Joe Lieberman treated his faith when he ran for vice president in 2000.

Both broke barriers as representatives of minority religions—specifically, as non-Protestants—in public life. But Kennedy made the case for
his own election on the grounds that his religion was *not important at all*
to his role as a politician. His central assertion, politically necessary at the
time, was that if ever his faith came into conflict with the Constitution or
the public interest, he would resign. And, in truth, few outside the most
anti-Catholic quarters (and certainly no one who actually knew Kennedy,
as Arthur Schlesinger Jr. noted) believed that was even remotely possible.

Joe Lieberman's approach could not have been more different. He
praised God in public. He thanked God for his new public role. He spoke
at length about the importance of his faith and about the legitimacy of a
politician bringing his or her faith to the public arena. Unlike Kennedy,
Lieberman said: *My religion is really, really important to me.* He joked that
as a result of all this, he became known as "Holy Joe," a title he said his
mother quite liked but that he did not like at all.

Notice: to win acceptance from Protestants, especially evangelical Protestants, it was absolutely essential for Kennedy to play *down* his faith. But
when Lieberman did the exact opposite by playing *up* his faith and speaking of God, his aim was seen as an effort to reassure and win over the
very same groups of evangelical Protestants (or perhaps their children and
grandchildren).

In truth, Lieberman was simply more religious than Kennedy was. But
their different approaches also reflected the different historical moments
in which they found themselves. In Kennedy's time, the fear to be addressed among conservative Protestants was that a politician was not Protestant. In Lieberman's time, the fear to be addressed among conservative
Protestants was that a politician was not religious enough. Thus a characteristic difference between the second and third stages.

This is a huge historical shift. There was once a time when the separation of church and state was a cardinal commandment of Southern Baptists and nearly all evangelical Protestants. For most of these Protestants,
to spend even a dime of public money on religious schools or church
programs was to assail the Founders, destroy religious freedom, and turn
God into a servant of the state. And it's worth recalling that a separationist
argument that now is allied with pluralism was once directed against it.

When Catholic immigrants began flooding into America from Ireland
in the 1840s, there was strong Protestant opposition to any government
assistance to the schools the Catholics were establishing. As John

McGreevy has documented in his magnificent history, *Catholicism and American Freedom*, separationism in this case was less about protecting government or religion than in opposing any expansion of "Popery." Similar fights broke out from the late 1940s through the 1960s over government aid to parochial schools. Eleanor Roosevelt carried out a famous and bitter public argument with New York's Cardinal Spellman on the issue.

What's striking now is that conservative Protestants who long opposed aid to Catholic schools now find themselves allied with a large share of Catholics in favoring government-financed vouchers for private schools.

For all the divisive political conflicts it has entailed, the third stage of America's experience of religious liberty—which is an attempt to honor *both* halves of the First Amendment, its free expression clause *and* its nonestablishment clause—has already borne some practical fruit.

An example of successful renegotiation was reflected in the 1995 federal guidelines to school administrators. They were designed to make clear that while government cannot impose religion, students cannot be forced to be secular against their will or silenced in their personal expressions of faith. Henceforth individual students could not be stopped from praying. Jewish students could not be barred from wearing yarmulkes. Children who wanted to talk about religion on school grounds had the right to do so. As President Bill Clinton said at the time, evoking language from the civil rights era, the Constitution "does not require children to leave their religion at the schoolhouse door."

Renegotiation has also worked in the area of the religious rights of federal employees. In 1997 the Clinton administration issued guidelines requiring government supervisors to respect individual expressions of faith by government workers. Christians, the guidelines said, can keep Bibles on their desks, Muslim women can wear head scarves, Jewish workers should be accommodated as much as possible in scheduling so they can honor the Jewish High Holidays.

This may have seemed like common sense, but it reflected an awareness that a desire to preserve religious freedom entails keeping the government out of the way *and* protecting the free expression of believers. And it underscored the difference between an American approach to religious toleration aimed at accommodating religious expression and the French style of toleration—known as *laicité*—that sought religious peace by clearing religion out of the public realm as much as possible. At this moment in history, which is the more promising approach?

Consider the 2003 controversy in France over the ban on Muslim head scarves and other conspicuous religious symbols in the country's public schools. President Jacques Chirac's stand on the issue called forth some startling ironies.

On a weekend in December 2003, the Iranian Foreign Ministry spokesman Hamid Reza Asefi condemned the Chirac government for "an extremist decision aimed at preventing the development of Islamic values" in France. Imagine being called "extremist" on a religious question by an official of the Iranian government! Meanwhile, thousands of French Muslims demonstrated in favor of the veil. The Associated Press reported at the time that some Muslim girls in France were thinking of attending Roman Catholic schools so they could continue to wear their head scarves. Astounding, no? The French government's heavy emphasis on secularism was, of course, deeply rooted in the country's history, in a reaction against Catholicism's dominance of the state before the French Revolution and the church's opposition to liberal values from the eighteenth century into the early part of the twentieth century. At the beginning of the twenty-first century, Muslim women were seeking to vindicate their religious rights through Catholic institutions.

And how often did the Bush administration have the opportunity to out-liberal the French? At the time, John V. Hanford III, the U.S. ambassador-at-large for international religious freedom, chided the French government and declared that students who wore visible religious symbols as "a heartfelt manifestation of their beliefs" have "a basic right that should be protected."

An anonymous French official who spoke to the *New York Times* said dryly of our country, "Very often there are debates on the Pledge of Allegiance or other religious issues in the schools. Never have you heard a French diplomat comment on an internal debate in the United States."

Chirac actually deserved more credit than he received at the time for linking his decision on head scarves with a necessary call for a renewed "fight against xenophobia, racism and anti-Semitism." He acted in response to both liberal and right-wing fears. French liberals worry about the rise of anti-Semitism, about the challenge that head scarves pose to women's rights, and, more generally, about the deeply antiliberal nature of certain forms of Islam. The French far Right had gained ground by exploiting prejudice against Muslim immigrants.

We Americans, moreover, could usefully exercise some humility before pretending that a simple imposition of the American model of pluralism would solve Europe's problems. Europe is seeking to accommodate a large and relatively recent wave of Muslim immigration at a moment when a violent strain of Islam has been gaining ground. As Ian Buruma demonstrates in *Murder in Amsterdam: The Death of Theo van Gogh and the Limits of Tolerance*, this is a challenge not simply to secularism, but also to every version of liberal pluralism. And before Americans crow, we should reflect on the fact of religious bigotry in our own history.

Nonetheless, there are decided advantages to the American approach. Both France and the United States see their respective governments as "secular" in the sense that they do not sponsor any particular faith. But as the historian Wilfred McClay has noted, there are at least two kinds of secularism. One is largely "negative," aimed at protecting religion from government establishment and interference. The other sees secularism as "an alternative faith" that "supersedes the tragic blindness and destructive irrationalities of the historical religions." People are free to act on their religious beliefs in private, McClay has written, "as long as they do not trouble the rest of us with them, or bestir the proverbial horses."

McClay is critical of this view and prefers the "negative" approach because it limits the government's claims and respects religion's contribution to the public realm. On the whole, the United States has operated within this pluralistic framework, while French secularism has been more aggressive in pushing religion to the margins.

The conflicts that confronted Chirac and face other Western nations suggest that America's form of secularism may, as McClay has written, provide "an essential basis for peaceful coexistence in a religiously pluralistic society." American-style secularism is rooted in a basic respect for religious traditions and not in hostility to religion. It has certainly eased the integration of new Muslim immigrants into the mainstream of American life. Neo-atheists have argued that religion has a natural tendency to monopolize power because of its claims to monopolize truth, and that the only sensible response is to insist upon the total secularization of the public sphere. This is a serious argument. But the American story, at least, suggests that despite the risks involved, respecting the public role of the many who believe, and who believe in diverse ways, is the more promising way to expand freedom's writ. The pressure that brought forth the third stage in America's debate over religious freedom was built into America's very particular form of secularism from the beginning.

The third stage means that religiously inflected arguments have been granted standing in a no-longer-naked public square. "We're no longer overlooked, persecuted, discriminated against, and misquoted in the mainstream media," an editorial in *Christianity Today*, the flagship evangelical magazine, declared in 2005. "So we've been mainstreamed, now what?" Now what?—exactly the right question.

V

With religion's public role accepted to the point that Democratic politicians from Hillary Clinton to Barack Obama and John Edwards have all explicitly appealed for the votes of "people of faith," is it possible to envision a radically new role for religious groups in American politics? This is not only possible but necessary, for the sake of our public life, and for religion's sake as well.

Conservatives like the religious landscape just the way it is—or, perhaps more accurately, just the way it was before conservatism started falling apart in the years after the 2004 election. That is why liberals should take on the challenge of rearranging that landscape and welcome the change that has already begun. "Fundamentalists rush in where liberals fear to tread," the political philosopher Michael Sandel has written. "A politics that brackets morality and religion too completely soon generates its own disenchantment."

Liberals should certainly not be complicit in this disenchantment. They should embrace unapologetically religion's contributions to a democratic, egalitarian spirit fostered by the equality of all souls before God, and the moral commitments that liberalism has underwritten.

Reflecting on the contributions of Niebuhr and historian and social critic Christopher Lasch, Richard Wightman Fox has written that religion can be seen

> both as a democratic social power—a capacity to build community— and as a tragic perspective that acknowledges the perennial failing of human beings to make community endure. . . . Religion allows people to grapple with the human mysteries that neither science nor politics

can address. But it also provides a force that science and politics can call on in their effort to understand and transform the social world.

All of us—liberal or conservative, moderate, libertarian, or socialist—should remember that religion's role can be both paradoxical and ironic. Religion can promote reaction or revolution, inclusiveness or exclusion, universalism or parochialism.

Liberals who are not believers cannot be asked to take up a faith they reject. Nor should liberals, whether believers or not, ever be silent about the abuses of faith or the dangers of religious fanaticism. In protecting personal freedom, liberals protect the believer and the atheist, the seeker and the agnostic, alike. And the last thing American politics needs right now are politicians who pretend to religious belief in pursuit of some critical swing vote. It was said in Hollywood that what you need is sincerity, and if you can fake that, you can do anything. But faking religious belief is one of the worst ideas I can think of.

Still, liberals should not be afraid to live up to their vocation of insisting that believers and unbelievers alike join in the quest Peter Berger described as "a common journey toward the truth." They do so accepting, as John Kennedy said, "that here on earth, God's work must truly be our own."

All religious traditions interact with their times. Some reject the spirit of their times. Some are swallowed up. Most traditions survive by finding a balance between preserving their integrity and adjusting to new conditions, and new revelations. The United Church of Christ nicely captured this dynamic process with its campaign built around the slogan "God is still speaking." To take the most obvious example: the Enlightenment waged war on the imposition of religion through force, and many religious traditions—often after some struggle, as we have seen in the case of the Catholic Church—eventually adapted to the lessons it had to teach.

It is usually forgotten that Pope Benedict XVI's 2006 address at Germany's Regensburg University that drew so much fire (including, it should be said, from me) for its comments on Islam included a powerful acknowledgment of the contributions of the Age of Reason and the Enlightenment to the Church and the world. Benedict argued that his "critique of modern reason" was a critique "from within" and

> has nothing to do with putting the clock back to the time before the Enlightenment and rejecting the insights of the modern age. The positive aspects of modernity are to be acknowledged unreservedly: we are

all grateful for the marvelous possibilities that it has opened up for
mankind and for the progress in humanity that has been granted to us.
The scientific ethos, moreover, is the will to be obedient to the truth,
and, as such, it embodies an attitude which reflects one of the basic
tenets of Christianity. The intention here is not one of retrenchment
or negative criticism, but of broadening our concept of reason and its
application. While we rejoice in the new possibilities open to humanity,
we also see the dangers arising from these possibilities and we must ask
ourselves how we can overcome them. We will succeed in doing so only
if reason and faith come together in a new way, if we overcome the self-
imposed limitation of reason to the empirically verifiable, and if we
once more disclose its vast horizons.

If Pope Benedict, that staunch defender of orthodoxy, is open and explicit in acknowledging his own tradition's debt to "the positive aspects
of modernity," doing so should not be so difficult for other believers.

Religion is, necessarily, both conservative and progressive. Religion is
rooted in tradition and survives through development and change within
the tradition. It applies old truths to new circumstances. It also reexamines
old truths in light of new circumstances. The conservative insists that the
tradition not be distorted merely to accommodate passing fads and fash-
ions. The progressive insists on purifying and clarifying the tradition by
freeing it from the distortions of cultural encrustations of the past. The
conservative keeps the tradition alive by honoring it. The progressive keeps
the tradition alive by adapting it, and sometimes by challenging it.

That is why religious conservatives and progressives should welcome
David Hollenbach's call to "intellectual solidarity." They need each other
more than they know. But it is hard for those on either side to realize this
when culture wars are said to be raging all around them.

2. Why the Culture War Is the Wrong War

RELIGION, VALUES, AND AMERICAN POLITICS

Is there a culture war in the United States? Of course. There always has been and always will be.

Those who battle today over gay marriage or abortion might usefully remember our unusual national experiment with banning the sale of alcohol, one of America's defining cultural moments. It pitted self-control (or puritanism) against pleasure (or self-indulgence), immigrants against the native-born, Protestants against Catholics—and, yes, Protestants against Protestants, the drinking Lutherans and Episcopalians against the abstemious Baptists and Methodists. This being America, even the moralists had a sense of humor about themselves. "They pray for Prohibition," went the ditty, "and then they vote for gin."

Of course we have culture wars, because there are so many different kinds of us. The Scots-Irish and the Yankees created very different cultures and different forms of politics: witness the long-standing historical differences between New Hampshire and Vermont. When Irish and Italian immigrants weren't battling each other, they were fighting the old-family English, a.k.a. the WASP establishment. When the establishment ran short on votes, it enlisted one immigrant group or another—the Italians in New York, the French Canadians in New England—to battle the Irish or some other rising culture.

Of course we have culture wars, because the great nation to our south is Spanish-speaking. Mexican Americans have been part of us from the beginning—from before the beginning, actually, since some of our country is conquered Mexican territory. They are thoroughly American, no less assimilated than Italians were a century ago. But they also have a culture and language of their own, and that makes some Anglos uneasy.

Of course we have culture wars, because we have always been a nation in which big-city values fight the values of the countryside. "Burn down your cities and leave our farms, and your cities will spring up again as if by magic," declared William Jennings Bryan, the Great Commoner who spoke for country folk. "But destroy our farms, and the grass will grow in the streets of every city in the country." Now, that's cultural warfare. Americans thinking of themselves as "modern" and "advanced" have always battled other Americans whom they wrote off as backward and parochial. The people dismissed as backward have always looked down on highfalutin big-city folks as hopelessly immoral. Today these battling types are all intermixed in suburbs and exurbs, though they try hard to congregate with their own kind.

And yes, we are black and white, and some of what passes for cultural warfare is also racial conflict. We are a country that waged a civil war over slavery and states' rights. Whether you explain that war in terms of the former or of the latter is still a sign, more than 140 years after it ended, of where your sympathies lie.

This history is important because we talk about the culture war as if it were a novel creation of the late twentieth and early twenty-first centuries, and only recently a factor in our politics. There is a hidden assumption that we were once a happy, homogenous nation that came apart only when hippies preached free love, the religious Right rose, secularists became more assertive, the Supreme Court began issuing liberal decisions, talk-show hosts began yelling, and intelligent designers began lobbying school boards.

Our perception of today's cultural battlefield is shaped by a view of the 1950s as conflict-free. So we forget that the seeds of modern feminism were planted in Ozzie and Harriet's day, with the rise of a large generation of well-educated women. We forget that the hippies of the 1960s were preceded by the Beats of the 1950s. *On the Road* was published in 1957, not 1967. Norman Podhoretz, who was to become a central figure in the rise of neoconservatism, gave hints of the battles to come when, as a liberal, he wrote a devastating attack in 1958 on the Beat sensibility of Jack Kerouac. Before the battles in the 1960s and 1970s to legalize abortion, there were fights in the late 1940s to legalize birth control. We think of today's conflicts over the display of monuments in honor of the Ten Commandments as the product of a uniquely fractious time. But Americans have always argued over the public role of the Ten Commandments. Several citizens died in Philadelphia after riots in 1844 over which version of the Bible (including which version of the commandments) should be used in the public schools.

So we should not be surprised today by battles over abortion and gay marriage, divisions between the more and the less religious, and fierce struggles over who should sit on the Supreme Court, how to settle the fate of those near the end of their lives, and whether or not the government should finance stem-cell research. We should not be surprised that these issues lurked so large in recent elections. The culture war is nothing new. It is also not exactly what we think it is.

II

The great virtue of the culture-war argument is also its great flaw: we can all use the debate to present our ideal visions or fierce criticisms of the United States, our pet views on human nature, our dreams about how politics (or the entertainment industry, the schools, or family life) should be organized. The empirical argument over whether there is a culture war is often lost in polemics about which side one should take.

My view (and it can be subjected to all these criticisms) is unapologetically Clintonian: yes, there is a culture war, and no, there isn't. It depends on what the meaning of "culture war" is.

If one looks primarily at the extremes of opinion (and I use "extremes" descriptively, not pejoratively), of course there is a deep cultural conflict in the United States. It is waged between the 15 to 20 percent of the country that is largely religious and staunchly conservative and the 15 to 20 percent that is largely secular and staunchly liberal. One can quibble about the exact numbers at each end; religious conservatives probably outnumber secular liberals, though the secular group is growing. But there is no doubt that these two groups exist, have very strong feelings, and on the whole can't stand each other. They regularly toss epithets across their divide. The godly attack the ungodly. The tolerant attack the intolerant. The cosmopolitan attack the parochial. The rooted attack the rootless. Moralists attack the permissive.

But whatever the numbers, those most ardently engaged on both sides of this fight, taken together, do not constitute a majority of Americans. I would reckon (and much social-science evidence supports this) that 60 to 70 percent of us fall at some middle point.

Those in the middle may tilt a bit left or a bit right, but they often have mixed or ambivalent views. Many defy stereotypes: right-to-lifers for gay marriage; prochoicers against assisted suicide; devoutly religious liberals; decidedly agnostic conservatives. And many simply run away at the first sign that a cultural battle is about to break out.

Network exit polls in the 2004 election suggested how broad the non-warring middle is. Asked about abortion, 21 percent of the voters said that it should always be legal, 34 percent that it should mostly be legal, 26 percent that it should mostly be illegal, and 16 percent that it should always be illegal. Viewed one way, respondents were "prochoice" by a margin of 55 to 42 percent. Viewed another way, 60 percent of the electorate gravitated to a "middle" position on abortion. There most certainly is a conflict akin to a culture war among the 37 percent of Americans—21 percent consistently prochoice, 16 percent consistently prolife—who were absolutely certain about where they stood on abortion. The rest of the population watches the battle from the sidelines, sometimes with sympathy for one camp or the other, but without anything like the engagement or commitment of the true warriors.

Meanwhile, the exit polls found that 25 percent of voters thought gays and lesbians should be able to marry legally, 35 percent favored civil unions, and 37 percent opposed any legal recognition for gay relationships. These findings could be used mischievously by either side in the argument. It can truthfully be said that 72 percent of voters opposed gay marriage. With equal truthfulness it can be said that 60 percent favored either gay marriage or civil unions.

A case can be made that journalists, and political activists trying to mobilize constituencies, are largely responsible for the idea that we are polarized. The political scientist Morris Fiorina is not being excessively cynical when he says that the notion of a culture war gives life to "useful fund-raising strategies" on the part of culture warriors.

"Certainly, one can find a few warriors who engage in noisy skirmishes," Fiorina wrote in *Culture War? The Myth of a Polarized Society.* "Many of the activists in the political parties and the various cause groups do, in fact, hate each other and regard themselves as combatants in a war. But their hatreds are not shared by the great mass of the American people—certainly nowhere near to '80–90 percent of the country'—who are for the most part moderate in their views and tolerant in their manner."

Rather provocatively, Fiorina added: "The bulk of the American citizenry is somewhat in the position of the unfortunate citizens of some third-world countries who try to stay out of the crossfire while Maoist guerrillas and right-wing death squads shoot at each other."

Here again the yes-and-no answer to the culture-war question provides a useful correction. Fiorina is quite right that many Americans want to stay out of culture wars, and that we are on the whole both moderate and tolerant. Yet as the numbers on abortion and gay marriage suggest, the proportion of us who care a great deal about these matters is rather larger than his metaphor of guerrillas versus death squads would imply. And arguments about these questions are passionately carried on well beyond the elite level of American life.

It is also obvious that cultural and religious differences have played a major role in recent elections, few more so than in 2004. Americans who attend religious services more than once a week voted overwhelmingly for George W. Bush in 2004. Those who never attend voted heavily for John Kerry. As William Galston and Elaine Kamarck showed in their recent work *The Politics of Polarization*, written for the organization Third Way, this particular religious divide is something new. The old divisions have not gone away: one of the largest voting gaps is between blacks and whites, and there is also a divide between Jews, who are strongly Democratic, and white gentiles, who tilt Republican. But an additional divide pits traditionalist or orthodox believers of almost all stripes (including Orthodox Jews but not African American Christians) against doubters, unbelievers, and more liberal or "modernist" believers. There is considerable truth to Michael Barone's suggestion that religion has become "the great divider" in American elections. Not all of the polarization in American politics can be explained by attitudes toward religious faith, but some of it certainly can.

James Davison Hunter, a sociologist at the University of Virginia who introduced the culture-war concept to a wide audience, defines the orthodox or traditionalist view as "the commitment on the part of adherents to an external, definable, and transcendent authority." In progressivism, on the other hand, "moral authority tends to be defined by the spirit of the modern age, a spirit of rationalism and subjectivism."

These conflicting worldviews play out across many issues related to religion and science, family life and sexuality. Pundits did not invent the battle over Terri Schiavo's case or the arguments over whether intelligent design should be taught as part of science curricula in the public schools. Karl Rove was not a fool for deciding to mobilize Christian churches on Bush's behalf in 2004.

But neither was Rove a fool for encouraging Bush to speak cautiously on these matters, lest he turn off too many of that mass of moderate and tolerant voters to whom Fiorina rightly calls our attention. During his debates with John Kerry in 2004, Bush emphasized his respect for "the culture of life," but he would never say flatly that he favored overturning *Roe v. Wade*. Because those prolifers who were genuinely engaged in the warfare over abortion allowed Bush to speak in code, he did not have to drag more-moderate voters into a war they wanted no part of. Kerry tried to choreograph a similarly intricate cultural dance on gay marriage. He sent strong signals of sympathy to the gay community and criticized Bush for pushing a divisive issue into national politics. But Kerry also said explicitly that he was opposed to gay marriage.

This strange approach to politics, involving nudges, nods, and winks on cultural issues, reflects the real division in the nation: between those who want to have a culture war and those who don't. At election time political candidates need simultaneously to "rally the base," which includes a heavy quotient of culture warriors, and to "appeal to the center," meaning the majority (often left of center on economic issues), which sees health care, education, jobs, taxes, and national security as central concerns trumping gay marriage or abortion. The result is a strained, dysfunctional, and often dishonest political dialogue based on symbolic utterances. Hot-button questions that rally particular sectors of the electorate—and draw listeners and viewers to confrontational radio and television programs—preempt serious discussion of what ails American culture and society.

III

The 2004 election will be seen as marking a high point of polarization around issues related to religion and culture. Other urgent matters—economic insecurity, foreign policy, terrorism, health care, and of course the

Iraq War—already began to displace cultural and moral questions as voting issues in the 2006 elections.

President Bush's departure from the White House will almost certainly ease polarization, particularly around questions of culture and religion. Bush came to embody some of the nation's deepest divisions, and his campaigns played cleverly on moral conflicts. Yet as the Bush presidency wound down, there were signs that Republicans, including conservative Republicans, were realizing that an us-versus-them style was reaching the end of its useful life for their cause.

The 2008 Republican presidential field was hardly made to order for evangelical conservatives. Rudy Giuliani was a thrice-divorced social liberal, even if he did win Pat Robertson's endorsement. John McCain had vociferously (and courageously) attacked the religious Right when he ran against Bush in the 2000 Republican primaries—and his efforts to conciliate with religious conservatives bore little fruit. Mitt Romney tried to present himself as the authentic representative of religious conservatism. But to do so, he had to reverse his past positions on abortion and gay rights, and his Mormonism was an obstacle for some evangelicals. Fred Thompson hoped to be the candidate who profited from the weaknesses of his opponents among religious conservatives, but his own past (including lobbying work on behalf of a prochoice group) was hardly philosophically pure. Perhaps most significantly, the obvious evangelical hero, former Arkansas governor Mike Huckabee, a Baptist minister with strongly conservative positions on social issues, took to broadening the evangelical agenda by speaking critically of Wall Street and linking his Christian commitment to concern for the poor and their access to education and health care. Huckabee understood that the religious conversation was changing.

All this is true. Yet because 2004 shaped so much of our current understanding of cultural and religious politics—and also called forth much new organizing on the religious center and left—it's important to understand what happened in that momentous election, and what didn't.

In 2004, as we have seen, the exit poll found that Americans who attend religious services more than once a week voted for George W. Bush over John Kerry by a margin of 64 percent to 35 percent. By contrast, those who said they never went to services backed Kerry, 62 to 36 percent. Case on religiosity closed?

Not quite. Taken together, these two groups account for only about three voters in ten—16 percent of American voters go to religious services more than once a week and 15 percent never go. What of the rest? Again, there is a definite relationship between Republican leanings and church attendance, but it is not as strong as one would assume looking only at the most and least religious. Weekly attenders backed Bush, 58 to 41 percent. Those who attended once a month split evenly, 50 percent for Bush, 49 percent for Kerry. Those who attended religious services a few times a year backed Kerry 54 to 45 percent.

Consolidating the categories among those who participate at least some of the time in organized religion, the four voters in ten who attended religious services once a week or more gave Bush 61 percent of their ballots; the four voters in ten who participated only occasionally gave Bush 47 percent, a difference of 14 percent.

Without question, these numbers are important, and they explain why Democratic strategists have spent so much time since 2004 pondering God, faith, and the attitudes of religious believers. There is good reason to think that some of the passion in the nation's current political polarization is religious passion. It reflects a clash between ardent believers and those who are less devout or highly skeptical.

But this is not the whole story. There are factors that matter even more than religious commitment in American politics, most notably race. And there are factors that compete with religious commitment in explaining the allegiances of voters, most notably class. There are local and regional factors that scramble class and religious differences. And in 2004 there was a question that mattered more to the electoral outcome than any of the issues related to faith: the war against terrorism.

Race has always been a factor in American politics, and since the 1964 election, fought in part around civil rights, the African American vote has been overwhelmingly Democratic. Despite small gains for Bush, that was the case in 2004. Where white voters backed Bush 58 to 41 percent, black voters supported Kerry, 88 to 11 percent. The black/white gap in support for Bush was 47 percent, a far larger difference than the divide between the most religious and the most secular voters.

Indeed, the impact of church attendance on voting decisions, while very strong among whites and noticeable among Latinos, was minimal among African Americans. Only 15 percent of African Americans who attend church weekly voted for Bush, whereas for whites and Latinos who attend church weekly, the percentages voting for Bush were 74 and 52, respectively.

It is striking that in all the talk about how Americans who are "religious" and "evangelical" are overwhelmingly conservative and Republican, so little attention is paid to African Americans. One of the most religious and evangelical groups in the nation, they are decidedly not Republican and are, on most issues, loyally liberal. It makes sense to argue that conservative Christianity is automatically allied with conservative politics, Andrew Greeley and Michael Hout note in their recent book, *The Truth about Conservative Christians*, "only if you want to exclude Afro-American Christians from the ranks of the religiously conservative." But ignoring African Americans, they write, "is a groundless exclusion. Their 'Evangelical' credentials are as good as anyone else's, in some cases marginally better." (Greeley and Hout explode other myths about conservatives Christians. For example, they found that conservative Protestants were marginally more likely to watch PBS news programs daily than other Americans— with the exception of those who say they have no religion, who watched at about the same rate. "If one finds the temptation irresistible to picture all 'Jesus people' as religious fanatics," Greeley and Hout write, "one should picture a fifth of them glued to PBS stations every evening.")

Republican strategists believe they can make inroads among blacks and Latinos by concentrating their attention on the most religious members of both communities. There is at least some evidence that church attendance modestly boosted Bush's share of the black vote, and this may have been especially important in Ohio. There, the Bush share of the African American vote—at 16 percent, according to the exit polls—was above his national average. The Bush campaign reportedly made a major investment in appealing to Ohio's African American voters, particularly around the issue of gay marriage, strongly opposed in the black churches. But even in Ohio, it was very hard to move African Americans away from loyalties that began developing during the New Deal and became firmly rooted during the civil rights years of the 1960s.

Religion played a large but complicated role in Bush's gains in the Latino community. Bush narrowly carried frequent churchgoers but lost among the less observant. Even more important was the sectarian divide among Latinos: a 2004 exit poll by the William C. Velasquez Institute found that Bush won 53 percent of the Latino Protestant vote, but only 30 percent of the Latino Catholic vote. The National Annenberg Election Survey produced similar results: 57 percent of Latino Protestants for Bush, compared with 33 percent of Latino Catholics.

Within the religious factor, there is also a strong regional factor. As data suggests, the South is more religiously observant than the rest of the United States. The West is considerably less observant. It cannot be stressed enough that the rise of the political influence of evangelicals in the Republican party is closely linked to the rise of white southerners as a key Republican constituency. Although evangelicalism has spread across the country, it still has a distinctly southern accent. A 2006 Pew Forum survey, for example, found that 52 percent of the nation's evangelicals live in the South, while only 31 percent of the rest of the population is southern. Evangelicals are much scarcer in the Northeast and in the West than in the country as a whole. Religious observance also varies sharply from state to state.

But analysis of data on religion, region, and race presents a classic chicken-and-egg problem. Southern whites are, all at once, more religious, more conservative, and more Republican than the rest of the country. This means that the national pool of frequent churchgoers includes a moderately disproportionate share of southerners. The Pacific Coast states are considerably less observant religiously than the rest of the country. It is thus important to disentangle the effects of region and race on religious observance and voting.

White southerners began to turn to the Republican party long before the rise of the religious Right, in reaction to the Democratic party's support for civil rights laws. Many conservative whites who switched sides were evangelical or fundamentalist Protestants, but their new voting behavior was not driven by religion. The conversion of white southerners into Republicans began with Barry Goldwater's campaign in 1964, continued with George C. Wallace as an independent conservative way station in 1968, and reached culmination in 1972, when Richard Nixon pursued his "southern strategy" aimed at whites in the South. The overlap between race and religion was underscored by the findings of Albert J. Menendez, a careful student of religious voting. He estimated that in 1972 Richard Nixon defeated George McGovern by a margin of thirteen million to three million among fundamentalists and evangelicals. In the nation's ninety-six most heavily Baptist counties, Menendez found that Nixon secured 75 percent of the vote. Jimmy Carter won back a good share of that vote for the Democrats in 1976, then lost it to Ronald Reagan four years later. (Menendez estimates that in 1980, Carter ran 18 points behind his 1976 showing in the most heavily Baptist counties; in the nation as a whole, Carter ran only 10 points behind his showing four years earlier). But it's significant that running in 1980, *after* the rise of the Moral Majority and the organized religious Right, Reagan received a share of the Baptist vote that was still 15 percent below Nixon's.

Many on the left argue that the corporate allies of the wealthy understood their inability to win a majority of the electorate for a program based solely on their economic ideas, which tilted government policies toward their own interests and away from those of the majority. These groups therefore formed alliances with social and religious conservatives in an effort to encourage working- and middle-class voters to cast ballots on the basis of "values" issues and against their economic interests. This is a simplified version of the argument made in Tom Frank's important book, *What's the Matter with Kansas?* This view suggests that white voters at the lower end of the income structure were *pulled* (or, in the eyes of some, manipulated) into a new, conservative political coalition.

Frank was building on years of scholarship and reporting on the decline of class politics in the United States, including such notable works as Thomas Byrne Edsall and Mary D. Edsall's *Chain Reaction: The Impact of Race, Rights, and Taxes on American Politics* and Jonathan Rieder's *Canarsie: The Jews and Italians of Brooklyn against Liberalism.* The Edsalls and Rieder are especially shrewd on the importance of racial politics in cutting the Democratic party's traditional advantage in the white working class. They, like Frank, showed how cultural issues, often linked to religion, broke the New Deal coalition by creating a new group of working-class conservatives, later known as "Reagan Democrats," who often found themselves reacting against upper-middle-class social liberalism. This, therefore, is not a new phenomenon. It was, after all, Richard Nixon's 1972 campaign that cast George McGovern's liberalism as being devoted to the causes of "acid [as in LSD], amnesty [for draft resisters], and abortion."

Kevin Phillips's seminal 1969 work, *The Emerging Republican Majority,* made a powerful and—judging by subsequent electoral results—successful case for a new conservative and Republican politics of class among whites. It was based, as Phillips wrote, on "public anger over busing, welfare spending, environmental extremism, soft criminology, media bias and power, warped education, twisted textbooks, racial quotas, various guidelines and an ever expanding bureaucracy." Note here the mix of racial issues ("busing, welfare spending") and so-called values issues ("twisted textbooks," "warped education.") At the heart of the Phillips view was a critique of "limousine liberalism," a term introduced into American politics by conservative New York Democrat Mario Procaccino in 1969, and a defense of "middle America," a clarion call for Nixon-era conservatives. This approach was the precursor to the religious Right, a reaction to the "modernist liberation" movements among the well-off, well-educated, and college young. Phillips's class analysis was so hard-edged that the conservative *National Review*—to Phillips's pleasure—later accused the writer, as he moved leftward on economics, of "country and Western Marxism." It was more prophetic than the magazine might have realized, given the way conservative politicians (even wealthy Yale-educated presidents) would later use country music and NASCAR races to cast theirs as a movement of "real people" against the upper-class snobs.

The argument received a certain intellectual heft when Irving Kristol and other neoconservatives introduced the idea of the "new class," borrowed from Milovan Djilas, a dissident Yugoslav Marxist. It was an elastic term that could refer to reform-minded intellectuals and bureaucrats generally and to specific groups ranging from Marxist professors and do-gooder social workers to activist lawyers and psychologists who defended permissive sexuality. Thus was born the idea of the "elitist liberal" that was to haunt Democratic candidates from McGovern to John Kerry.

Again, it's important to put today's arguments in historical perspective: the rightward shift among white voters, particularly in the South, was first noticed more than three decades ago. Put another way: *the movement of white evangelical southerners into Republican ranks was fueled initially by civil rights and a reaction against liberalism on nonreligious grounds, not by religious fervor itself.*

This factor must be taken into account in any analysis of religion's role in subsequent elections. From 1948 to 1972—long before Falwell or Robertson—the Democrats lost 25 percentage points among lower-status whites, as Everett Carl Ladd Jr. and Charles D. Hadley reported in their 1975 work, *Transformations of the American Party System.*

Thus the prelude to the rise of the religious Right in the late 1970s and early 1980s. Religious conservatives, ignited by court decisions on school prayer and abortion and reacting against what they saw as the depredations of trashy magazines, movies, and television programs, decried the growing "secularization" of America and engaged in what sociologist Nathan Glazer has called a "defensive offensive." It was meant to restore the consensus on values that existed—or at least seemed to exist—before the 1960s. The Christian conservatives cast themselves as a beleaguered minority.

In light of this history, the remarkable fact is that in the 2004 election, class (measured by income) had *not* disappeared as a key determinant of voting decisions. Nearly four decades of conservative mobilization around the issues of race, culture, and religion has certainly dented the Democrats' appeal to middle- and lower-income whites. But the facts suggest that claims about the death of class politics have been exaggerated.

To take the most extreme ends of the income structure: Bush received 63 percent of the votes from voters who earned over $200,000 annually but only 36 percent from those who earned under $15,000. Bush won 57 percent from voters in the $100,000 to $200,000 a year range, but only 42 percent among those earning between $15,000 and $30,000. To consolidate the various income groups: Bush won 44 percent among voters earning less than $50,000 a year but 56 percent among those earning over $50,000. This 12-point gap is certainly not as robust as the class divide that was so important in the Democratic victories of the 1930s and 1940s. But the divide persists.

In fact, political scientist Larry Bartels offers evidence in a 2006 article in the *Quarterly Journal of Political Science* that among white voters, income divides have become *more* important in our most recent elections. Bartels finds that "since the 1970s, there has been a large and fairly consistent gap in partisan preferences between richer and poorer white voters regardless of whether or not they happen to have college degrees." He goes on: "In the white working class, as in the electorate as a whole, net Republican gains since the 1950s have come entirely among middle- and upper-income voters, producing a substantial gap in partisanship and voting between predominantly Democratic lower income groups and predominantly Republican upper income groups."

The income split is reinforced by the rift between Americans who belong to unions and those who don't. Bush received 38 percent of the votes of union members, but 54 percent among nonmembers. It is, of course, a problem for Democrats that union membership is in a long-term decline. This has reinforced a weakening of class politics, as has the steady drop in manufacturing employment. Nonetheless, the story, again, is of the persistence of class politics—and the loyalty of union members to the Democrats has grown stronger, not weaker, in recent elections.

If class remains important, so does region. The gap between black and white voters is large across the country. But again, it's necessary to stress southern particularism. The voting gap across racial lines is 24 points larger in the South than in the East, 15 points larger in the South than in the Midwest or West.

While it is possible to make too much of these differences, it's worth noting that the "religion gap" is much larger in some states than in others. According to the 2004 exit polling, the gap barely exists in Louisiana but is enormous in Minnesota and Washington State. California appears to be the only state in which Bush failed to secure a majority among weekly churchgoers. In all these cases, racial and ethnic factors explain at least some of the differences. In Louisiana, the Democratic share among regular church-attenders is boosted by African Americans and, to some degree, Cajun Catholics. Minnesota and Washington have relatively small African American populations—and African Americans, as we have seen, are the most Democratic group among loyal churchgoers. In California, the Democratic share among those who attend religious services once a week is boosted by a large Latino vote—and the fact that California's Latinos are, on the whole, more Democratic than their counterparts elsewhere.

Over half of the voters in Georgia and Louisiana attended religious services at least weekly—and a quarter to a fifth more than once a week. Only 7 and 8 percent of voters in these states, respectively, claimed never to attend religious services. By contrast, in California and Washington, over half the voters attended religious services occasionally or never—including a fifth to a quarter who never attend. The contrast between the religious patterns in the Deep South and on the Pacific Coast offers important clues as to the different political cultures of these regions.

It is particularly difficult to generalize about Latinos without taking into account regional, ethnic, and even state-by-state differences. While Bush carried a substantial majority of frequent church-attenders among southern Hispanics, Kerry carried a substantial majority of Latino church-attenders in the East and the West. This contrast reflects the presence of a large number of Cuban Americans, a Republican-leaning group, in the southern sample, and the fact that Mexican Americans in California are more staunchly Democratic than Mexican Americans in Texas.

These findings suggest the need for care and subtlety in discussing the religious factor among Latinos because distinctive religious forces are at work in their community. For example, a Pew study in 2007 found that among Latino Catholics, 48 percent identified themselves as Democrats, while only 17 percent identified themselves as Republicans. Latino Protestants, on the other hand, gave Republicans a 37 percent to 32 percent advantage. The Catholic-Protestant divide is far greater among Latinos than among non-Hispanic whites. Since nearly two-thirds of Latinos are Catholics, Democrats enjoy a healthy overall advantage among Hispanic voters. (I deal with the Catholic vote in more detail in chapter 6.) Since Protestantism has made substantial inroads among Latinos, Republicans may have new opportunities to gain ground—though a strong reaction against Republican congressional opposition to immigration reform in 2006 and 2007 threatened to wipe out the GOP's progress among Protestant and Catholic Latinos alike. Dramatic evidence of a decline in Latino voting for Republicans was already visible in the 2006 elections.

In sum: the religion gap exists. But it varies by region, and it varies by state. Republican strength in the South, already strong, is enhanced by the region's religious commitment. Democratic strength in the West, particularly on the Pacific Coast, is enhanced by the region's relatively low levels of formal religious participation. Religious commitment and region interact. The polarization in American politics is partly a religious phenomenon, partly a regional phenomenon. And race remains far more divisive in American politics than religion.

IV

Before leaving 2004, it's important to note that for all the proper attention given to the role of religion, there was a tendency to exaggerate its role in the final outcome. In the end, John Kerry was *not* defeated by the religious Right. He was beaten by moderates who voted—reluctantly in many cases—for President Bush. This was hard for many Democrats to take. It was easier to salve their wounds by demonizing religious conservatives. But in the 2004 election, Democrats left moderate votes on the table that could have created a Kerry majority. By contrast, Democrats built their 2006 majorities by scooping up many of these voters whose disenchantment with Bush had grown.

Consider these findings from the 2004 network exit polls among voters who took middle-of-the-road positions on cultural issues. Some 38 percent of those who thought abortion should be legal in most cases went to Bush. Bush got 22 percent from voters who favored gay marriage and a rather astonishing 52 percent among those who favored civil unions. Bush even managed 16 percent among voters who thought the president paid more attention to the interests of large corporations than to those of "ordinary Americans." A third of the voters who favored a government more active in solving problems went to Bush.

True, 22 percent of the voters said that "moral values" were decisive in their choice. But 71 percent picked some other issue, including 34 percent who mentioned either Iraq or terrorism, and 37 percent who mentioned the economy, health care, taxes, or education. (The remainder exercised their right to decline to answer pollsters' questions.)

All this means that Bush won not because religious conservatives are on the march, not because there is a right-wing majority in the United States, but because the president persuaded just enough of the nonconservative majority to go his way. Even with their increased numbers, conservatives still constituted only 34 percent of the 2004 electorate. The largest share of the American electorate (45 percent) called itself moderate. The moderates went 54 to 45 percent for Kerry—good, but not enough. And 21 percent of the voters in 2004 called themselves liberal, which means that liberals can win only in alliance with a large share of moderate voters. This suggests that polarized politics may be of more help to conservatives than liberals and that liberals have an opportunity to gain ground as a reaction to polarization sets in.

The numbers of 2004 do not lend themselves to a facile ideological analysis. The populist Left can fairly ask why so many progovernment, anticorporate voters backed Bush. The social liberals can ask why so many socially moderate and progressive voters stuck with the president. The centrist crowd can muse over the power of the terrorism issue. The exit polls found that perhaps 10 percent of Al Gore's 2000 voters switched to Bush. Of these, more than eight in ten thought the war in Iraq was part of the war on terrorism.

Everyone should notice that the Bush campaign knew it could not win without moderates. When Karl Rove went after the red-hot right-wing vote, he did so largely through person-to-person contact, mailings, and conservative talk-meisters. As we've seen, Bush always spoke in code to this group, reducing the risk of turning off the middle. Rove and Bush won the 2004 election on decidedly old strategies that had nothing to do with ideas. These included the attacks on Kerry for being weak, and the claim, apparently subscribed to by a majority, that Bush would be tougher on the bad guys. It was familiar, Cold War-era stuff.

To get a sense of how the war on terror and other factors may have played a larger role than religious affiliation in the 2004 outcome, consider where Bush made gains over his 2004 vote. According to the 2004 exit polls, Bush increased his vote by only 1 percentage point among voters who attended religious services more than once a week or weekly. But he gained 4 points among monthly attenders, 3 points among those who attend a few times a year, and 4 points among those who never attend religious services. Put simply, *the swing to Bush was higher among the less religiously observant than among the more religious.* This fact is always overlooked in analyses seeking to explain the 2004 results primarily through the prisms of religion, culture, and morality.

None of this disproves the importance of religious commitment in influencing voter decisions, or Bush's success in boosting turnout among religious conservatives. But it does suggest that even in the polarized climate of 2004, religion was not the only significant factor and may have been less important to the final outcome than other factors. The 2004 election, in other words, contained the seeds of the 2006 realignment.

V

Writing on November 26, 2006, *Philadelphia Inquirer* reporter Thomas Fitzgerald began a front-page analysis of the role of religion in the midterm election with these arresting words: "A minor miracle occurred this month: The 'God Gap' in American politics narrowed."

But ten days earlier, the Pew Research Center had issued a postelection report by analyst Scott Keeter that was just as definitive in declaring: "The 'God Gap' Widens."

Who was right?

Both accounts were based on fact, not speculation. "While the most religious voters in recent years have tended to favor Republicans, a slice of them voted Democratic in the Nov. 7 midterm congressional elections," Fitzgerald wrote. "The shift has raised eyebrows among pollsters and strategists." He reported that "Democrats took back the Catholic vote they lost in 2004" and "trimmed the GOP advantage among weekly churchgoers, and even gained ground with the most loyal segment of the Republican base: white evangelicals."

"In this year's campaign, same-sex marriage and abortion were less dominant issues than they were two years ago," Fitzgerald wrote. "Postelection analyses also suggest that many religious voters were concerned most about the war in Iraq and corruption in Washington."

The *Inquirer* writer naturally focused on the U.S. Senate contest in Pennsylvania, where Democrat Bob Casey, an economic progressive and an opponent of abortion, defeated Republican incumbent Rick Santorum, an across-the-board conservative. Fitzgerald noted that Casey "got 59 percent of the Catholic vote against fellow Catholic Santorum, and the Democrat also won a narrow majority of all those who said they attend religious services weekly. Casey won 29 percent of self-described evangelicals."

He added that while Bush "carried the Harrisburg television market, which encompasses much of the state's conservative middle, by 34 percentage points over Democratic Sen. John Kerry in 2004," in 2006, "Santorum won that essential Republican turf by just 10 percentage points over Casey, a 24-point shift."

By contrast, Pew's Keeter found that the Democratic party's gains in the election were "concentrated among non-Christians and secular voters, suggesting that there was a larger political divide between Christians and the rest of American society." Keeter offered ample support for this view:

> The GOP held on to voters who attend religious services at least once a week (55% voted Republican versus 58% four years ago). But less frequent churchgoers were much more supportive of Democrats than they were four years ago. Among occasional churchgoers, 59% voted Democratic. In 2002, just 51% did so. And among those who never go to church, 67% voted Democratic—four years ago, only 55% did so. Thus, the gap in Democratic support between the most and least religious has grown from 16 percentage points in 2002 to 24 points today.

Republicans, he said, "did very well among white evangelicals: 72% voted Republican in races for the U.S. House nationwide, and they gave strong support—about two thirds or more—to Republican Senate candidates in several key states including Tennessee, Pennsylvania, Ohio, Missouri, and Virginia." These levels of support, he noted, are comparable to those registered by evangelicals in 2004 and in 2002 (about 75 percent for Republican candidates).

As for Bush, his approval rating among evangelicals on Election Day, 2006, "was 70%, far higher than in the general electorate." That was down 10 points from its level two years earlier, Keeter noted, "but the decline was no greater among evangelicals than among the rest of the electorate." Evangelicals were clearly more inclined to vote on the old moral issues than other voters. While 59 percent of these voters said that "values issues such as gay marriage and abortion" were "extremely important" to their vote, just 29 percent of other voters said this.

Lest there be any doubt about who drove the Democratic victory, Keeter added this: "In fact, the Democratic Party's gains came largely among non-Christians. Democratic House candidates gained 25 points among Jews and 7 points among those of other non-Christian faiths, compared with 2002. They also picked up 10 points among secular voters."

That two intelligent analysts could reach such starkly different conclusions suggests how slippery and controversial the matter of religion and voting has become. But reconciling the two views is not that difficult. Remember, the *Inquirer's* Fitzgerald claimed only that "a slice" of the religious vote had gone Democratic. Democrats did, in fact, post gains among religious voters in 2006, including white evangelicals. But, as Keeter suggested, Democrats gained even more from less religiously inclined voters. A fair way to summarize the results is that Keeter is quite right in asserting that the gap between the more and less religious voters actually widened between 2004 and 2006; but the religious gap turned from being a disadvantage to the Democrats into an advantage. They modestly cut their losses among more religious voters (all that new organizing among voters of faith paid off at least to some degree) while at the same time vastly expanding their advantages in the rest of the electorate. Put another way, Republicans did so badly among less religious voters in 2006 that their continuing, if slightly diminished, advantage among the more religious was not enough to save them.

In his thought-provoking 2007 book, *The Faith Factor: How Religion Influences American Elections*, John C. Green, one of the nation's best students of religious voting patterns, parallels the Galston-Kamarck analysis in distinguishing what he calls the Old Religion Gap, based on differences among adherents to distinctive religious traditions, and the New Religion Gap, based on differences in behavior (frequency of attendance at religious worship is one key marker) and the depth of religious belief. The Old Religion Gap involved the significant political variations in political behavior among—to list some of the largest groups—mainline Protestants, evangelical Protestants, Catholics, and Jews. The New Religion Gap crisscrosses these older divides and is rooted, as Green puts it, in "the politics of behaving and believing."

In the 2006 election, Green notes that both the Old and the New Religion Gaps were in play. He shares Keeter's view that the New Religion Gap expanded, and did so in the Democrats' favor. But the Old Religion Gap reappeared because Democrats restored their majorities among Catholics while expanding their already large majorities among Jews. Latinos, including Latino Catholics, gave Democrats substantially larger majorities in 2006 than they had to John Kerry, in part because of the tough anti-immigration stance of one wing of the Republican party. Non-Latino Catholics also moved the Democrats' way, notably, as Fitzgerald pointed out, in the critical Pennsylvania Senate race between Bob Casey and Rick Santorum.

Because so much has been made of the 2006 Democratic victories in Ohio, Virginia, and Pennsylvania—since the first two states supported Bush over Kerry in 2004 and since Pennsylvania saw the nomination of a Catholic Democrat opposed to legal abortion—it's worth examining how much (and also how little) the religious gap changed from the first election to the second.

Ohio, the state on which Bush's electoral college victory hung, saw a massive swing toward the Democrats, fueled by local Republican corruption, the sharp decline in manufacturing jobs, and the same discontent over Iraq and the Bush administration that affected much of the rest of the nation. Ohio had significant races for both governor and the U.S. Senate, and both jobs shifted from the Republicans to the Democrats. The Democratic nominee for governor, Representative Ted Strickland, was a moderate and also a Methodist minister who spoke often of his faith. He opposed Secretary of State Ken Blackwell, closely and proudly aligned with the religious conservative movement. In the Senate race, a staunch liberal and tough critic of free trade, Representative Sherrod Brown, opposed Mike DeWine, the moderately conservative incumbent.

Both Democrats swept the state, Strickland with 60 percent of the vote, Brown with 56 percent. Much was made of Strickland's strength among religiously active voters. He won 38 percent among Ohio voters who attended religious services more than once a week, a 7-point gain over Kerry's showing, and 55 percent among those who attended religious services weekly, a 19-point gain. But he did best of all among voters who said they never attended religious services, winning 81 percent of their ballots, an 18-point gain over Kerry. Strickland also did well among occasional church-attenders, winning 68 percent in this group, an 11-point gain on Kerry.

In other words, even though Strickland gained substantial ground on Kerry among religious voters, the "religion gap" was actually higher in 2006 because of profound Republican weakness among nonreligious voters. The patterns were similar in Brown's victory, although the gains were generally smaller. Brown did gain as much ground as Strickland did among those who attended religious services more than once a week, somewhat less in the other groups. Interestingly, Brown, the more liberal candidate, ran 7 points *behind* Strickland among voters who never attended religious services—partly, perhaps, because nonreligious voters were more inclined to cast ballots against the conservative and openly devout Blackwell than against the more moderate DeWine.

In Pennsylvania, as Fitzgerald's account suggests, Democrats were very pleased with the staunchly Catholic Casey's success over the equally staunchly Catholic (and much more conservative) Santorum. But the evidence suggests that Casey's strong showing was built by moderately religious voters or voters who were not religious at all. Casey actually *lost* marginally from Kerry's showing among voters who attended religious services more than once a week, down 3 points (though this was within the margin of error). He gained 7 points among weekly attenders, but 12 points among occasional attenders and 10 points among those who said they never attended religious services. Casey, like Strickland and Santorum, did best among the nonobservant, securing 78 percent of their ballots. As we have seen, Casey did improve the Democrats' share of the Catholic vote by 8 points, to 59 percent. But he also gained 6 points among Protestants, and a remarkable 14 points among the roughly one-tenth of the voters who said they had no religion. As in Ohio, a strongly anti-Republican secular vote played an important role in the Pennsylvania result.

The key Virginia contest between incumbent Republican Senator George Allen and Democrat Jim Webb underscores how political change in 2006 cannot be ascribed simply to religious shifts. Allen, the heavy favorite at the beginning of the contest, came under fire during the summer for directing what appeared to be a racial epithet at an Indian American filming one of his events on behalf of the Webb campaign. Allen's candidacy never fully recovered, and he faced subsequent questions about his sympathy for the Old Confederacy.

Webb, a former Reagan Republican who became a Democrat because of his intense opposition to the Iraq War, made few specific appeals to religious voters. He ran instead on the war and economic populism, casting himself as an Andrew Jackson Democrat. Webb won a 50 to 49 percent victory, defeating Allen by just over 7,000 votes out of more than 2.3 million cast. After Election Day, Virginia's was the last contest called, and Webb's victory gave the Democrats control of the Senate.

What's striking about the Virginia race is how *minor* the religious shifts were between 2004 and 2006. Allen's support among white evangelical Christians in the home state of Pat Robertson and Jerry Falwell was as solid as George W. Bush's had been two years earlier. White evangelicals voted 80–20 for Allen, and his performance was a statistically insignificant single point better that Bush's two years earlier. Allen ran slightly better than Bush among those who attended religious services more than once a week, slightly worse among weekly attenders. Webb, like Democrats in the other states, gained the most ground on Kerry among the least religiously observant—those who attended religious services a few times a year, or never.

Visible in all these contests was a sharp shift in the issue agenda between 2004 and 2006. The "values" issues so touted two years earlier were never as important as the press clippings suggested, and they were overwhelmed as voting issues in 2006 by Iraq, by the economy, and by a general disaffection with the performance of Republicans in Washington. In Virginia, for example, the group most disposed to Webb was those voters who said they strongly disapproved of the Iraq War. They constituted 37 percent of the electorate and gave Webb 91 percent of their ballots.

In 2006 Americans seemed tired of culture wars, tired of polarization around moral questions, and tired of religion's use as a political weapon. While religious divisions endured (and in some ways strengthened), a large majority of Americans—including many who are religious—decided that electoral campaigns may not be the best arena for settling religious differences, and that the proper focus of politics was on the large questions that would affect the future of their nation: war and peace, national security, economic justice, competence and honesty in government. The greatest irony of the first years of the twenty-first century may be that the Republican party sought power in part by championing "moral values" and then lost it because of a voter backlash against corruption on its watch.

VI

Why Can't They Be Like Us?, the title of Father Andrew Greeley's 1971 book, is a very old American question that was at the heart of electoral conflict during the Bush era. It was by no means the only period in which politics was defined by hostility and incomprehension between and among groups, even if the definition of "us" and "them" can vary from decade to decade. Yet in our history, we have often answered the question by ignoring it. Sometimes we even acknowledge that "they" are more like "us" than we want to admit. Occasionally we'll notice that the culture war rages inside individuals at least as much as between groups. Spotting this fact is one of the sociologist Alan Wolfe's great contributions to the culture war debate.

Prohibitionists sometimes pray for gin. Cultural liberals are as appalled as anyone else that their children might watch X-rated movies or cruise dangerous Web sites. Cultural conservatives who have gay friends cannot abide prejudice against homosexuals. Opponents of abortion often cannot find it in themselves to condemn a woman they know who has had an abortion for a reason they understand. Some supporters of abortion rights find the issue morally troubling nonetheless and might never choose to have an abortion themselves. Many, in short, long for freedom but understand freedom's limits. Many long for orthodoxy yet want it to bend a bit on matters related to their own sense of freedom, or justice.

The past decade or so may have seen the U.S. economy send many well-paying jobs abroad, but it has been very good for those in the business of producing cultural jeremiads. A partial list includes *The Closing of the American Mind, The De-moralization of Society, The Corrosion of Character, Slouching Towards Gomorrah, Bowling Alone, The Death of Outrage, The Great Disruption,* and *Egotopia: Narcissism and the New American Landscape.*

All these books speak, albeit in very different ways, to a sense of cultural and moral unease. It is an unease not bounded by ideological categories.

On the contrary, people on the left and on the right are equally forceful in decrying self-centered individualism, consumerism, new pressures on the family, and the decline of community. Analysts left, right, and center are sensitive to how technological and economic changes have altered the rhythms of family life and lifted up certain virtues and values at the expense of others. In *The Great Disruption*, Francis Fukuyama, a freethinking neoconservative, argues that the new knowledge-based economy will transform the social world of the twenty-first century—how we raise our children, where we live, what we value—as much as the Industrial Revolution altered the organization of life in the nineteenth and early twentieth centuries. Fukuyama sees the knowledge economy as placing a high premium on radical individualism and a lower value on solidarity.

From the left Richard Sennett argues that the new, highly flexible capitalism has ended the concept of loyalty at work and therefore undermined it in society. "Character is expressed by loyalty and mutual commitment, or through the pursuit of long-term goals, or by the practice of delayed gratification for the sake of a future end," he writes in *The Corrosion of Character*. But in the new economy, he insists, there is no long term. He asks, "How do we decide what is of lasting value in ourselves in a society which is impatient, which focuses on the immediate moment? How can long-term goals be pursued in an economy devoted to the short term? How can mutual loyalties and commitments be sustained in institutions which are constantly breaking apart or continually being redesigned?" How, indeed?

Not all intellectuals attribute cultural and moral unease to social and economic changes. The writings of Gertrude Himmelfarb (and also William Bennett) place a strong emphasis on *individual* virtue and its alleged decline. But Himmelfarb, a sophisticated conservative historian, is alive to how "manners and morals" are embedded in a society (she is partial to the way the Victorians managed this), not created out of thin air by individuals. She shrewdly notes the shift away from talk of "virtues" to an analysis of "values." The word "virtue," she writes, "carried with it a sense of gravity and authority, as 'values' does not." Values, Himmelfarb says, "can be beliefs, opinions, attitudes, feelings, habits, conventions, preferences, prejudices, even idiosyncrasies—whatever any individual, group, or society happens to value, at any time, for any reason." She adds, "One cannot say of virtues, as one can of values, that anyone's virtues are as good as anyone else's, or that everyone has a right to his own virtues."

Sennett and Himmelfarb disagree profoundly about politics, yet they both see a cost to the decline of old virtues in a highly individualistic society. Himmelfarb worries about what happens to morality in a world in which values can be picked and chosen as one might buy a peach or a cantaloupe at the supermarket. Sennett wonders how individuals can live meaningful moral lives in an economy that so often wars against loyalty, commitment, and solidarity.

Beneath the clamor of the politicized and televised culture war, in other words, is a more measured debate between libertarians and communitarians, between individualists (moral or economic or both) and those who would emphasize some version of a common good. This, too, is an old American argument. As Robert Bellah and his colleagues wrote in *Habits of the Heart*, the history of our country might be seen as one long debate over how to balance the joys of individual freedom against the satisfactions of community and commitment. But this is a hard argument. It's much easier to scream across barricades about abortion, gay marriage, or Terri Schiavo's fate.

It has long been fashionable in American political discussion to separate "social issues" from "economic issues." But the two, as Sennett and Fukuyama would insist, are intertwined. Most Americans, no matter which cultural battle they choose to fight (or avoid), understand this. Family life is powerfully affected by work arrangements—and by the ability to find a decently paying job. Community life is shaped by how we build our homes and neighborhoods, by how long people's commutes are, and by how much time is left over from the struggle to make a living. Our culture is shaped in large part by commercial forces that, paradoxically, promote a permissiveness in entertainment and advertising that conservatives who in theory revere the market in fact deplore.

The counterculture has become the over-the-counter culture. Liberals and conservatives alike are vexed by this. Liberals desperately do not want to be blue-nosed or judgmental. Yet they are uneasy with a consumerist, individualistic culture that often violates their sense of community, decency, and mutual obligation. Benjamin Barber's 2007 book *Consumed* provides ample evidence of this disaffection. Conservatives who dread economic regulation and defend capitalism at every turn often find the cultural fruits of capitalism bitter and distasteful. Liberals and conservatives may battle over gay marriage or abortion and yet agree wholeheartedly about which television programs their children shouldn't watch, which

Web sites they shouldn't visit, and which video games they shouldn't play. Both are likely to be critical of mall culture, and for some of the same reasons.

Yet everyone tries to cope, and our coping has been remarkably successful. The exurbs, so disliked by opponents of sprawl, produce their own kinds of community through religious congregations, kids' sports leagues, mothers' groups, school organizations, business clubs—and political activities on both sides of the cultural divide.

Fears of moral decay may be pervasive, but crime, teen pregnancy, abortion, and divorce have declined since the early 1990s. Feminism, which conservatives once feared as an assault on family life, has proved its compatibility with updated versions of old-fashioned family arrangements. Every father of a daughter, no matter his politics, is a feminist when it comes to her education and her ambitions. Most conservative parents of gay or lesbian children, however uneasy they may be with homosexuality, will stand up for their kids against bigotry. Most liberal parents, however open in theory they may be to cultural experimentation and rebellion against accepted norms, lay down the law to their children on many matters ranging from homework, dating practices, and the dangers of drunk driving and drugs.

We would be better off if we challenged the culture-war metaphor and, in the process, the self-understandings of liberals and conservatives. One need not be a cultural pessimist to share the concerns of Sennett, Himmelfarb, and Bellah over the state of our common life. One need not be a wild-eyed optimist to see signs that—for all the disruptions wrought by the new economy, for all the moral disturbances created by wardrobe and other cultural malfunctions—Americans, as individuals and in their families, are trying to create new forms of community and new ways of transmitting old values (and, yes, virtues).

The culture war exploits our discontents. The task of politics is to heal them.

3. What Are the "Values" Issues?

ECONOMICS, SOCIAL JUSTICE, AND THE
STRUGGLE OVER MORALITY

The tasks of easing the culture war and healing our discontents have been especially difficult because we underestimate the extent to which politics has invaded our discussions of religion and morality. To a remarkable degree, the core divisions among religious Americans, and particularly Christians, are no longer defined by theological issues. The splits are political. The friendly (or at least usually friendly) arguments among believers over back fences and at kitchen tables or backyard barbeques tend not to focus on the Virgin Birth, the real presence of Jesus in the Eucharist, infant baptism, or the nature of the Trinity. More often, they are about questions such as abortion and gay marriage—and also attitudes toward government.

This has led to a peculiar kind of ecumenism discussed earlier. Old divisions—between Protestants and Catholics, Christians and Jews, Methodists and Baptists—have largely passed away. Now, conservative Catholics, Protestants, and Jews often ally together against liberal Catholics, Protestants, and Jews. As Grant Wacker, a professor of church history at Duke Divinity School, has said, "One of the most remarkable changes of the 20th century is the virtual evaporation of hostility between Protestants and Catholics. I don't think it's because Baptists have come to have a great respect for Tridentine theology. It's because they see Catholics as allies against graver problems. There's a large reconfiguration going on now."

Wacker was speaking mostly of the conservative side of politics, but his words apply to moderates and liberals as well, and his analysis fits with John Green's distinction between the Old and New Religion Gaps. Alan Wolfe has written pointedly about the triumph of political concern over religious commitment. Politics, not "religion itself," Wolfe argues, explains far more about our current situation than many who stress the importance of faith would like to believe:

> It may be true that some people attach so much importance to their views on abortion, capital punishment, or gay marriage that they seek allies in other religious traditions. But if so, it is their political views—their take on public policy—that they are putting first, while their theology or religious practice comes second. At earlier periods in American history, people have argued over which Bible should be read in schools and how it should be interpreted. Those were debates that put theology first. The people who fight today's culture war, by contrast, put politics first. It is not their stance on what God wants that determines the party for which they vote. They know what they believe on political matters, and they pick a party just as they pick a denomination.

Wolfe goes on to ask some blunt questions:

> At some point, people who line up this way and begin to put their political convictions ahead of their theological beliefs will have to scratch their heads and ask, "Is this what we are really about? We came to religion to express our spirituality and find out about the nature of the divinity, yet here we are being urged by our pastors to vote for tax cuts and the war in Iraq?" Such a shift in priorities cannot be all that satisfying to a genuine religious believer.

Of course, tax cuts and the war were not necessarily at the top of the list for conservative preachers, even as they urged their flocks to support candidates for whom these *were* the top priorities. It has been far more common for the preachers to talk about gay rights and abortion. The gay rights issue in particular has led to great contention within many of our Protestant denominations. Less prominent in media accounts, but at least as important, is the sharp difference among believers over government's role in dealing with major social challenges. The split over government is the Overlooked Schism.

The argument within both the Christian and Jewish traditions is not, for the most part, about the individual's obligation to charity toward the least among us nor, in principle, about the biblical call to justice. The Old and New Testaments are abundantly clear in demonstrating what the Catholic Church has called "a preferential option for the poor." As Jim

Wallis has long argued, for Christians to ignore Jesus's preaching about the poor is to eviscerate the Gospel message, and the message of the Old Testament prophets.

But there is a powerful dispute over what modern government, as against individuals, should do to lift up the poor. There is contention over the relative importance of social and individual responsibility. There is disagreement over whether the economic marketplace, untempered by regulation and redistribution, can create a just social order. If religious progressives tend to criticize government for being insufficiently generous toward the poor, religious conservatives argue that too much government assistance promotes dependency.

Consider the Tale of Two Methodists. George W. Bush is an occasional Methodist by marriage; Hillary Clinton, a Methodist from birth. Each might be seen as standing in for very different aspects of the Methodist tradition and, by extension, for different sides of the broader religious debate over the obligations to justice, and to lifting up the poor.

Bush is a plausible representative of the self-perfecting, self-improving, pious side of the argument; Clinton, of the side that speaks for social change, social activism, and social justice.

On the one side is a view that accepts a communal role in resolving poverty but often locates that role outside of government. It highlights the importance of individual, personal transformation and conversion as the essential elements in curing social ills.

On the other is a concern for the common good embodied in an economically progressive (or social democratic or New Deal liberal) view that emphasizes the social and structural causes of poverty and inequality, and the social responsibilities that fall on both individuals and the government to heal them.

The Bush view—let's call it compassionate conservatism—typically locates the causes of poverty in individual shortcomings or failures, rather than in social or economic injustice. The emphasis is on drug addicts who must free themselves from dependency, former offenders who must transform their hearts, parents who need to learn to be more faithful toward each other in marriage and more loving and responsible toward their children. What we see here is a communal language put to the service of what is, in the end, a serious but individualistic way of solving social problems.

Bush offered some very strong words about the poor in his first inaugural address. He said, "In the quiet of the American conscience, we know that deep persistent poverty is unworthy of our nation's promise and whatever our views of its cause, we can agree that children at risk are not at fault." At that point, he had everybody with him from left to right.

Bush went on to say, "Abandonment and abuse are not acts of God, they are failures of love, and the proliferation of prisons, however necessary, is no substitute for hope and order in our souls."

Now given Bush's record on law-and-order issues, it was moving to hear him raise the proliferation of prisons as a problem. Yet what's noteworthy here is where he locates the cause of these social difficulties: abandonment and abuse are the problems for these poor children; hope and order in our souls is the solution to the problem of criminality.

Later in the speech, Bush declared, "Compassion is the work of a nation, not just a government, and some needs and hurts are so deep that they will only respond to a mentor's touch or a pastor's prayer, church and charity, synagogue and mosque lend our communities their humanity and they will have an honored place in our plans and in our laws."

Again, there is a lot here most would applaud, but, whatever it is, it is not exactly the old Social Gospel, and it surely is not the New Deal.

In the case of Hillary Clinton, on the other hand, we know that her emphasis is elsewhere. *It Takes a Village*, the title of her book on how to nurture children, comes from Africa. But it could well arise out of the Christian and Jewish social justice traditions. Clinton, in fact, believes in many of the old virtues, and her religious faith seems to be an important part of her life. It is no accident that the late Michael Kelly's famously acerbic 1993 *New York Times Magazine* article on her was entitled "Saint Hillary." Kelly, no friend of the Clintons, argued that Hillary Clinton's political approach reflected "a generally 'progressive' social agenda with a strong dose of moralism, the admixture of the two driven by an abundant faith in the capacity of the human intellect and the redeeming power of love." Way back then, she was preaching "an ethos of individual responsibility and caring," a society that "makes us feel that we are a part of something bigger than ourselves." She was calling for the reinvigoration of "intermediary institutions" such as families, local communities, and voluntary groups—an idea put forward forcefully in the late 1970s by Peter Berger and Richard John Neuhaus, hardly hard-core liberals, in their justifiably famous essay, *To Empower People*. She also declared that "there is no—or should be no—debate that our family structure is in trouble" or that "our children need the stability, the predictability of a family." As Peter Steinfels wrote of a speech and a series of interviews in which Clinton offered these observations, they sounded "sometimes like Vaclav Havel, sometimes like Martin Luther King Jr., and sometimes, well, like George Bush with his 'vision thing' and a thousand points of light." (Steinfels, of course, was talking about the first President Bush.)

Yet Hillary Clinton's view of the village clearly encompassed not just families and churches but also government itself—the "progressive" part of her agenda that Kelly referred to. She has spoken often of the government's obligations to universal health care, education, family leave, income supplements, and child care. In that sense, Bush and Clinton embody two distinct traditions.

It's worth recalling, as we saw in chapter 1, that the emphasis on self-improvement and self-control that is part of the Bush story was once in our history intimately linked to the cause of social reform itself. This connection was visible not only in the Prohibition movement, but also in the early trade-union movement, which put heavy emphasis on education and self-help, even as it preached organizing and solidarity. It was powerfully present in the civil rights movement. In his brilliant book, *Radical Equations: Math Literacy and Civil Rights*, the legendary civil rights leader Robert Moses captures the magic of that moment. "The civil rights movement of the 1960s," he writes, "was less about challenges and protests against white power than feeling our way toward our own power and possibilities—really a series of challenges by ourselves, and our communities, to ourselves." This was a movement that placed demands on society *and* on individuals.

Now in speaking with genuine respect for the self-denying side of our religious traditions, I certainly don't want to pretend to a false piety. I have no special sympathy for the cause of Prohibition, and have I have always thought "Roosevelt and Repeal" was a one of the finest slogans in American political history: right on both counts.

But to understand the current moment, it's essential to confront a new division that has arisen between those who advance the cause of personal moral improvement and those who seek social and economic transformation. Two causes that were once allies in our nation's politics now often face off against each other as adversaries.

II

A few years ago I was fortunate to edit a volume called *Lifting Up the Poor*, in which two of the nation's leading voices on welfare policy debated the religious underpinnings of their disagreements. In an especially thoughtful and searching way, they hit upon the essentials of so many of those back fence debates among religious believers.

Mary Jo Bane, a liberal Catholic and an assistant secretary of health and human services in the Clinton administration, supported a strong government role in social provision. Her view was rooted in a sensibility she described as "hopeful rather than despairing, trusting rather than suspicious, more generous than prudent, more communitarian than individualistic." While acknowledging that the scriptures "do not enlighten us much on the questions of who is obligated to provide what for whom under what conditions," she was unabashed in endorsing communal provision.

"My moral argument," she wrote, "asserts that the community is obligated to provide basic levels of subsistence, health care, and education to all its members. The obligation is based on the preciousness of every human being and on the belief that God's plan desires the flourishing of every person."

Lawrence M. Mead, a moderately conservative evangelical and a professor of politics at New York University, sees the Gospel's call for salvation as restoring individuals to full moral agency. Economic poverty, as he sees it, is not the paramount concern of Christ's preaching. "There is no preference for the poor," he insists, "only a lively concern for them as well as other people in trouble. Jesus does help the needy and commands his followers to do so, but he has other concerns which are not economic, and he is not undemanding toward those he helps."

The key for Mead is to overcome a culture of poverty that he describes as a "defeatist culture." This culture has many effects. "Unwed pregnancy and drug addiction would appear to be self-defeating, irrational behaviors for those who adopt them," Mead writes. "The idea that people 'choose' these lifestyles attributes to them more power to control their lives than, inwardly, the seriously poor appear to have." Mead advocates an unashamedly "paternalistic" approach to the poor based on the idea that "if you receive some benefits, you accept some obligations in return."

Mead is not unconcerned about the poor, and Bane is not unconcerned about personal responsibility. Yet note the difference in emphasis: Bane tends to emphasize the structural causes of poverty; Mead, individual shortcomings rooted in a flawed culture.

This is the central divide among religious Americans over government's role in alleviating poverty. It is a schism just as rooted in values as the more publicized debates over abortion and gay marriage. It has large implications for the poor. Progressives cannot ignore it, partly because conservative religious Americans who so often demonstrate abundant financial generosity toward the poor in their personal acts of charity ought, in principle at least, to be the allies of liberals and moderates in the cause of creating a more socially decent society.

Can this breach be healed—or, more modestly, can the combatants at least learn to address each other with the same passion for mutual understanding that animated the Bane-Mead dialogue?

It's already clear that a central argument of this book is the urgency of reforging the link between social and personal responsibility. The poor suffer from high rates of teen pregnancy, fatherless families, and family breakup, *and* they suffer from unjust social structures and large changes in the economy that produce greater inequality. In the case of African Americans and Latinos, they also suffer from racism. There is no reason for progressives to be silent about either half of this argument, and no reason for conservatives to deny the second half. By speaking out for personal responsibility, religious progressives can challenge their conservative friends to get serious about social responsibility.

Barack Obama's sense of urgency about linking these two lines of argument is one of the reasons he emerged as a major force in American politics—even if, as we've seen, Hillary Clinton was making parallel arguments. Speaking to the religious progressives gathered in June 2006 at the "Call to Renewal" conference in Washington, DC, Obama was unapologetic about the demand for social justice embedded in the great faith traditions. He thus took a swipe at those who would repeal the estate tax, saying this entailed "a trillion dollars being taken out of social programs to go to a handful of folks who don't need and weren't even asking for it."

But he insisted that social improvement also requires individual transformation. When a gang member "shoots indiscriminately into a crowd . . . there's a hole in that young man's heart—a hole that the government alone cannot fix." Contraception can reduce teen pregnancy rates, but so can "faith and guidance," which "help fortify a young woman's sense of self, a young man's sense of responsibility and a sense of reverence that all young people should have for the act of sexual intimacy."

And if you think this sounds preachy, Obama has an answer: "Our fear of getting 'preachy' may also lead us to discount the role that values and culture play in some of our most urgent social problems."

Obama's talk was inevitably read as a road map for Democrats struggling to speak authentically to people of faith. Thus did the Associated Press headline its early stories about the speech with the words: "Obama: Democrats Must Court Evangelicals."

Well, yes, Obama did indeed criticize "liberals who dismiss religion in the public square as inherently irrational or intolerant." But a purely electoral reading of his words missed the invitation he offered all parties to think differently about the power of faith—an invitation addressed no less to conservatives than to others. "No matter how religious they may or may not be," Obama said, "people are tired of seeing faith used as a tool of attack. They don't want faith used to belittle or to divide. They're tired of hearing folks deliver more screed than sermon." There have been few more accurate descriptions of the current state of our debate over religion and public life.

Without issuing screeds of their own, religious progressives do need to challenge the core conservative contention that government help for the less fortunate inevitably produces "dependency." Our nation moved closer to "equality of opportunity" because of extensive government efforts to offer individuals opportunities to develop their own capacities (and to offer minorities and women protection against discrimination). As legal philosopher Stephen Holmes has pointed out, it was the intellectual father of the free market, Adam Smith, who favored a publicly financed, compulsory system of elementary education. After World War II the government's investment in the college education of millions through the GI Bill simultaneously opened new opportunities for individuals and promoted an explosive period of general economic growth. "Far from being a road to serfdom, government intervention was meant to enhance individual autonomy," wrote Holmes, who went on to cite John Stuart Mill's view of publicly financed schooling as "help toward doing without help."

Progressives also need to challenge a core conservative view—or hope—that private and religious charity is sufficient to the task of alleviating poverty. That is simply not true. In a 1997 article in *Commentary* magazine—hardly a bastion of liberalism—William Bennett and John DiIulio made the crucial calculations: "If all of America's grant-making private foundations gave away all of their income and all of their assets, they could cover only a year's worth of current government expenditures on social welfare." What would happen the next year?

They cited a study by Princeton's Julian Wolpert of 125,000 charities, each with receipts of $25,000 a year or more. Among them, they raised and spent $350 billion annually. This sounds substantial until you realize that the sum is only one-seventh of what is spent each year by federal, state, and local governments.

Bennett and DiIulio, neither of them enthusiasts of the old welfare state, concluded, "It is unlikely that Americans will donate much more than their present 2 percent of annual household income, or that corporate giving will take up any significant proportion of the slack in the event of future government reductions." The title of their article was "What Good Is Government?" Their answer was clear.

But religious progressives also need to engage in a dialogue with conservatives on the most basic questions related to values and virtues. Religious conservatives and liberals share an aversion to excessive materialism. They agree that the market should not be the only arbiter of values. They agree that not everything can or should be bought and sold.

We do not, for example, believe that justice in the courts or votes and public offices should be bought and sold. We do not now (though many Americans once did) believe that human beings should be bought and sold. But these do not exhaust the instances in which free people might decide to limit the writ of money and the supremacy of the market. As political philosopher Michael Walzer has argued, one of the central issues confronting democratic societies concerns which rights and privileges should not be put up for sale.

As an abstract proposition, we reject the notion that a wealthy person should be able to buy extra years of life that a poor person cannot, since life itself ought not be bought and sold. Yet the availability of health care affects longevity, and making health care a purely market transaction comes close to selling life and death. This was the primary argument for Medicare and remains the central moral claim made by advocates of national health insurance. Similarly, we do not believe that children should be deprived of access to food, medicine, or education just because their parents are poor—or, for that matter, irresponsible. As Holmes has asked,

"Why should children be hopelessly snared in a web of underprivilege into which they were born through no fault of their own?"

The relationship between the moral and economic crises in our society can be seen most powerfully in families where the need to earn enough income forces both parents to spend increasing amounts of time outside the home. One of the great achievements of the last century was "the family wage," which allowed the vast majority of workers to provide their families with both a decent living and the parental time to give their children a decent upbringing. The family wage was not simply a product of the marketplace. It was secured through a combination of economic growth, social legislation, agitation, and unionization. If the marketplace becomes not simply the main arbiter of income, as it will inevitably be, but the *only* factor determining living standards, then all social factors, including the need to strengthen families and improve the care of children, become entirely irrelevant in the world of work.

The moral crisis so many conservatives talk about thus grows not primarily from the "countercultural" or "permissive" ideas that developed in the 1960s. Its roots lie deeper, in a society that threatens to allow market values to crowd out all other values. The result, as Richard Sennett argued, is a steady erosion of the bonds of solidarity, morality, and trust. This affects the values put forward by the popular culture, the organization of family life, and the aspirations of the next generation—all questions of vital concern to religious conservatives.

My friend the late Father Philip Murnion regularly offered his friends in the Catholic social justice community a powerful insight from the time he spent as a child on welfare after his father died. In his day, Murnion said, poor children could count on three basic forms of support: some money from government, love and nurturing within the family, and moral guidance from churches and neighbors who lived in relatively safe and orderly communities. In recent years, he argued, poor children came under threat in all three spheres: government help is in danger; many of the poorest children live in difficult (and at times dangerous) family situations; and the moral order and physical safety of many neighborhoods has collapsed.

Social justice requires economic support from government, a concern for family life, and serious efforts to strengthen community institutions and to protect public order. Religious progressives may find their vocation in insisting that our society needs to grapple with each of these issues. At the heart of their arguments should be two principles: compassion is good, but justice is better; and while government certainly cannot solve all problems, what government does—and fails to do—matters enormously.

III

But how does one define justice? That question is central to sorting out what government's role in the marketplace should be. Here again, one of the most important debates among religious people has been buried beneath a mound of media reports about sexually charged questions that are presumed to appeal to a wide audience. And perhaps the editors and producers know what they're doing: unlike economics, matters involving sexuality have never been dismissed as being part of a "dismal science." Yet some of the most exciting theological controversies in recent years— from liberation theology and the Vatican's reaction to it to Pope John Paul II's own reflections on economic justice—have arisen from the interplay between religious tradition and the realities of global capitalism.

Take John Paul's *Centesimus annus*, which has to rank as one of the most successful papal documents in history. The highest compliment to the pope's 1991 social encyclical lay not in the fact that so many were eager to say they agreed with the pope, but that partisans of so many different viewpoints in the Church insisted that the pope had agreed with *them*.

Such consensus is often reached with fuzzy language, artful compromises, and a high level of generality. But that was not true with *Centesimus annus*. The pope was specific about the principles Catholics (and others who care about justice) should embrace in assessing economic systems. He was clear as to how various systems—socialist, capitalist, welfare state liberal—failed to live up to his criteria.

But John Paul wisely chose not to build a political and economic system from top to bottom and declare his creation the one and only Catholic or Christian way. The pope's principles rule out certain approaches (including dictatorships, highly centralized command economies, capitalism without social safety nets and safeguards) while leaving open a broad area for debate and experimentation. The pope's approach was principled but not ideological; broadly egalitarian without being a demand for absolute equality; open to the advantages of markets and the positive uses of government.

Precisely because the pope seemed more open to the capitalist market than were many of his predecessors, his encyclical was greeted with great enthusiasm in conservative Catholic circles in the United States. Catholic advocates of the market such as Michael Novak, Richard John Neuhaus, and George Weigel were given credit for their role in influencing the pope down this road.

Without claiming explicit credit, Neuhaus was one of the first out of the blocks with his sweeping analysis of the meaning of the John Paul's words. His op-ed piece was published on May 2, 1991, the day after the encyclical became public, on the opinion pages of the *Wall Street Journal,* which have a certain canonical authority among conservatives, if not all Christians. The headline was arresting: "The Pope Affirms the 'New Capitalism.'" Neuhaus's two key assertions were arresting as well: "Capitalism is the economic corollary of the Christian understanding of man's nature and destiny," and "The present encyclical must surely prompt a careful, and perhaps painful, rethinking of conventional wisdoms about Catholic social teaching." Neuhaus took specific aim at the American bishops' 1986 pastoral letter, "Economic Justice for All," which had been highly critical of unrestrained capitalism. That document, Neuhaus said provocatively (and intentionally so), "must now be recognized as unrepresentative of the church's authoritative teaching." Neuhaus later published a somewhat more nuanced view of the matter in a book called *Doing Well and Doing Good: The Challenge to the Christian Capitalist.*

In fact, it is hard to sustain Neuhaus's claim that the 1986 pastoral letter was in any way "unrepresentative" of the core principles of the pope's encyclical, let alone some of John Paul's earlier attacks on "imperialistic monopolies" or his insistence that "the needs of the poor must take priority over the desires of the rich, and the rights of the workers over the maximization of profits."

The basic orientation of the American bishops' approach was reformist, quite in line with John Paul's overall economic view. Consider this rather balanced view of the American economy:

> The U.S. value system emphasizes economic freedom. It also recognizes that the market is limited by fundamental human rights. Some things are never to be bought or sold. This conviction has prompted positive

steps to modify the operation of the market when it harms vulnerable members of society. Labor unions help workers resist exploitation. Through their government, the people of the United States have provided support for education, access to food, unemployment compensation, security in old age, and protection of the environment. The market system contributes to the success of the U.S. economy, but so do many efforts to forge economic institutions and public policies that enable *all* to share in the riches of the nation. The country's economy has been built through a creative struggle; entrepreneurs, business people, workers, unions, consumers, and government have all played essential roles.

The letter also asserted a set of principles consistent with John Paul's:

The fulfillment of the basic needs of the poor is of the highest priority. . . . Increasing active participation in economic life by those who are presently excluded or vulnerable is a high social priority. . . . The investment of wealth, talent, and human energy should be specially directed to benefit those who are poor or economically insecure. . . . Economic and social policies as well as organization of the work world should be continually evaluated in light of their impact on the strength and stability of family life.

In fact, the bishops' 1986 pastoral letter was a high point of progressive Catholicism in the United States, one reason why conservatives were so critical of it. It placed the Church squarely on the side of the staunchest advocates of social justice and in opposition to many of the policies of the Reagan administration.

Before the pope's 1991 encyclical, American Catholic conservatives were quite willing to take issue with some of John Paul's own teachings. Anticipating the American bishops' letter, a group of conservative Catholics led by Novak and former Reagan treasury secretary William Simon issued a detailed economic statement of their own in 1984 that not only challenged the more liberal bishops but also took issue with the pope's repeated assertions of the "priority of labor over capital." The conservatives' report declared, by contrast: "The fact of widespread unemployment shows beyond a doubt that, as an efficient cause, labor is not prior to capital but, on the contrary, requires new investment as its own prior cause." This was a statement of what might be called supply-side Christianity.

A defense of the spirit of enterprise was central to the conservatives' argument. Their statement insisted that the Catholic Church's social thought "remains relatively underdeveloped in its conceptions of how new wealth is produced." Enterprise is "a virtue relatively neglected by theologians," their statement said, and the Church placed insufficient emphasis on "the practical insight of the entrepreneur." It defended "economic activism" and declared that the "use of economic talents is as much a Christian vocation as political activism."

The polemics of the mid-1980s explained the eagerness of conservatives to interpret the pope's 1991 encyclical as a triumph for their side and, as Neuhaus's *Wall Street Journal* article suggested, as a defeat for their progressive adversaries inside the American church. Perhaps the best statement of their point of view was Novak's 1993 book, *The Catholic Ethic and the Spirit of Capitalism*. Because of the comprehensive nature of Novak's account, his book provides a useful focus for the argument about economic justice among Christians generally, and not just Catholics.

Novak's starting point, appropriately, is *Centesimus annus*, and it should be said that his comments two years after the encyclical's release are rather more careful than some of the polemics that animated the early conservative reaction. He accepted that the pope's encyclical "gives encouragement to social democrats and the moderate Left, *as well as* to persons who share my own proclivities, *and* to those further to my right. It is not a party document." (The emphasis here, and in all subsequent quotations, is Novak's.) An enthusiast for capitalism, Novak nonetheless went out of his way to make clear that his claims were limited. "No democratic capitalist regime should pretend to be the Kingdom of God," he wrote at one point. "The market principle is a good one," he said at another, but then added: "It is not an idol."

Yet for all of Novak's welcomed caution, he had a particular case to make that did, indeed, square with the broader conservative argument (and the conservatives' polemics of the 1980s). The encyclical, Novak insisted, marked a major shift in Catholic social thought because it offered not only a negative definition of capitalism, common enough in the history of Catholic social analysis, but also a positive take rare in papal documents. John Paul, he argued, not only understood the efficiencies bred by market economics, but also the important role markets play in rewarding creativity and invention. Novak saw this as a large advance over traditional

Catholic efforts to find "a third way" between capitalism and socialism. The pope pointed toward the idea that "the threefold combination of democracy, capitalism, and religious liberty is the 'middle way.'"

Novak drew his title from Max Weber's book about the Protestant ethic and argued that Weber defined the spirit of capitalism too narrowly, attributing to Calvinism certain attitudes that were more broadly shared among many varieties of Christian and Jewish thinking. But Novak's argument with Weber was secondary to his broader goal of offering a history of Catholic attitudes toward capitalism, and a celebration of where the church came out.

Many of Novak's assertions about the importance of civil society and the institutions of church and family reflected a consensus that had taken hold across the political spectrum, something to which the words of both Hillary Clinton and Barack Obama offered testimony. Significant parts of the Left, and virtually the entirety of the religious Left, would agree with Novak's assertion that "[t]he best thing government can do, in a positive way, is to catalyze the efforts of civil society, so that the citizenry at large will bring its many diverse talents and resources to the assistance of the needy."

Still, Novak could not resist scoring points. He argued, for example, that "the first response of the American Catholic Left to *Centesimus annus* was shocked silence, followed less by an exposition of its theme than by an attack on neoconservatives for 'hijacking' the encyclical." It's quite true that liberals expressed unhappiness over the conservatives' hijacking operation. But "shocked silence" hardly characterizes their reaction. A handful of particularly dogmatic critics of capitalism may well have been unhappy with the very parts of the document Novak liked most. And some on the Catholic Left were more enthusiastic about the pope's earlier formulations on social questions (especially *Laborem exercens*, which included the stress on the priority of labor over capital).

But most progressives accepted the central themes of *Centesimus annus*. Its conclusions were summarized well in the liberal Catholic magazine *Commonweal* by the Rev. J. Bryan Hehir, one of the prime movers behind the bishops' 1986 letter. Hehir argued that the pope's assessment "takes the market reality seriously and acknowledges values in it that John Paul's predecessors may have assumed but did not assert." At the same time, Hehir added, the pope saw moral limits on the market, notably that "many human needs are not met by the workings of the market," that "there are whole groups of people without the resources to enter the market," and that "there are goods that cannot and must not be bought and sold."

That's a fair reading. In the meantime, some conservatives were quite uncomfortable with many of the things the pope said. One contributor to a *National Review* symposium on the encyclical saw parts of it as "endorsing socialism in its currently fashionable form of corporatism." Milton Friedman saw "much for left-liberals" in the document. Those, of course, are precisely the sentiments that conservatives expressed toward the American bishops' pastoral.

Perhaps the largest gap between Novak and the Left lay in his attempt to redefine "social justice" as a personal virtue. Arguing that the concept existed in a "conceptual fog," Novak cited Hayek in asserting that "social justice has become the chief battle cry of those who would expand the role of government, particularly in questions of redistribution."

Well, yes. A libertarian like Hayek disliked the concept of social justice precisely because he rejected on principle the idea that one should worry about social, as against individual, outcomes. Those who question a libertarian view would assert that social justice is relevant precisely because market outcomes do not automatically produce a just society. The antilibertarian argument is familiar. Within many large corporations, for example, executive salaries, pensions, and "golden parachutes" are usually determined by political factors related to how corporations are governed. They bear a tenuous relationship at best to a company's market performance. This raises questions of "social justice." So, too, does the plight of a steel worker who devoted himself loyally to his firm for a quarter century only to find himself unemployed because of shifts in the world market for steel. Wherever one stands on trade, this is a social as well as an individual reality, and it most definitely raises issues of justice.

The difficulty with Novak's view—and that of others even less sympathetic than he is to notions of a social safety net—is that it tends to sweep aside questions about the inequitable distributions of power that unchecked capitalism can produce and downplays the enormous dislocations that the system, especially in its new global form, can create. In particular, capitalism can be highly disruptive of those ties of "family, work, and neighborhood" that conservatives extol and point to as the solution to many of our problems. Of course social justice is bound to be a highly contested concept. That is also why it is so useful.

Novak's desire to define "social justice" as a virtue applying to individuals does, however, have certain advantages. "The practice of social justice means activism, it means organizing; it means trying to make the system better," he wrote. No progressive would argue with that—it sounds, in fact, like an excellent argument for trade unionism—or with the idea that Christians have a personal obligation to expand what political scientist Robert Putnam has referred to as our pool of "social capital."

Ever since he published *The Spirit of Democratic Capitalism* in 1982, Novak has been urging us to embrace what he calls "a tripartite system" involving a market economy, a democratic polity, and a "moral cultural system" that would nourish the "virtues and values" on which free economies and societies depend. (Note that this is very close to the same system he ascribes to the pope's view.) Most who call themselves progressives, liberals, or social democrats broadly accept some version of this system. Progressives obviously embrace democracy, few of them these days are suggesting that the market can or should be scrapped, and most want a "moral cultural system" as independent as possible from both the state and the market.

The difficulties arise over the interaction among these three systems. The largest difference in view is over the relationship between democracy and the market. Novak is not a pure libertarian; he accepts the need for social safety nets organized both by the state and by private institutions. But he would severely circumscribe the state's economic role. Novak traces the hostility to capitalism he perceives among intellectuals as related to what he calls "the aristocratic biases of modern intellectual life." As a result, he argues that intellectuals "overlooked the self-reforming capacities of capitalism when the latter is embedded in powerful democratic and moral-religious traditions."

Yet far from being friends of aristocracy, many critics of pure capitalism are democrats who insist that the market works best—and on behalf of the largest number of citizens—when it is constrained and improved by the workings of democratic government. The "self-reforming" capacities of democratic capitalism are in significant part due to democracy, not to the inner workings of capitalism itself. Most of the social reforms in the capitalist countries were the product of New Dealish and social democratic movements.

Even on the level of economic performance, government intervention has often been needed to keep the free market from running off the rails. A global economy that produces substantial job shifts from high-wage to low-wage countries requires energetic government to ease the transitions of millions of workers. Even if it can be asserted that, on balance, global trade lifts the standard of living within poor countries—its record on this is more complicated than defenders of free trade often allow—the global trading system tends to have its most negative effects on the *least advantaged* within the wealthiest societies. Corrections to these imbalances will inevitably come from outside the system. One could multiply these examples, but the point is clear enough: capitalism has often been saved by its democratic critics.

This raises the broader question of the Christian's proper attitude toward any political or economic system. Novak does not deify capitalism. But many who see his enthusiasm for capitalism as excessive act not out of a blindness to its benefits, but from a view that Christians have a particular obligation to be critical of the failures, imperfections, and injustices in "this world." The critical posture stems from the Christian's vocation to live in dynamic tension with whatever system or society he or she happens to participate in, to be, in John Paul's evocative phrase, "a sign of contradiction."

Novak would agree with this analysis in principle, but argue that many on the Left take this "prophetic stance" in the wrong direction by dismissing the moral and practical advantages of the market system—and, if they are Americans, the achievements of their country. Personally, I welcome criticisms of self-righteousness and reflexive anti-Americanism on the left, as long as they are accompanied by criticisms of the self-righteousness that plays a more than ample role on the right. But few on the left deny the market system's capacity to encourage creativity and enterprise. Throughout the world, the democratic Left is committed to reforming and improving the market system, not to dismantling it.

And so if capitalism's critics, even some of the self-righteous ones, have been responsible for the very process of self-correction that Novak celebrates, and if Christianity has nurtured that critical spirit and encouraged impatience with injustice, is there not much to celebrate? To put it in the market's own terms, don't the benefits of this stance far outweigh its costs?

IV

But let us assume for a moment that Michael Novak is closer to the truth than I am, and that Lawrence Mead's approach to poverty is more morally persuasive than the view that Mary Jo Bane and I broadly share. Where I agree with Novak and others who have celebrated John Paul's economic vision is that there is broad room for constructive argument among Christians—indeed, among all who share a democratic moral vision—over what constitutes a moral economy and how our duties of justice for the poor and the dispossessed should be discharged.

But there is a moral obligation to have that argument in the first place. What is so disturbing about the recent definitions of "values voters," "moral issues," and "religious concerns" is that we have continued to narrow the nature of our public moral discourse. We have defined economic and foreign policy issues as involving something other than "moral" concerns. Consider that famous 2004 exit poll that found 22 percent of voters listing "moral values" as decisive in their vote. The flaw in the question is that it cast "moral values" against other choices involving economics and taxes, terrorism and Iraq, education and health care. The poll sent an unintentional message: that voters who checked boxes for any of these issues, instead of for "moral values," were not really worried about morality. Voters who had a moral commitment to universal health care or to improved education or economic redistribution to the poor were not counted as "moral values" voters. Why? For that matter, voters who had a moral commitment to a less intrusive government and lower taxes or to seeing through the war in Iraq were not counted as "moral values" voters, either. Why?

The narrowing of our moral and religious vision is one of the great tragedies of American politics since the late 1970s. Our traditions, most certainly Christianity and Judaism, teach us that we should not lie, cheat, or steal, and that we are supposed to love our neighbor. Shouldn't the question of how such moral rules apply to our economic and social policies be a matter of lively debate within our political system? It is simply absurd to say that religious voices can be heard on family life, but not on the economic underpinnings of the family; on personal responsibility, but not on the responsibility of great economic actors; on generosity of the spirit, but not on the economic works of mercy. "If one's faith is to infuse all parts of one's life," the economist Rebecca Blank has written, "it is hard to argue that community has meaning in one's religious life but no meaning in economic life. Religious life cannot be easily separated from religious activities."

The current separation of economics from "values issues" owes a great deal to the particular needs of the conservative coalition built around Ronald Reagan, and rebuilt around George W. Bush. In 1979 a group of conservative activists led by Paul Weyrich of the Free Congress Foundation and Morton Blackwell, a Republican National Committee member from Virginia, approached the late Rev. Jerry Falwell, urging him to organize what became the Moral Majority. Their primary goal was not religious but political: to enlist evangelicals, many of whom had eschewed political activism altogether, behind conservative Republican candidates. Blackwell candidly called evangelicals "the greatest tract of virgin timber on the political landscape."

The activists reaped a mighty load. Ronald Reagan was the first major beneficiary of this organizing, and his own trajectory is revealing. Having signed one of the most liberal abortion laws in the nation as governor of California in the early 1970s, he switched sides on the abortion issue. By the late 1970s he had become one of the nation's most eloquent advocates of the right-to-life position, and a hero to the anti-abortion movement. At a Religious Roundtable meeting in 1980, David Von Drehle and Thomas B. Edsall wrote in the *Washington Post*, Reagan noted "that the ministers might not feel comfortable endorsing a candidate. But the applause was thunderous when Reagan added: 'I endorse you.'"

The role of the Moral Majority and evangelical Christians more generally in Ronald Reagan's defeat of Jimmy Carter in 1980 has often been exaggerated. But Jeffrey Bell's 2007 political obituary for Jerry Falwell in the *Weekly Standard* captured the importance so many in the conservative movement ascribed to the revolution among religious traditionalists. Bell noted that whereas Democrats had enjoyed a 25-point margin among theologically conservative white Protestants in 1976—the year a born-again southern Baptist named Jimmy Carter was elected—Republicans had a 62-point lead in Ronald Reagan's reelection in 1984. The swing among these religious conservatives, Bell observed, was much larger than the overall shift between the elections, from a 2-point Carter victory in 1976 to an 18-point Reagan advantage eight years later.

As for the Christian Coalition, which arose after the decline of the Moral Majority, its inspiration was equally political. Emerging from Pat Robertson's unsuccessful bid for the 1988 Republican presidential nomination, it sought to advance his influence in the party. Later, Ralph Reed, the Coalition's executive director, helped Karl Rove roll the evangelical political apparatus into a near-formal relationship with the Republican party.

The political goals of these conservative activists would not be advanced by a broader moral agenda—many white evangelicals back in 1980 still had considerable sympathy for New Deal economics, and many evangelicals, as we've seen, still have considerable sympathy for the poor. The Christian Coalition's interests lay in declaring certain issues decisive and "nonnegotiable." If abortion and gay marriage and stem-cell research were the preeminent moral issues, voting based on a narrow definition of "values" became a moral imperative. Thus were many economically moderate or even populist religious voters pried away from old loyalties and turned into reliable allies of the conservative movement.

The unnatural division between a limited set of moral issues and all other moral concerns could not be sustained indefinitely. George W. Bush profited politically as long as this split was maintained. But it was an approach that became increasingly untenable during his second term. We turn next to that part of the story.

4. Selling Religion Short

WHEN IDEOLOGY IS NOT ENOUGH

George W. Bush's open religiosity, so attractive to his evangelical followers, has led many of his opponents to believe that he is bent on establishing a theocracy.

Consider the following presidential remarks on Saint Paul's letter to the Ephesians. "Ephesians says we should speak the truth with our neighbors for we are members one of another," the president said. "I believe that. I think that is the single most important political insight, or social insight, in the Bible. And I think it is what should drive us as we behave together."

Then he got to his compassionate God-talk. "Is my destiny caught up in yours?" he asked. "Are we part of the same family of God? It's not enough to say we are all equal in the eyes of God. We are all also connected in the eyes of God."

And the crowd applauded.

Those bothered by the president's religious talk should consider that the uplifting thoughts just cited were offered not by President Bush, but by President Bill Clinton at Washington's Metropolitan Baptist Church in December 1997.

There are many things for which George W. Bush deserves intense criticism. But in the way he has spoken of God, Bush is much more typically presidential than he is painted, especially by our friends abroad.

Much commentary in 2003, for example, focused on this passage from the president's State of the Union address: "The liberty we prize is not America's gift to the world, it is God's gift to humanity. We Americans have faith in ourselves, but not in ourselves alone. We do not claim to know all the ways of Providence, yet we can trust in them, placing our confidence in the loving God behind all of life and all of history. May

He guide us now, and may God continue to bless the United States of America."

Now this passage was classic Bush, as interpreted by his gifted chief speechwriter Michael Gerson, but it would not be hard to imagine these same words coming from Clinton or Ronald Reagan—or from John F. Kennedy, who insisted in his inaugural address that "the rights of man come not from the generosity of the state, but from the hand of God."

Yet Bush's religious rhetoric certainly bothered many people. "Such America-with-God-on-its-side language smacks of the type of religiosity and fundamentalism that is at the root of the terrorist conflict in the first place," Diane Francis wrote of that State of the Union speech in Canada's *National Post*. "Such mentality is neither helpful, nor accurate, nor does it accurately reflect the views of most Americans."

Of course, a similar line of criticism might also be directed against the Declaration of Independence, written by a skeptical deist named Thomas Jefferson. Recall its assertion that "all men are created equal, that they are endowed by their Creator with certain unalienable Rights, that among these are Life, Liberty and the pursuit of Happiness."

Yet the president's effusive godly talk caused consternation well beyond the ranks of nonbelievers. Even religious people worried when Bush suggested he sensed a religious calling to his moment in history, to the challenges of terrorism, and to the cause of Iraq. It's common for Christians to speak of a calling. But it did not help Bush or his country for the world to wonder—even unfairly—if an American president waging war was inspired not only by his own utter certainty but also by God's. The very nature of the conflict, steeped as it is in religious feeling, required Bush to be even more careful than his predecessors in his invocations of the Almighty.

Still, the fact that Bush, like other presidents, spoke often of God was not the problem. The difficulties with religiosity in the Bush era were quite different. They lay, first, in the sense Bush often conveyed that religion was primarily about feeling—what was in his "heart"—and that while his religious convictions could be used for electoral purposes, they could not be subjected to serious intellectual or moral inquiry. A revealing illustration occurred during a 1999 presidential debate in Iowa, when candidate Bush responded to a question about who was his favorite philosopher. Bush replied, "Christ, because he changed my heart." In one sense, Bush was providing information to voters who, after all, have a vital interest in knowing if a candidate's public policy positions are influenced by his or her faith. This can be a useful form of democratic knowledge. If Jesus's teachings matter to a candidate, the voters should know it. The troublesome aspect of Bush's answer came later. Bush did not explain how Christ's teachings affected his view of policy. When asked how Jesus had "changed his heart," he replied, "Well, if they don't know, it's going to be hard to explain."

This approach, perfectly acceptable in conversations among friends, misses the point of public democratic discourse. Bush was telling voters, in effect, that if they had not had his specific kind of religious experience, he couldn't possibly explain it to them, and they wouldn't understand anyway.

Conservative evangelicals were quick to defend Bush's remarks after the Iowa debate. "That's how we talk about our faith," said a Southern Baptist friend who is a staunch Democrat and otherwise had no use for Bush as a presidential candidate. "Bush," said Michael Cromartie, vice president of the Ethics and Public Policy Center and a conservative evangelical himself, "was describing a personal, existential subjective experience that was real for him, but was put in language and terminology unfamiliar to the Jewish religious experience and the Catholic religious experience."

But one obligation for political candidates in a free, pluralist society is to express personal religious views in ways that are accessible to all—believers and unbelievers alike—and to explain how those views have a bearing on how they would govern.

"Religion is certainly about the heart, but it's about more than the heart," said Father Bryan Hehir, one of the country's most influential Catholic spokesmen on public questions. "It's about an intellectual structure of belief, and a candidate needs to explain what that intellectual structure is about. And that was totally missing from Bush's answer."

A second problem with Bush era religiosity was a sharpening of the argument that religion is closely and necessarily aligned with the entire conservative agenda. Any religious person who dared suggest that faith might lead to a concern for the environment, support for government help to poor, or opposition to the Iraq War was deemed inadequately faithful. These developments have been simultaneously bad for public life and harmful to religion.

This was the view of the Rev. Joel Hunter, who in November 2006 walked away from the job of heading the Christian Coalition because, he

said, the group seemed unhappy with his proposals to highlight environmental and antipoverty issues rather than focus on purely "moralistic"
issues such as abortion. Hunter said his decision to go—and, it should
be said, the group's decision to want him to do so—reflected "a basic
philosophical difference."

"I saw an opportunity to really broaden the conversation and broaden
the constituency," he said. "I'm really over this whole polarization thing."
In his book *Right Wing, Wrong Bird: Why the Tactics of the Religious Right
Won't Fly with Most Conservative Christians*, Hunter, the pastor of Northland Church, just outside Orlando, Florida, argued that "Conservative
Christians need to be more ambidextrous than just 'right' or 'left' ori-
ented." In 2007 he told the *Orlando Sentinel*'s religion writer Mark Pinsky,
a close student of the evangelical world, that groups such as the Moral
Majority, the Christian Coalition, and Focus on the Family "almost demand a more strident tone to raise money or media ratings." Rank-and-
file pastors, he added, "don't have the same pressures on us. We work
with people. We know what it takes to be patient and motivational and
encouraging." Because of a disaffection with the politics of polarization,
Hunter argued that the evangelical vote was now a "jump ball."

Shortly after Hunter and the Christian Coalition severed their ties, Rick
Warren was asked about the controversy on Fox News's *Hannity & Colmes*.
While affirming his own stand in opposition to abortion, Warren insisted
on a broad agenda for Christians. "Jesus' agenda is far bigger than just one
or two issues," Warren said. "We have to care about poverty, we have to
care about disease, we have to care about illiteracy, we have to care about
corruption in government, sex trafficking. There are whole kinds of issues
that are far more than just the few that evangelicals have been most known
for. I care about those."

Bush era religiosity has also been associated with a form of absolutism
and ideological litmus testing that came in the way of practical solutions
to problems recognized by religious and nonreligious citizens alike. Right-
to-life politics was defined by the quest for an absolute legal ban on abortion, however ineffective it might prove to be, rather than by a search
for policies that might reduce the number of abortions. An insistence on
abstinence as the only solution to the problem of teenage pregnancy got
in the way of programs that might reduce teen pregnancy by *combining*
abstinence education with programs promoting contraception. "Family
values" became a slogan directed against gays and lesbians rather than an

affirmative call for responsibility on the part of heterosexual couples with children. This narrowing of the moral conversation carried a price for the public interest, and it eventually carried a price for the conservative movement.

II

I struggled to figure out the relationship between Bush's faith and his politics while working on a long profile of him for the *Washington Post Magazine* published in 1999. In the period leading up to the 2000 election, Bush was genuinely skilled in the way he addressed the religion question—and yet he left a large mystery in his wake. He would let his interlocutor know that *he* knew how embarrassing it would be if he laid it on too thick. He suggested that his religious experiences are not something he likes to talk about. And then he would, if asked to, talk about them.

The way Bush spoke of his faith during the 2000 campaign solved three problems at once. Emphasizing compassion toward the poor took the hard edges off his conservatism. It allowed him to relate easily to Christian conservatives without having to spend too much time on the difficult issues—abortion, gay rights, creationism—that turned off moderates. And his conversion allowed him to draw a sharp line between his self-described "young and irresponsible" past and his presidency-seeking present. He became the prodigal son, the repentant sinner, the transformed man.

When I presented Bush with this compact, all-purpose, and, I admit, somewhat cynical theory, he gave me a steely look. "People will see through that in a minute," he said.

No one I have ever met, including Bush's enemies, doubts the sincerity of his conversion, the apparent seriousness of his faith, or the fact that his life *did* seem to change when he turned forty in 1986. But the content of his faith has always been harder to pin down. The evidence, especially of his own words, is that it was less an intellectual calling than a matter of feelings and will. When I asked him in the late 1990s about his favorite passages in the Bible, for instance, his answers were surprisingly vague and general. "Well, the Beatitudes are great. I mean a lot of the Bible."

"Religion is a very personal matter to me—as it should be to everybody," he said. "I also understand that everybody comes to have religion different ways. All I know is—I know the pathway for me is what I know.

And I'm not going to try to tell you the pathway for you." This is a very nonjudgmental, end-of-the-century, good-vibes religion. Yet compassionate conservatism Bush-style has always been rooted in his personal experience, in the notion that religious faith offers the most effective path to solving problems—private and public. At times, he seemed to be promising a Faith-Based New Deal or Great Society: help for every American who wanted a religious experience to have one. It was the Ultimate Political Pledge.

"I ask the question, Does it work?" he said back then. "And to answer your question, from firsthand knowledge I know that changing your heart can work. It's worked for me. Will it work for everybody? Probably not. But, for example, if in fact we've reduced recidivism by changing hearts first, the state of Texas and, for that matter, America ought to say, 'Thank you, Lord, let's do more.'"

Religious language enabled Bush to take hard, controversial political questions and move them to the soft, friendly ground of personal obligation and faith. He has never talked much about social justice, minimum wages, unions, or monopoly power. In a sense, he has preached everybody's obligation to live up to his earthly father's creed: to be kinder and gentler and to create a thousand points of light.

"Getting tough on crime is easy compared to loving our neighbors as ourselves." said the man who always boasted about his aggressive anticrime laws in Texas. "The truth is, we must turn back to God and look to Him for help."

Bush's compassion talk before he was elected—and this provided an important clue to how he would govern—was never about the failure of the economic system, or the rights of those who are poor, or systematic injustices. He always came back to individuals.

"I know many conservative thinkers and people who adhere to the notion of heralding the individual and individualism and less federal government are people who really do care about the future," he said. "Because they know what I know: Government can't make people love one another. There have really been a lot of false promises over the last 30 years as well: 'Oh don't worry, you know, we'll make you love each other.' Well, unfortunately it doesn't happen that way. Love comes from a more powerful source."

He was proposing God, not government. It was how he squared his talk about compassion with his insistence on small government. How small? In

Texas, at least, it was pretty small. In one legislative battle with the Democrats in his final term as governor, Bush wanted to limit the number of poor children covered by a federally financed health care program. Eventually the governor compromised, but the larger point was made: compassionism, as perhaps it should be called, was never liberalism—not even close. Although it sometimes sounded moderate, it wasn't even that. And that was a problem when Bush took office.

III

In principle, Bush had a point when he began pushing his faith-based initiative. The idea that government might partner with religious organizations was not new. Not only did Bill Clinton's administration encourage such efforts; Omar McRoberts, a sociologist at the University of Chicago, has traced such cooperation back to the New Deal, with Franklin Roosevelt paying close attention to the needs (and political power) of the African American churches. McRoberts offers the arresting image of a painting unfurled at a 1936 Democratic pre-election rally in Madison Square Garden, organized by a group that was targeting the African American and labor vote, celebrating three liberators—Jesus Christ as liberator from sin, Abraham Lincoln as liberator from bondage, and FDR as liberator from social injustice. The moment, McRoberts said, revealed how New Deal era political organizers were "thinking about religious symbols, working with them, actively inserting them into black religious settings."

Nor did religious partnerships with government need to skirt or run over the line protecting religion from state interference or government from excessive religious entanglement. Many religious groups—Lutheran Services, African American churches, Catholic Charities, and the Jewish federations, among others—have long joined in partnerships with government to lift up the poor.

And Bush's "compassion agenda" did not have to become a partisan issue. Consider this statement: "I've seen the difference faith-based organizations make. I believe the lesson to the nation is clear: In those instances where the unique power of faith can help us meet the crushing social challenges that are otherwise not possible to meet . . . we must explore carefully tailored partnerships with our faith community." Or this one: "I'm a supporter of these programs in which faith-based organizations help the government serve public purposes. If a drug addict or a prisoner or a homeless person can find inspiration and strength within himself to deal with his or her problem, then don't we all gain from that?"

The first statement was made by Al Gore in a May 1999 speech; the second by Joe Lieberman, Gore's running mate, during a February 2000 appearance on ABC's *Nightline.*

But despite the historical precedents and the strong potential for bipartisan support, it all came to naught. The money that flowed to the various faith-based initiatives of the Bush administration was miniscule compared with the money that went to tax cuts for the wealthy—and the war in Iraq. Bush resisted more spending on core commitments to the poor, including, as he had done in Texas, for children's health care, the source of a major battle with congressional Democrats in the fall of 2007. Bush's budgets simply did not support his soaring words.

The shame of this can be discussed in moral terms. But there was also a great loss for public life. Putting aside cynicism or political calculation— and the bitterness over the Supreme Court decision that anointed Bush the winner of the 2000 election—most religious progressives at the beginning of Bush's term were willing to work with the administration to expand partnerships between government and religious groups to help the poor. There was a moment early in Bush's term when the bitter polarization in both political and religious life might have been resisted. It was not to be.

Disappointment with the Bush administration's failure to deliver on its compassion agenda was at least as important to the rise of an organized movement of religious progressives as was the reaction against the religious Right, or the disappointment with the 2004 election results.

In June 2003 a group of religious leaders sent Bush an open letter asking how he could square his fine talk about the poor with the priorities of his budgets. The signers, an ecumenical group led by Jim Wallis, noted that many in their ranks had "supported your faith-based initiative from the beginning of the administration" and "the proposals of your administration to strengthen marriage and family as effective antipoverty measures."

Citing the president's kind words about the "good people" in community groups that help the poor, the signers offered these sobering thoughts: "Mr. President, 'the good people' who provide such services are feeling overwhelmed by increasing need and diminished resources. And many are feeling betrayed. The lack of consistent, coherent and integrated domestic policy that benefits low-income people makes our continued support for your faith-based initiative increasingly untenable. Mr. President, the poor are suffering, and without serious changes in the policies of your administration, they will suffer more."

The failure of the Bush compassion agenda was perhaps best exemplified by the poignant story of David Kuo. I got to know Kuo in the 1990s, and more than anyone else, he led me to take compassionate conservatism seriously. An evangelical Christian who worked in President Bush's Office of Faith-Based and Community Initiatives, Kuo never saw compassionate conservatism as a political ploy. For him, it was a profound commitment. He had hoped its rise would encourage a dialogue across the lines of party and ideology about what an authentic commitment to lifting up the poor would look like. When I asked Kuo in 1998 to write an essay for a book I edited on community and civil society, his title was characteristic: "Poverty 101: What Liberals and Conservatives Can Learn From Each Other." Kuo, it might be said, was a compassionate conservative before compassionate conservatism was cool.

And so when John DiIulio asked Kuo to join him at Bush's Faith-Based Office, Kuo naturally accepted and became its deputy director.

Kuo eventually left his post deeply disheartened. In a 2005 article for Belief.net, he announced his break. "From tax cuts to Medicare, the White House gets what the White House really wants," Kuo wrote. "It never really wanted the 'poor people stuff.'"

The very fact that it took David Kuo's 2006 book, *Tempting Faith: An Inside Story of Political Seduction*, to put President Bush's faith-based initiative back into the news proved his thesis right. The White House, he said, never put much money or muscle behind compassionate conservatism. It used the faith-based agenda for political purposes and always made tax cuts for the wealthy a much higher priority than any assistance to those "armies of compassion" that Bush evoked so eloquently. As a result, the faith-based initiative was off the public radar for years.

The headlines that came Kuo's way focused on the author's claims that White House staffers ridiculed some of their evangelical supporters as "nuts" and "goofy" and that public events surrounding Bush's faith-based initiative were geared toward Republican electoral fortunes. It might have made some evangelicals wonder whether their alliance with political conservatism has actually made the world more godly from their own point of view. What were evangelicals actually getting out of this partnership?

Were they being used by a coalition that, when the deals were cut, cared far more about protecting the interests of its wealthy and corporate supporters than its churchgoing foot soldiers?

There will come a time when liberals who care about the poor will be less squeamish about building stronger alliances between government and those engaged in religiously based social action. Conservatives will hasten that day by acknowledging that liberal worries about excessive entanglements between church and state and fears of the consequences of pushing too hard against the limits set by the First Amendment reflect not a dogmatic secularism but a genuine concern about protecting religious liberty, the rights of religious minorities, and religion itself from state interference. There are appropriate and inappropriate partnerships between religious institutions and government. We would do well to seek consensus on the proper forms of cooperation. For while government has the resources to accomplish things that religious and community groups cannot, religious and community groups can draw on a spirit that allows them to achieve things that government might not even contemplate.

In the meantime, it is heartening that many conservative evangelicals seem to be taking to heart Kuo's warning that there's something wrong with "taking Jesus and reducing him to some precinct captain, to some get-out-the-vote guy."

IV

The faith-based initiative was a relatively recent lost opportunity for a less politicized and less polarized approach to religious engagement in public life. The debate over abortion is one of the longest standing sources of acrimony in American politics. It did not have to be this way, and it does not have to stay that way.

When the Supreme Court ruled in *Roe v. Wade* that the right to an abortion could not be denied by legislatures, opponents of abortion were understandably enraged. If those who believed passionately in abortion rights saw the 1973 decision as a kind of Magna Carta for women's liberties, abortion opponents saw it as a political gag order that removed the abortion issue from the normal give-and-take of democratic decision making. *Roe* struck down abortion laws in forty-six states and the District of Columbia, and the decision represented, as legal scholar Jeffrey Rosen has noted, "one of the few times in history that the Court leaped ahead of a national consensus." Ironically, a new, moderately prochoice consensus was already being formed in the country at the time *Roe* was decided. Key states with Republican governors (notably California under Ronald Reagan and New York under Nelson Rockefeller) had broadly legalized abortion. It is likely that had the Court left more discretion to the states, the gradual trend toward legalization would have continued, even if some states would have resisted it.

Initially, reaction to *Roe* did not fall neatly along party lines, partly because prominent conservatives (including Reagan) favored legal abortion and many liberals in the New Deal tradition, particularly Catholics, opposed it. Yet in the long run, *Roe* proved to be of great benefit to the Republican party. Attacking *Roe* fit in well with conservative Republicans' attacks on "judicial activism" (even though what they actually opposed were liberal court decisions; conservative judicial activism would suit them just fine later on as conservative strength on the bench expanded). The abortion issue, as noted earlier, allowed Republicans to make deep inroads into previously Democratic constituencies, particularly Catholics and white southerners—and to sustain gains they began to make in these groups in 1968 and 1972 on the basis of other issues, including a reaction to civil rights. Over time, Republicans came to be broadly identified as the prolife party, Democrats as the prochoice party.

The increasing partisanship around the issue had many unfortunate side effects. Abortion involves genuinely difficult moral questions, including the obvious ones: When does human life begin? Does the fetus have a different moral status in the first weeks of pregnancy than it has in the final month? What are the relative rights of the mother carrying the fetus (or the unborn child) and those of the unborn child (or the fetus)? Is the choice to have an abortion more morally justifiable in some circumstances than in others? Such are the questions individuals grappling with the issue regularly ask themselves. Yet political campaigns tend to reduce abortion to a simple litmus test. They demand a firm "Yes" or "No." Answers such as "Maybe," "It depends," "I'm not sure," "It's complicated," or "Yes, sometimes, and no other times" are unacceptable.

The emergence of abortion as a partisan cause has had a particularly unfortunate effect upon presidential campaigns: a subject on which politicians claim to be expressing their most deeply held moral convictions is often the issue on which they seem especially opportunistic and unprincipled.

In a little over a decade Mitt Romney, the former Massachusetts governor, moved from strong support of abortion rights (when he was running for Ted Kennedy's Senate seat in 1994) to a point where he said he made "no apology for the fact that I am pro-life" (when he was seeking the 2008 Republican presidential nomination).

Rudy Giuliani finally settled on reaffirming his prochoice position in the spring of 2007, but only after he gave a rather convoluted answer to an abortion-related question in a Republican presidential debate. When asked if it would be "a good day" for America if *Roe v. Wade* were overturned, Giuliani replied, diffidently, "It would be okay." He then added that it would also be okay if "a strict constructionist judge viewed it as precedent, and I think a judge has to make that decision." In other words, Giuliani would take any position as long as he could paste the stale and meaningless phrase "strict constructionist" over it—and shuck off responsibility to a judge. He knew this position could not stand and eventually declared himself in favor of abortion rights.

Reappraisals and conversions are not confined to Republicans. Both Al Gore and Richard Gephardt, the former House Democratic leader, altered their positions on abortion over the years to bring their views into line with those of Democratic primary voters who predominantly support abortion rights.

But there is something systematic about the willingness of politicians to adapt their views on abortion to suit the preferences of whatever electorate they are facing at any given time. The reason: our political system has created strong incentives for candidates to be less than candid about what they really think.

Candidates are rarely willing to say outright what's true for so many of them: that they do not consider abortion the most important issue in politics, and that it is not the reason they entered public life. Of course there are exceptions such as Rep. Chris Smith, a New Jersey Republican who began his political career as executive director of the New Jersey Right to Life Committee. But Smith's case is unusual. Many Democrats entered politics primarily because of a mix of commitments related to social justice, poverty, labor rights, health care, civil rights, and the environment. Many equally principled Republicans were animated largely by skepticism of government interference in the marketplace, support for lower taxes, and, in many cases, a belief in an assertive foreign policy.

Yet politicians who told the truth by saying that abortion was not one of their driving concerns would be denounced, oddly enough, as unprincipled. Opponents of abortion would argue that failing to see abortion as a central issue now is akin to denying the importance of slavery in the 1850s. Supporters of keeping abortion legal, for their part, would see such a politician as shamefully defective in his or her commitment to women's rights. As a result, politicians pretend to be deeply committed to a view even when they're not.

Making abortion a party issue has encouraged this dissembling. In Britain and Australia, a politician's stand on abortion is accorded "free vote" status, disconnected from party discipline. And why not? It's perfectly consistent for a progressive committed to broad public provision for the poor to believe that abortion is wrong. It's equally consistent for a conservative opposed to government meddling in the marketplace to support a woman's right to choose.

In theory, our parties do not enforce a single line on abortion, and there are many prolife Democrats and prochoice Republicans. The 2006 campaign represented a modest but healthy loosening of informal discipline on the subject. But presidential candidates searching for primary votes know they must hold to each party's version of political correctness. Giuliani's moderately prochoice stand will test whether this is as much of a straitjacket as the demands of a party whip.

Finally, we don't make it easy for politicians to admit, as most voters do, that abortion is an agonizing question. It's not hard to share the concern of right-to-lifers for the value of life from the moment of conception. It's not hard to share the concern of abortion rights advocates that a legal ban could endanger the health and the lives of women by driving abortions underground without much reducing their number.

And it is strange to make abortion a litmus test issue when partisans on both sides know perfectly well that an absolute ban on abortion is never likely to become law in the United States. In deeply Republican and staunchly conservative South Dakota, an Election Day referendum in 2006 saw voters turning back a law passed by the state legislature that would have prohibited all abortions, excepting only those to save a mother's life. The anti-abortion movement itself acknowledged the importance of the defeat. "You'd better take a hard look at these election results and ponder what they mean," Judie Brown, president of the American Life League, wrote in the conservative magazine *Human Events.* "South Dakota is not the liberal West Coast nor the ultra-liberal East Coast. It is part of America's heartland."

Especially striking in South Dakota was the strong vote in many Republican counties against the sweeping abortion ban. The Associated Press noted that in heavily Republican Pennington County—which includes Rapid City—61 percent of the voters rejected the abortion ban; in Custer County in the conservative southern Black Hills, 66 percent voted against the ban. Interestingly, as the AP noted, one of the more Democratic counties in the state, Minnehaha County—which includes Sioux Falls—voted against the ban by what the news agency called "a lesser landslide," 57 percent to 43 percent.

The import of the victory for prochoice forces in South Dakota should not be exaggerated. The South Dakota law was defeated in part because it was far too severe. Many voters who might take a rather restrictive view of abortion could not stomach a ban that did not allow exceptions in the cases of rape or incest.

The vote was also significant because it marked a change in strategy for prochoice forces. Rather than seeking to overturn South Dakota's ban in Court, the typical course of action for the prochoice movement since *Roe,* abortion rights advocates decided to appeal to the electorate. The very fact that voters and not judges made the final decision reduced the likelihood of a popular backlash—and the ability of conservatives to charge the abortion rights movement with antidemocratic elitism. There were certainly tactical considerations in the decision to fight the issue in a referendum campaign. Abortion rights advocates know that higher federal courts have moved away from a strict interpretation of *Roe*—an assumption confirmed in 2007 when a 5 to 4 Supreme Court ruling upheld the ban on "partial birth" abortion. But the South Dakota result also validated a broader intuition that the democratic process will often yield moderate results on difficult moral and social questions.

Indeed, some in the prolife community predicted long before the South Dakota results that a state law aimed at challenging the Supreme Court to overturn *Roe* would court a popular rebuke. The *Aberdeen American News* noted that in March 2006, when the ban was signed into law by South Dakota Governor Mike Rounds, Daniel McConchie, director of public policy for Americans United for Life, predicted that a "frontal assault" would just "inflame the pro-choice movement and help them raise lots of money." Which it did.

Is there an alternative to no-win abortion politics in which the abortion rate stays high even as advocates of abortion rights live in fear that the right to choose will be taken away? Is there a more honest approach that might allow politicians to express their moral doubts about abortion—and also their worries that severe restrictions on the practice, particularly in the early weeks of pregnancy, could be both unworkable and dangerous to the health of women?

One of the most heartening developments in politics in recent years has been the movement to use noncoercive approaches to achieve sharp reductions in the number of abortions. Consider the case of Thomas R. Suozzi, the county executive of Long Island's Nassau County, a churchgoing Catholic who believes that abortion should remain legal, and a Democrat who thinks that government should take concrete steps to make it easier for women to choose against abortion.

In May 2005 Suozzi tried to move the national abortion debate to more constructive ground in a speech at Adelphi University. "As a Democrat, I do not often find it easy to talk with other Democrats about our need to affirm our commitment to the respect for life and how we need to emphasize our party's firm belief in the worth of every human being," he said. "As a Catholic, I do not often find it easy to talk with other Catholics about my feeling that abortion should and will remain safe and legal, and that we should instead focus our efforts on creating a better world where there are fewer unplanned pregnancies and where women who face unplanned pregnancies receive greater support and where men take more responsibility for their actions."

Suozzi spoke directly to the cultural contradictions that push many women toward abortion. Women, he said, are "unfairly judged regardless of the choices they make." To wit: "Women who choose abortion have their morality questioned. Women who choose to put a baby up for adoption have their maternal instincts questioned, and women who carry an unplanned pregnancy to full term when unmarried or financially insecure are often labeled irresponsible."

Suozzi asked questions that politicians on both sides of the issue often slide by: "Why do women choose abortion in the first place? Fear of the stigma or the economic burden of single motherhood? Concerns regarding the effect of the child on career or life plans? Worry about affording good prenatal medical care or housing? These are all valid questions—and if we can answer them with more specificity, perhaps we will do more to reduce the necessity for abortions."

When prochoice Democrats say anything about reducing the abortion rate, cynics say that they are looking at the election returns and trying to cut the party's losses among prolifers. Some of Senator Hillary Clinton's statements on abortion that paralleled Suozzi's view ran into this line of attack. But Clinton and Suozzi are, in fact, challenging the right-to-life movement no less than their own side. "A decade ago," Suozzi said in an interview, "I was attending Mass and a priest said that abortion would probably stay legal for the rest of his life. It struck me at the time that maybe we should stop arguing about the legality of abortion and try to figure out how to reduce the number of abortions." As for supporters of abortion rights, Suozzi said, "The left needs to prove that it's pro-choice and not just pro-abortion by supporting the other choice."

Surprisingly, given the habit of polarization, Suozzi's proposal won some initial sympathy from Long Island's Roman Catholic bishop, William Murphy, who called the speech "important and, on the whole, very helpful." It is, in fact, very hard to dispute Suozzi's reading of the public's moral sense on this question. "Most people," he says, "say that abortion should remain legal, but wish there weren't so many of them."

"Anyone who really wishes to reduce the number of abortions," Suozzi added, "has an obligation to help those women who choose not to have an abortion yet find themselves alone."

Some months later, Suozzi put money behind his words by announcing nearly $1 million in county government grants to groups ranging from Planned Parenthood to Catholic Charities. He proposed to support an array of programs—adoption, housing, sex education, and abstinence promotion—to reduce unwanted pregnancies and to help pregnant women who want to bring their children into the world. Note that the grants went to groups on both sides of the usual culture-war frontiers. At his news conference announcing the grants, he was flanked by representatives of both ends of the abortion debate.

True, Suozzi's support for abstinence programs made some liberals nervous. But as the National Campaign to Prevent Teen and Unplanned Pregnancy has long argued, the best approach to the problem involves neither abstinence-only nor contraception-only programs but a combination of the two.

It's worth pausing to notice that the problem of teen pregnancy is an area where real progress has been made by putting aside culture-war arguments in favor of a focus on what works. As it turns out, what works in this case conforms to the moral and practical intuitions of most Americans, including most parents.

The best available research suggests that abstinence-only programs do not reduce teen pregnancy, and a widely publicized study released in the spring of 2007 suggested that such programs appear to have little effect on teenage sexual activity.

What the data do suggest, according to Doug Kirby, one of the nation's most careful students of teen pregnancy statistics, is that the programs that work best *combine* abstinence messages with contraception as a backup. "What a large majority of American sexuality educators and a large majority of Americans are pushing for is abstinence plus," Kirby says, meaning "you give real weight to abstinence, you give it serious attention, you say that abstinence is the only method that is 100 percent effective against pregnancy and sexually transmitted diseases. But then you also talk about condoms and contraception in a balanced and accurate manner."

Perhaps the least surprising but also least remarked-upon finding is that age and sexual experience of the teens involved in any given program also matters. "If you only have 5 or 10 percent of the youth in a grade level who have had sex, then the abstinence-only message is fine, it's appropriate," Kirby says. "When a larger percentage have had sex, I think we have a moral obligation to give them accurate information about condoms and contraception."

It doesn't always happen this way, but in the case of teen pregnancy, the discoveries of the researchers match what most Americans believe is the sensible approach: a majority of adults believe that teens should avoid sex until they get out of high school, and nearly three-quarters support programs that provide information on both abstinence and contraception.

Religious polarization has been fostered by the idea that American society is in steep moral decline, that dark forces have undermined traditional values, that only radical changes in behavior and politics can set things right. Yet American culture has already begun a slow process of healing itself without taking any sharp turns. Indeed, it's striking that the 1990s—coinciding with the Clinton era and a period of broadly shared economic growth and optimism—marked the beginning of this turn around. That was certainly true in the cases of teen pregnancy and abortion. According to the National Campaign to Prevent Teen and Unplanned Pregnancy, the birth rate for those aged fifteen to nineteen declined 35 percent from 1991 to 2005. The birth rate for African Americans in that age group fell 48 percent between 1991 and 2006. At the same time, the abortion rate has dropped steadily since a peak reached in 1981.

Such figures point to the promise of the abortion reduction approach— *it proposes a concrete goal that can be achieved through a combination of moral and cultural change, economic opportunity, and practical public policy.* That is why abortion reduction politics has now also won champions in Congress.

Shortly before the 2006 elections, a group of twenty-three prochoice and prolife Democratic House members introduced what they called the "Reducing the Need for Abortion and Supporting Parents Act." The unlovely title nonetheless made the bill's point. Sponsored by Tim Ryan, an abortion opponent from Ohio, and Rosa DeLauro, an abortion rights supporter from Connecticut, the bill bridged the gap between those in the prochoice movement who prefer programs encouraging effective contraception and those in the prolife movement who favor programs designed to help women who choose to carry their children to term.

The proposal sought to create or expand programs aimed at reducing teen pregnancy, promoting contraception, and encouraging parental responsibility. But it also included strong measures offering new mothers full access to health coverage, child care, and nutrition assistance. The public debate usually ignores the fact that abortion rates are closely tied to income. As the Guttmacher Institute has reported, "the abortion rate among women living below the federal poverty level . . . is more than four times that of women above 300 percent of the poverty level." The numbers are stark: 44 abortions per 1,000 women in the lower-income group, 10 abortions per 1,000 women in the higher-income group.

In other words: *those who seek fewer abortions must be concerned with the circumstances of poor women.* This has implications for members of both parties, and for those on both sides of the abortion question. Liberal supporters of abortion rights should be eager to promote a measure that does not make abortion illegal but embraces goals, including help for the poor, that liberals have long advocated. Opponents of abortion should acknowledge that even the victories they have won do little to reduce the number of abortions. Rachel Laser, director of the Third Way Culture Project, has pointed out that those who would ban late-term or "partial-birth" abortions need to recognize that very few are performed, meaning that these laws do little to reduce the overall abortion rate. According to one study cited by Laser, far fewer than 1 percent of abortions are performed in the third trimester. Parental consent laws affect fewer than a fifth of all abortions—those obtained by teenagers 17 or younger—and it is not clear how many abortions these measures stop, since some studies suggest that many parents favor rather than oppose abortion in such circumstances. In other words, the "gradualist" approach to banning abortion being pursued by the right-to-life movement may save far fewer fetal lives than the reduction approach proposed by Suozzi, Ryan, and DeLauro.

There is also the politics of the issue. In her study, Laser pointed to a group she called the "abortion grays," that is, the six voters in ten who do not see the issue in black-and-white terms. This group tilts prochoice but does not believe abortion should always be either legal or illegal. For Democrats, this means taking into account that while most of the new members they elected in 2006 favored abortion rights, the party's freshmen included strong opponents of abortion—among them Senator Bob Casey and about a half-dozen of their new House members. Democrats are a party with a prochoice majority, a significant prolife minority, and a lot of grays. Republicans are the more anti-abortion party but include many prochoice voters and grays in their ranks. They face a broadly prochoice country and now have to battle a right-wing image that drove many moderate and independent voters away from their party in the 2006 elections.

If there has been movement toward conciliation on the abortion question among Democrats, there are also signs of change among Republicans, even among the party's strongest opponents of abortion who are increasingly inclined to recognize that a commitment to life entails far more than the abortion question itself.

"The pro-life movement has often been castigated for its focus on the child in the womb, and once the child got out of the womb, he was on his own," Mike Huckabee, a 2008 Republican presidential aspirant and staunch abortion foe, told the *Washington Post*'s Sridhar Pappu in an interview published at the end of August 2007.

"My point," Huckabee continued, "is for us to show true credibility, we must show as much compassion for the child sleeping under the bridge or in the back seat of the car as we do for the one in the womb.

"That's what pro-life really means," he said. "It is really about understanding the value of each individual life as having intrinsic worth. So whether that life is in the womb or is an 89-year-old invalid in long-term care, what we value is the individual and respect the dignity and value of that person."

And as we've seen, after trying to fudge his position on abortion for the benefit of conservative Republican primary voters, Rudy Giuliani, the leader at the time in the polls for his party's presidential nomination, eventually reaffirmed his prochoice position. What's intriguing is that he did so while embracing the DeLauro-Ryan approach.

"I think we can agree, all of us on this stage, that we should seek reductions in abortion," Giuliani said during a debate at the University of South Carolina in mid-May 2007. "I ultimately do believe in a woman's right of choice, but I think that there are ways in which we can reduce abortions. Abortions went down 16 percent when I was the mayor. Adoptions went up 133 percent during the eight years that I was mayor, compared to the prior eight years. So there are ways in which we can work together and achieve results that we all want."

Taking substantial steps to reduce the abortion rate will never settle the larger moral and ethical argument over when human life begins. But it could give religious Americans—liberal, conservative, moderate, and apolitical—a worthy rallying point. And pursuing that goal could show that politicians are capable of living up to their highest calling, which is to seek practical forms of moral seriousness.

V

Pursuing such an approach has been especially difficult on the issue of gay marriage. I should say at the outset that while I have come to support gay marriage for reasons I'll explain, I certainly understand those who oppose it because I once shared their view.

The first time I wrote about the subject was in a laudatory 1995 column about Andrew Sullivan's powerful book *Virtually Normal: An Argument about Homosexuality*. I admired Sullivan's book for many reasons, not the least being his sense that so many public arguments about the rights of gays and lesbians cast it as a fight "between 'perverts' and 'bigots.'" Sullivan's desire to avoid stereotyping those who might disagree with him stood in admirable contrast to a politics of false choices that insists on seeing

every issue in either/or terms. As a conservative himself, Sullivan appreci-
ated that his philosophical tribe was in principle committed to "allowing
individuals considerable freedom of moral action" while also "protecting
the fabric of society that makes such liberties possible in the first place."
Anything involving "the fabric of society" is a public issue. But from the
standpoint of gays and lesbians, the issue is necessarily public for another
reason: denying people basic rights of citizenship (such as the right to serve
in the military) because of their sexual preference is refusing them the
most basic right of all, the right to be honest about who they are.

Sullivan offered his own synthesis aimed at correcting the flaws he perceived in the four major arguments typically made about homosexuality—
he called them "prohibitionist," "liberationist," "conservative," and "liberal." He argued against civil rights laws aimed at banning discrimination
in "private" matters such as housing and employment, but he insisted on
an end to all public discrimination. By this, he meant an end to the ban
on gays in the military and all other government institutions, an insistence
on the repeal of all sodomy laws that applied only to homosexuals, and the
opening of marriage to homosexuals. It's worth noting that when Sullivan
wrote, gay marriage was not remotely near the top of the gay rights agenda.
It was contested not only outside the gay and lesbian communities but
also within. Yet Sullivan insisted on gay marriage for both impeccably
liberal and impeccably conservative reasons. Marriage, he argued, is a right
granted by the state as a "social and public recognition of a private commitment" and therefore, on liberal grounds, could not be denied to same-sex
couples. And marriage promoted commitment and fidelity, virtues dear to
the conservative heart.

Here is what I wrote about Sullivan's argument in 1995:

> In the end, I had both "conservative" and "liberal" qualms about Sulli-
> van's argument. He is surely right about basic rights, such as military
> service, and has a point about the value of publicly recognizing commit-
> ted homosexual relationships. I am less convinced by his insistence on
> the word "marriage" to apply to them. That word and the idea behind
> it carry philosophical and theological meanings that are getting increas-
> ingly muddled and could become more so if it were applied even more
> broadly. And while Sullivan makes some telling points against the "lib-
> eral" gay rights project involving laws against housing and employment
> discrimination, I think he undervalues the usefulness of such mea-

sures—not to "educate" but simply to prevent the most egregious forms of discrimination.

I still hold the same view of civil rights laws as I did then, but I now support gay marriage. I have come to believe that on the latter question, Sullivan is right and I was wrong. Why?

The short answer is that I have found the *conservative* case for gay marriage persuasive. That argument has been made not only by Sullivan but also by Jonathan Rauch in his thoughtful book *Gay Marriage: Why It Is Good for Gays, Good for Straights, and Good for America*, and by conservative *New York Times* columnist David Brooks. This view emphasizes that society has an interest in building respect for long-term commitment and fidelity in sexual relationships. Gay marriage, far from undermining that goal, underscores how important commitment is.

Consider Brooks's argument, offered in a November 2003 column, that

even in this time of crisis, every human being in the United States has the chance to move from the path of contingency to the path of marital fidelity—except homosexuals. Gays and lesbians are banned from marriage and forbidden to enter into this powerful and ennobling institution. A gay or lesbian couple may love each other as deeply as any two people, but when you meet a member of such a couple at a party, he or she then introduces you to a "partner," a word that reeks of contingency.

You would think that faced with this marriage crisis, we conservatives would do everything in our power to move as many people as possible from the path of contingency to the path of fidelity. . . .

The conservative course is not to banish gay people from making such commitments. It is to expect that they make such commitments. We shouldn't just allow gay marriage. We should insist on gay marriage. We should regard it as scandalous that two people could claim to love each other and not want to sanctify their love with marriage and fidelity.

Brooks is a married man with two children. Rauch is gay (and, I might note, he is, like Brooks, a friend whose views differ from my own on many other issues). Rauch has written:

A solitary individual lives on the frontier of vulnerability. Marriage creates kin, someone whose first "job" is to look after you. Gay people, like straight people, become ill or exhausted or despairing and need the comfort and support that marriage uniquely provides. Marriage can strengthen and stabilize their relationships and thereby strengthen the communities of which they are a part. . . . society benefits when people, including gay people, are durably committed to love and serve one another.

Yes, letting same-sex couples wed would in some sense redefine marriage. Until a decade ago, no Western society had ever embraced or, for the most part, even imagined same-sex marriage. But until recently, *no Western society had ever understood, to the extent most Americans do today, that a small and more or less constant share of the population is homosexual by nature.* Homosexuals aren't just misbehaving heterosexuals. Fooling straight people into marrying them is not an option. *Barring them from the blessings of marriage is inhumane and unfair, even if that is a truth our grandparents did not understand.*

So today's real choice is not whether to redefine marriage but how to do so: as a club only heterosexuals can join or as the noblest promise two people can make. To define marriage as discrimination would defend its boundaries by undermining its foundation. (Emphasis added)

I do not expect social conservatives or religious traditionalists to accept these arguments immediately or without qualms. Indeed, to the extent that I still agree with what I said on this subject in 1995, I understand how hard it is for people who live traditional lives (as, in fact, I do) to accept gay marriage. I worry, as they do, about the problems marriage confronts. I agree with them entirely that for all its problems, the two-parent family is, in most cases, still the best mechanism we have to raise children, and that family breakdown is the enemy of economic equality. It is a central theme of this book that caring about social justice requires caring about family values, and that caring about family values—in light of the economic pressures on families—requires caring about social justice.

But Sullivan, Rauch, and Brooks make the essential point: gays and lesbians seeking marriage are not the primary cause of family breakdown. Heterosexuals who walk away from their own marriages in pursuit of other heterosexual relationships bear the primary responsibility. I confess that watching self-proclaimed conservative traditionalists who divorced one, two, or three times profess their loyalty to "traditional marriage" by opposing gay unions made me highly cynical about their supposed fealty to family values—and more sympathetic to gay marriage. In 2007, the conservative writer Kate O'Beirne quipped that among the front-running Republican presidential candidates at the time, the only one with only one wife was the Mormon, Mitt Romney.

Indeed, it was remarkable how eager conservative publications and think tanks were to criticize homosexuals, while remaining remarkably reticent about the obligations of heterosexuals to their own marriages. David Boaz, vice president at the libertarian Cato Institute, wrote a powerful article in 1994 documenting this problem. Boaz wrote:

> Children need two parents, for financial and emotional reasons. Children in fatherless homes are five times as likely to be poor as those in two-parent families. Single mothers also find it difficult to control teen-age boys, and such boys have made our inner cities a crime-ridden nightmare.
>
> Conservatives have taken note of that problem, and many of them have correctly indicted the welfare state. But with a few exceptions—notably Dan Quayle—they seldom put a high enough priority on condemning single parenthood.
>
> And they pay almost no attention to the effects of divorce—every year more children experience divorce or separation than are born out of wedlock. Those children are nearly twice as likely as those from intact families to drop out of high school or to receive psychological help. Conservatives overlook that because they are too busy attacking gay men and lesbians.

Boaz then offered the data on conservative magazines. He noted that the *American Spectator* had run ten articles on homosexuality in the previous three years, compared with two on parenthood, one on teenage pregnancy, and none on divorce. *National Review* had printed thirty-two articles on homosexuality, five on fatherhood and parenting, three on teenage pregnancy, and just one on divorce. Boaz looked at an index of the publications of the Family Research Council, a leading conservative group, and found that "the two categories with the most listings" were "homosexual" and "homosexuals in the military"—he found a total of thirty-four items, plus four on AIDS. The organization, Boaz said, has shown some interest in parenthood—"nine items on family structure, 13 on fatherhood and six on teen pregnancy"—yet there were "more items on homosexuality than on all of those issues combined." He added, "There was no listing for divorce." It's possible that things have changed in the years since Boaz did his research, that there is more discussion of the costs of divorce; but it's also true that the cause of opposing gay marriage became more central to the conservative social agenda over time, particularly in 2004.

The notion that social conservatives might be more interested in stopping gays from marrying than in reducing the divorce rate should be genuinely troubling for authentic believers in traditional values. At least one prominent social conservative, former education secretary William Bennett, understood that this was a problem. Speaking to the Christian Coalition in 1994, Bennett said, "I understand the aversion to homosexuality. I understand the difference between approval and tolerance. But if you look in terms of the damage to the children of America, you cannot compare what the homosexual movement, the gay rights movement, has done with what divorce has done to this society."

It is highly unlikely in the short run that gay marriage will become a popular cause—even if, in the long run, it will be. One of the most extraordinary changes in American public attitudes over the last generation is increasing openness, connectedness, and empathy toward homosexuals. William G. Mayer, one of the most careful students of public opinion and the author of *The Changing American Mind: How and Why American Public Opinion Changed between 1960 and 1988*, sees this as the most important liberalizing change in American attitudes in the pre-Bush era. This has happened because so many heterosexual Americans discovered, as their gay and lesbian friends and relatives came out of the closet, that people they liked and loved were homosexual. The second most important determinant of attitudes toward gays and gay marriage is whether someone has a close gay friend or relative. The most decisive determinant, among evangelical Christians as in the rest of the population, is age. The two findings are related, since young people are far more likely to know and be comfortable with homosexuals.

In the short run, it may ask too much of traditionalists, whose attitudes toward gays and lesbians are so much more open than they used to be, to leap into support for gay marriage. Many uncomfortable with gay marriage are quite willing to give gay and lesbian couples legal rights effectively equal to those granted heterosexual couples. Thanks to the debate on gay marriage pushed by Sullivan, Rauch, and gay rights activists around the nation, a majority of the country has moved to what now seems to be the "moderate" position of supporting civil unions that grant gay couples legal equality, though not formal marriage. The path toward legalized gay marriage will, in most states, pass through civil unions as our religious traditions come to terms with whether gay unions constitute capitulation to a permissive culture or, on the contrary, reflect our culture's profound belief in commitment and fidelity.

And advocates of gay marriage have an obligation to deal with the fear of conservative churches that legal recognition of such unions would compel traditions opposed to gay or lesbian unions on theological grounds to bless them. This is a groundless fear—the government cannot impose its will on churches in this way, a view shared by many civil libertarians who support gay marriage. Nonetheless, it is essential to reassure religious institutions and denominations that nothing the government does to recognize either civil unions or gay marriage would require them to change their theology of marriage or their own practices. There have already been battles on this issue within both the Christian and Jewish traditions. Such arguments will go on no matter what state or local governments do on this question—and our national history of constitutional respect for the integrity of our religious traditions demands that the government not interfere with these debates.

There is so much work to be done to battle against family breakdown and to encourage husbands and wives to strengthen their commitments to each other and to their children. It is, at best, odd and troublesome that religious traditions that have contributed so much to the just ordering of our public life should expend so much energy fighting the desire of homosexuals to have their own committed relationships respected by government, and their rights enshrined in law.

VI

If Bush and the Republicans profited politically from their opposition to gay marriage, particularly in 2004, there was an important battle they lost, and lost decisively, in 2005. It's not possible to understand the backlash against the most strident wing of the religious Right (and, ultimately, the Republican leadership in Washington) without touching on the tragic case of Terri Schiavo.

Politically, the Schiavo case was critical because it marked the collapse of the careful management of the politics of moral issues by Bush and Karl Rove. As we saw in chapter 2, their approach had been shrewd. It involved showing the religious conservatives that the president was with them, but in ways that did not alienate moderates. In the Schiavo case, the administration and its allies turned out to be well to the right of the national consensus on end-of-life issues and were widely perceived by moderates as bending to the far Right.

Morally, the case involved a vast overreach by the federal government, political usurpation of the role of the courts, political pandering of the most overt sort, and a manipulation of both religion and medical science for the purposes of constituency management.

Schiavo's fate had long been a major cause for part of the right-to-life movement. Schiavo had suffered severe brain damage after a potassium imbalance caused a heart attack in 1990, and she went on life support. From 1998 on, Michael, her husband, and Schiavo's parents had battled in court over whether the feeding tube should be removed. Nearly a score of judges were involved in the case, and the decisions ultimately came down on the side of the husband's desire to end artificial life support. Her parents, backed by conservative activists, led the appeals to keep her alive and ultimately brought their case to Congress.

The remarkable denouement came on the morning of March 21, 2005. Called back by its leaders for an emergency session during its Easter recess, Congress empowered federal courts to step into the case, override state rulings, and reinsert Schiavo's feeding tube. At 12:42 a.m. the House passed the bill already approved by the Senate. Bush, who had flown back from his Texas ranch to act on the matter, signed the bill into law at 1:11 a.m. and declared: "I will continue to stand on the side of those defending life for all Americans, including those with disabilities."

Some Democrats spoke out against the bill, with Representative Barney Frank of Massachusetts arguing: "Every aggrieved party in any similar litigation now will . . . come to Congress and ask us to make a series of decisions." He added: "This is a terribly difficult decision which we are, institutionally, totally incompetent to make." But in the end, only fifty-eight House members opposed it, and Senate Democratic leaders declined to use the powers they had to delay a vote on the bill. "Our folks are nervous about this," a high-ranking House Democratic aide told the *Washington Post* at the time. Both parties misread the country's mood on the issue, but Republicans, having pushed the bill through, paid the political price.

And, it turned out, to no practical effect. The federal courts, including ultimately the Supreme Court, did not overturn the state court judgments. Schiavo's tube was never restored, and she died at age forty-one on March 31, 2005.

Why did Congress feel an obligation to turn Schiavo's tragedy into a federal case? President Bush's answer was, on its face, compelling: "In a case such as this, the legislative branch, the executive branch ought to err on the side of life." One did not have to be a religious conservative to agree with that view, or to worry about prematurely allowing someone to die. But what, exactly, did "a case such as this" mean? Did it refer to one that received widespread publicity and became a major national cause for the right-to-life movement? Did it mean any case in which the parents and the spouse disagree about the fate of a loved one?

For as Frank noted in the debate, there are countless decisions made every week when a family member removes someone they love from life support. Shortly before Congress acted on the Schiavo case, a five-and-a-half-month-old baby named Sun Hudson had died after doctors at Texas Children's Hospital removed the breathing tube that had kept him alive. It was removed *over his mother's opposition* under the provisions of the 1999 Texas Advance Directives Act signed by then governor George W. Bush.

Democrats such as Representative Debbie Wasserman Schultz of Florida argued at the time that Bush's decision to sign the bill protecting Schiavo's life was inconsistent with his earlier decision to sign a law designed to rationalize the way end-of-life decisions are made. But whether Wasserman Schultz was right about this or not, there was still the question of why Schiavo's case was a national cause and Sun Hudson's wasn't. Perhaps there were medical and moral distinctions to be made, but how many bills would Congress have to pass to ensure that in every close medical call around the country, we "err on the side of life"? How many courts would have to be involved? That's why it was not surprising that even a conservative-leaning Supreme Court chose to stay out of the Schiavo controversy.

Whatever the merits of the 1999 Texas bill, Bush's decision to sign it was an acknowledgment that end-of-life issues in an age of advanced medical technology must be confronted, however wrenching they are. Facing up to those questions and drawing distinctions is especially important for those who oppose doctor-assisted suicide, as I do. Preventing euthanasia requires the drawing of a very bright line between the withdrawal of artificial life support and the affirmative act of putting a patient to death. My own biggest surprise during the Schiavo controversy was the extent that some in the right-to-life movement were willing to blur this line, which in the long run will weaken, not strengthen, the position of those—again, including me—who see outright "mercy killing" as dangerous.

Nor did those who spoke up so forcefully for keeping Schiavo alive acknowledge how her health care was financed in the fifteen years after her heart attack. The available information suggested that some of the money had come from one of those much-derided medical malpractice lawsuits, and that the drugs she needed had been paid for by Medicaid. The irony was not lost on Democrats. Just a few days after most Republicans in both houses of Congress had supported cuts in federal funding of Medicaid, they voted to err "on the side of life" in a single case. The same issue has come up in Florida, where then governor Jeb Bush, a strong supporter of keeping Schiavo alive, had been proposing cuts of his own in Medicaid spending.

Republicans cried foul when any link was made between the Schiavo question and the Medicaid question. "The fact that they're tying a life issue to the budget process shows just how disconnected Democrats are to reality," harrumphed Dan Allen, a spokesman for House Majority Leader Tom DeLay.

In fact, reality required acknowledging the close link between life issues and money issues. Those who lack access to health care because they can't afford insurance often die earlier than they have to—with absolutely no national publicity and with no members of Congress rising up at midnight to pass bills on their behalf. What did it mean to stand up for life in an individual case but not confront the cost of choosing life for all who are threatened within the health care system—or, perhaps more often, by their lack of access to it?

By raising the central question—what does it mean to be prolife?—the Schiavo case forced issues to the fore that badly need a more searching discussion. And it did more than that: it suggested the terrible distortions of both morality and science that can occur when a genuinely difficult question is transformed into the stuff of sound-bite politics and pandering. We are entitled to our moral, ethical, and philosophical commitments. We are not entitled to our own facts.

On June 15, 2005, the autopsy for Terri Schiavo was made public. It found, as the *Washington Post* reported, that she had "suffered severe, irreversible brain damage that left that organ discolored and scarred, shriveled to half its normal size, and damaged in nearly all its regions, including the one responsible for vision."

I offer these gruesome details because they directly contradicted the claims made by so many politicians in the heat of the Schiavo debate. It's important to acknowledge that the autopsy report did not settle all the moral issues in the Schiavo case. It was certainly legitimate (if, I believe, mistaken) to argue on philosophical grounds that every medical decision in a circumstance such as Schiavo's should be made on the side of keeping the sick person alive. But those who supported an extraordinary use of federal power to force their own conclusion against the judgment of state courts knew that philosophical arguments would not be enough. Most Americans were uneasy about compelling Schiavo's husband to keep his wife alive if—as the state courts had concluded and as the autopsy confirmed—she had suffered irreversible brain damage and was incapable of recovering.

So the political advocates for the case had to invent a story. They had to insist that they knew more about Terri Schiavo's condition than did the doctors on the scene. They had to question Michael Schiavo's motives and imply that he wanted to, well, get rid of her.

"As I understand it," Senate Majority Leader Bill Frist said on the Senate floor, "Terri's husband will not divorce Terri and will not allow her parents to take care of her. Terri's husband, who I have not met, does have a girlfriend he lives with and they have children of their own." The innuendo here was breathtaking.

Frist, a highly respected surgeon before he entered politics, did not just make his case as a prolifer. He invoked his expertise as a member of the medical profession. "I close this evening speaking more as a physician than as a U.S. senator," Frist had said during the debate on the bill forcing a federal review of the case. Proffering references to medical textbooks and journals, Frist led his colleagues through to his conclusion. He argued that "a decision had been made to starve to death a woman based on a clinical exam that took place over a very short period of time by a neurologist who was called in to make the diagnosis rather than over a longer period of time." Dr. Frist, in other words, was offering a second opinion.

In an appearance on ABC's *Good Morning America* after the autopsy, Frist insisted: "I raised the question, 'Is she in a persistent vegetative state or not?' I never made the diagnosis, never said that she was not."

That depended on the meaning of the word "diagnosis." In the midst of his impressively detailed medical review during the earlier debate, Frist had declared flatly: "Terri's brother told me Terri laughs, smiles, and tries to speak. That doesn't sound like a woman in a persistent vegetative state."

As for House Majority Leader Tom DeLay, he did not pretend to be a doctor. But he was expert enough to know what was wrong with the news reports. "Mrs. Schiavo's condition, I believe, has been at times misrepresented by the media," DeLay had said in pushing for the bill to take control of the case from state courts. "Terri Schiavo is not brain-dead; she talks and she laughs, and she expresses happiness and discomfort. Terri Schiavo is not on life-support."

The awful irony is that in the course of the Schiavo case, right-to-life politicians did terrible damage to their own cause. They claimed to know what they did not, and could not, know. They were willing to imply, without proof, terrible things about a husband who was getting in their way. Instead of making the hard and morally challenging case for keeping Terri Schiavo on life support, they spun an emotional narrative that they thought would play well on cable TV and talk radio.

And, finally, they violated nearly all their other stated principles to impose the federal government in a situation that had, traditionally, been the prerogative of state governments and state courts. This drew the ire not just of liberals, but also of many conservatives who themselves sympathized with the right-to-life movement. Writing in the *New York Times*, Adam Liptak cited the honest anguish of Douglas W. Kmiec, a well-known conservative law professor at Pepperdine University, over Congress's action: "I would be naturally inclined to Terri Schiavo's part in this enterprise," Kmiec told Liptak. "This is, however, a benignly intended but tragically mistaken law. It contravenes almost every principle known to constitutional jurisprudence." It bothered Kmiec, Liptak reported, that Congress had been so quick to assume the worst of Florida's state judiciary. "There seems to be a very troubling supposition in this law that the state courts were biased or prejudiced or incompetent," Kmiec said. "Yet state judges are men and women of training who have taken an oath to uphold the Constitution."

Religious and moral commitments cannot be trumped by scientific and legal expertise, but neither can those offering religious and moral arguments freely distort science or contort their own legal and political principles in defense of what they see as a higher law. The scriptures tell us that the truth shall make us free. Religious activists in politics should hold themselves to the same standards against twisting the truth that they rightly insist upon applying to their fellow citizens of a more secular inclination. From the Schiavo case, they should learn the dangers of a moral arrogance that will, ultimately, defeat the very causes they would advance.

VII

The narrowing of the focus of religious engagement in politics to abortion, gay marriage, end-of-life questions, and a handful of other cultural issues is—it's a strong word, I know—a sin. It limits the reach of faith. It suggests to some who might otherwise contemplate belief that religion is primarily about right-wing politics and drives many such people away. In the case of Christianity, it radically confines a tradition that through history has had much of importance to say about the just ordering of political, economic, and social life.

That is why a rebellion against this selling out of a great tradition is now under way. The case of Rich Cizik, vice president for government affairs at the National Association of Evangelicals is inspiring. In March 2007 Cizik faced down right-wing partisans as the board of the National Association of Evangelicals reaffirmed its own view, and Cizik's, that solving global warming is an important moral cause.

Cizik, who combines his opposition to abortion with a firm commitment to human rights, the poor, and the environment, came under attack from a gang of ideologues who would freeze evangelicals on a political course set more than a quarter-century ago.

"This tussle over the issue of climate change is part of a bigger tussle over the definition of evangelicalism and who speaks for evangelicals," Cizik says. Calling on evangelicals to "return to being people who are known for our love and care for our fellow human beings and the Earth," Cizik warned that "if you put the politics first and make it primary, I believe that is a tragic and fateful choice."

The political maestros who threw in their lot with Republican politics could not abide any serious evangelical Christian daring to broaden the agenda beyond the limited set of issues that kept the faithful voting for the GOP. Cizik was a threat, so they attacked him in a March 1, 2007, letter to the NAE board. It was signed by such conservative luminaries as Paul Weyrich, James Dobson of Focus on the Family; Don Wildmon of the American Family Association, Tony Perkins of the Family Research Council, and Gary Bauer, who ran for the 2000 Republican presidential nomination.

"Cizik and others," they said, "are using the global warming controversy to shift the emphasis away from the great moral issues of our time, notably the sanctity of human life, the integrity of marriage and the teaching of sexual abstinence and morality to our children."

Worse, they smeared Cizik because he had expressed concern about the size of world's population in a speech last year at the World Bank. "We ask," they wrote, "how is population control going to be achieved if not by promoting abortion, the distribution of condoms to the young, and, even by infanticide in China and elsewhere?"

To suggest that Cizik, given his record, favored abortion or infanticide was scandalous. "My wife shows up in church," Cizik lamented "and people ask her, 'Is your husband pro-abortion and in favor of abortion as birth control?'" It was also unpersuasive. The board of the NAE, with only a single dissenting vote, backed Cizik and the organization's earlier stand on the importance of "creation care" in dealing with climate change.

What made the fight strange is that Cizik is no liberal. On the contrary, he supported Ronald Reagan twice and George W. Bush twice. He is still proud of his role in drafting the invitation to Reagan that led to the former president's 1983 speech before the NAE calling the Soviet Union an "evil empire."

Cizik simply rejected the idea that his environmental commitment ran contrary to his support for the antiabortion movement: "Tell the parents of children who are mentally disabled because of mercury poisoning—tell them that the environment is not a sanctity-of-life issue," he says. "We should be primarily concerned with what the Gospel says, not whether you're getting off some political train." Those are the words of the New Reformation. Many evangelicals are boarding a new train. It runs along tracks defined by the broad demands of their faith, not by some party's political agenda or some ideology's very particular demands.

But the struggle within the evangelical movement was just one part of a broader argument raging among American Christians. The Catholic Church, with its well-articulated views on so many public issues, was also challenged by the intense partisanship of the Bush years. And its engagement in politics was shaped by two Europeans—a charismatic Pole and a brilliant German intellectual—whose impact on American politics was profound.

5. John Paul, Benedict, and the Catholic Future

It is at odd moments that you realize the peculiar (yet often important) impact of the religious tradition in which you're raised. I had one of those realizations about my Catholicism back in 1986 when I was covering the Vatican and found myself drawn to a speech in which Pope John Paul II was defending the idea that angels existed.

The pope was very careful to say that believing in angels was not a central tenet of the faith and acknowledged that "confusion at times is great" on the subject. Indeed. Yet a small piece of me inside cheered when the pope insisted: "The angels are those creatures which are unseen. They are invisible, for they are purely spiritual beings." And as was his way, he rebuked "materialists and rationalists" for denying their existence and insisted that angels were "collateral yet inseparable from the central revelation."

I confess that some of my enthusiasm for the pope's comments reflected my immediate awareness that I would be surprising the mostly rationalist readers of the *New York Times* by confronting them with a story about angels as they drank their morning cups of coffee. (My love of the movie *It's a Wonderful Life*, in which an angel plays a prominent role, may also have conditioned my view.)

But I also rather liked what I saw as a specifically Catholic tendency to try to give elaborate (and, occasionally, I'll acknowledge, even contorted) intellectual support to the idea of a spiritual realm apart from the material—to the notion, as I wrote in my story at the time, that there is more to life than, well, *this* life. I quoted a priest in the Vatican as saying of John Paul: "He's trying to get people to appreciate the spiritual dimension of human existence. If you believe, as the Pope does and as I do, that this is not the only world, you have to think about what links there are between this world and the other world."

And then my informant added: "If the Pope can't talk about these things, who can?"

I offer this tale by way of explaining that the next two chapters about the Roman Catholic Church are, at once, analytical and personal. It is impossible to discuss religion and American politics without paying close attention to the role of Catholics, a quarter of the electorate and growing, and of a church that has been so outspoken on public matters from abortion and war to economic justice and immigration. Catholic social thought has been influential beyond Catholic or even Christian circles, and it is a brute political fact that Catholics are, along with mainline Protestants, two of the country's most important swing voting blocks. It is also impossible to discuss the American Catholic Church without understanding the influence of popes John Paul II and Benedict XVI. But as I explained at the outset, this chapter and the next also reflect my own passions, engagements, and interests.

I learned covering the Vatican for *New York Times* in the mid-1980s that it was quite possible for me as a Catholic to be—and I know this is a contested word—unbiased in my coverage of the Church in the sense that I could write with some distance on the intellectual, political, and theological currents shaping Catholicism at that moment. My Catholic background was more helpful in this task than not, since I had learned as a matter of course from the time of childhood about Catholic doctrine and could understand from the inside why Catholics might believe in the Virgin Birth or transubstantiation, or angels. (I also understood easily enough why many others found these doctrines strange or even irrational.) I had also learned a great deal, almost without trying, about Catholic history. And—most usefully, given the controversies of that moment—I had learned about many of the progressive tendencies in theology, including the theology of hope and the theology of liberation, as a college undergraduate.

It was also easy enough to understand that the Vatican was, in many obvious ways, a political organization, even if the Church's mission was spiritual and, in principle, other-worldly in its focus. I would sometimes tell friends that I often tried to cover the Vatican as if I were still covering the New York State Legislature. There are competing forces in the Vatican and in the Church, as there are in a legislature or any other political body. Part of the job was to try to identify the different factions and voices, and to get inside the thinking of those involved in the contests that would define the future of Catholicism.

And it was certainly easy during Pope John Paul II's papacy to understand that part of the job was to cover an astonishing world-historical figure who was shaping his church but also his times. Yes, John Paul was many of the things people said he was: a charismatic, shrewd, tough, intelligent leader who took the long view and had a strategy for the Church and the world. This was a man who mastered modernity's tools in the name of challenging a fair share of modernity's assumptions. So much of the confusion about him stems from his complex and paradoxical relationship to the modern world. For John Paul, modernity's attitudes on everything from sex to business—and above all its skepticism about the spiritual realm—were in need of radical change. His use of modern language and modern communications did nothing to hide the message. Yet many were understandably perplexed that a figure so resolutely up-to-date in certain ways was so forcefully opposed to the spirit of his times in others. Trying to unravel that mystery was one of the joys of being a journalist at the Vatican in the mid-1980s, when John Paul was at the height of his energies. I saw my task not as trying to propagate the faith—or my own religious views—but rather as trying to explain this man and his purpose, this church and its role in the world.

Yet, of course, I was also a Catholic. I would often take a break from writing my stories during papal masses in Africa or South America or India to receive Communion. My conversations with Vatican officials, particularly the people I got to know well, often involved not simply questions of a journalistic sort but also inquiries on just why this church we both belonged to taught and acted as it did. (Many intellectually curious non-Catholic journalists also had conversations of that sort; covering the Vatican gave everyone so inclined an excuse to ponder the Big Questions.) I couldn't resist pressing the usual "North American" questions: Why did the church not allow women or married men to become priests, why did it oppose "artificial" birth control, why was power so centralized in a church that now preached the merits of democracy? Over time, such queries, particularly the ones related to women and sexuality, became a useful litmus tests that informed my journalism by telling me how different individuals thought about things. *How* people went about answering my questions, and not just whether they took the orthodox line, taught me a great deal about who they were, how they thought, and how the issues I might raise were discussed inside the Vatican itself. There were, as well, discussions of "South American" questions related to liberation theology, elements of which the Vatican was condemning at the time, and how one should properly read the views of the pope and the Church on social justice.

The odd thing was that the *less* Catholic I felt, the *easier* I found it to be sympathetic to John Paul's (and, then-cardinal Joseph Ratzinger's) view. From a distance, I could see how, given John Paul's analysis of modernity's corrosive effects on the Church, the task of proclaiming an uncompromising doctrine with great clarity and free from ambiguity was an urgent priority. And it was also obvious that the pope confirmed many progressive departures that began with John XXIII and the Second Vatican Council, even as he blunted others. Yet the more I thought of myself as a Catholic— a Catholic of a liberal sort—the more inclined I was to worry about the course John Paul and the Church were taking.

Several tensions thus run through the discussion in the next two chapters: what I hope is a dispassionate discussion of the role of Catholics in American politics stands side-by-side with my own views as a liberal Catholic. My analysis of John Paul II and Benedict XVI reflects both admiration and unease. And I conclude with a defense of the liberal Catholic worldview that I believe—despite the many setbacks described here— remains surprisingly robust.

II

Do you think of John Paul as the man who condemned "luxurious egoism" and "imperialistic monopoly"? Do you remember him as the friend of workers who asserted "the priority of labor over capital"? Do you honor him as the first Pope who visited a synagogue, who told Catholics to embrace Jews as "our elder brothers," and who condemned anti-Semitism "at any time and by anyone"? Do you regard him as the hero of human rights who helped bring down Communist dictatorships and battled the death penalty?

Or do you think of John Paul as the man who presided over the condemnation of theologians who questioned the Church's teachings or preached liberation theology? Do you see him as intransigent in refusing to allow questioning of the all-male celibate priesthood? Do you note the extent to which he transformed the Church by appointing conservative bishops and by naming a College of Cardinals likely to keep Catholicism on a traditionalist path?

"A sign of contradiction" was a favorite John Paul phrase, and it might be said to define his papacy.

One cannot understand the pope apart from his native Poland. Yet nothing rankled John Paul or his supporters more than the tendency to reduce him to his Polishness.

Although he rejected the dialectical materialism of Marxism, John Paul himself might be called a dialectical spiritualist. He was relentless in his attacks on Marxism, seeing in it not only a rebellion against God but also a violence against the dignity of the individual, which comes directly from God. But there were also those fiery speeches criticizing capitalism.

John Paul was an intellectual. But he was dedicated to the intellectually unfashionable symbols of popular Christianity: those angels, relics, and statues, devotions to the saints and, above all, the Blessed Virgin Mary.

He consistently subordinated the political to the spiritual in principle, but he vastly increased the political influence of the Church.

He always and everywhere called himself a pope of the Second Vatican Council. Yet his critics contended that he sought to roll back the reforms of Vatican II.

He was the most universal of popes, sensitive to cultural diversity inside the Church. Yet he did more to centralize authority in the Vatican than any pope since the Council.

In his effect on Roman Catholicism's relationship to the world, John Paul's achievement will be judged largely as liberal. But his impact on the Church he led has to be seen as conservative. These terms are vexed, and John Paul himself would probably reject them—he'd insist on his own consistency in opposing both the Marxist and capitalist forms of materialism, in arguing that the spiritual is always primary, and in asserting the Church's obligation to doctrinal clarity. But the pope's version of consistency does not necessarily match that of the world that is judging him. That's one of the many paradoxes at the heart of his papacy.

Take first John Paul's approach to the outside world. Before the Second Vatican Council and the papacy of John XXIII, the Church decried modernity and liberalism, which many in the Church leadership condemned simply as "a sin." As Peter Steinfels has noted, Pope Pius IX used the terms "pernicious," "perfidious," "perverse," and "a virus," to refer to liberal

Catholicism. The pre–Vatican II Church, especially in the 1930s, was inclined toward authoritarian governments and worried that embracing religious liberty meant tolerating "error."

Vatican II changed that, marking a truce with the modern world and, for many Catholics, an opportunity to embrace it. The Church sided with religious tolerance, democracy, and human rights. It was a stance at once moral and practical. Moral, for what are obvious reasons to modern lovers of liberty. Practical, because the Church was beginning to grow in parts of the world where it found itself in the minority. Anyone who belongs to a group that finds itself in the minority learns the value of minority rights.

It's also important to see John Paul as, at least in part, building on the legacy of Pope John XXIII, who believed profoundly in taking the world as he found it—which meant grappling creatively with modernity. "Distrustful souls," he wrote in December 1961, "see only darkness burdening the face of the earth. We prefer instead to reaffirm all our confidence in our Savior who has not abandoned the world which he redeemed. Indeed, we make our own the recommendation of Jesus that we learn to distinguish 'the signs of the times,' and we seem to see now in the midst of so much darkness more than a few indications that augur well for the fate of the church and of humanity." As Father Joseph A. Komonchak, the premier historian of the Second Vatican Council, has noted, "The conviction that God was still present and active in the world, as in the church, lay behind his frequent remark that the church is not a museum of antiques but a living garden of life."

John Paul confirmed the historic shift that John initiated and Pope Paul VI sustained. Precisely because John Paul is seen as a conservative, his acceptance of these changes almost certainly makes them irreversible. One can make a strong case that, one hundred years from now, John Paul's best-remembered achievements will be the "liberal" ones. He insisted upon the dignity of every human person and thereby campaigned for human rights, for social justice, and for the rights of workers and the poor. At Yad Vashem, he apologized for "the hatred, acts of persecution, and displays of anti-Semitism directed against the Jews by Christians." There was some debate over whether he had said enough. For Jews and Catholics of a certain age, what he said was a breathtaking relief.

And his experiences reaffirmed, as the Second Vatican Council and John had understood, that religious tolerance had practical benefits for a Church taking root in the world's non-Christian regions. His visit to India in 1986 was a striking lesson in the importance of religious liberty to the future of the Church. Walls in Madras carried anti-Christian graffiti, including "Go with Christ. Go get crucified." No wonder John Paul praised the "precious principle" of the Indian constitution, which "specifically includes the right 'to profess, practice, and propagate religion.'"

John Paul lived in dynamic tension with modernity. That is different from outright opposition. And he was obviously skilled at adapting a two-thousand-year-old Church to the realities of his times. He realized that a centralized papacy provided him with a platform no other religious leader could claim. The pope may have no divisions, as Stalin once sneered, but boy, could he command media attention.

And on economic questions, as we've seen, the pope was, in the broadest sense, a progressive who may have understood the market's benefits better than earlier popes but also understood its limits. Not only *Centesimus annus* but also *Loborem exercens* remain touchstones for those who rally to movements for social justice and stand up for the rights of labor.

If John Paul's story stopped here, his papacy would be about the triumph of liberal Catholicism. But that is not how we understand it, because, if so much of what the pope did in relation to the world outside the Church was progressive, so much of what he did inside it was conservative. His was a centralizing papacy, a papacy that insisted upon a strict—his critics would say narrow—view of orthodoxy. John Paul closed off debate on the nature of the priesthood, refusing discussion of expanding its ranks to women and noncelibate men despite the great shortage of priests. In a Church that had relied on the work of nuns, many middle-class, educated women—especially in the United States—went into rebellion. He cracked down hard on dissent, dealing blows to what conservatives might call the North American heresies (about sex and birth control) and the South American heresies (about Marxism).

This did not go down well with theologians who insisted there was nothing heretical about their convictions. The Reverend Charles Curran, a well-liked, respected (and tenured) professor of moral theology at Catholic University, was condemned in the mid-1980s and told to leave the faculty for his critique of the Church's stance on—among other things—birth control. Liberal Catholic scholars feared the threat to academic freedom. Curran's home bishop backed him strongly. "If Father Curran's status as a Roman Catholic theologian is brought into question," said Bishop Matthew Clark of Rochester, "I fear a serious setback to Catholic education and pastoral life in this country."

The Vatican condemned liberation theology, which emphasized Christians' obligation to shake up or overthrow unjust social structures. It was understandable that the pope might see it as a kind of Christianized Marxism, given his profound mistrust of a system of thought that had left his native Poland in chains. Yet many progressive Latin American bishops at the time begged to differ. "[L]iberation theology is not a theology of violence or one that pushes toward violence," insisted Bishop Jose Ivo Lorscheiter of Santa Maria, Brazil. "It is not a theology that assumes or justifies Marxist ideology."

The battle over liberation theology reflected the break—at once large and subtle—between the spirit of John XXIII's papacy and the spirit of John Paul's. John XXIII quite consciously sought to create an opening to the left for Catholicism. His papacy paved the way within Italian politics for coalitions between the Christian Democrats, the traditional Catholic party, and democratic socialists. But the implications of his policies were felt well beyond Italy. John XXIII's key encyclicals in the early 1960s, *Pacem in terris* (Peace on Earth) and *Mater et magistra* (Mother and Teacher), urged Catholics to work in broad alliances for peace and justice and freed them to be more open than in the past to ideas that came from hostile shores, including Marxism. Conservatives understood the threat. *National Review*, William F. Buckley Jr.'s magazine, rejected the even more radical second encyclical with the cheeky line, "Mater, Si, Magistra, No."

Freed by John XXIII, Catholic theologians, notably the Rev. Johannes Metz in West Germany, began friendly philosophical dialogues with Marxists and, in Metz's case, began creating what he called a "political theology." The ferment in Europe resonated in Latin America in the late 1960s, when continued Church support for dictatorships and oligarchies seemed increasingly untenable, especially after Vatican II.

At a meeting in 1968 in Medellin, Colombia, the Latin American bishops adopted a document that has had profound effects. Latin Americans, they said, "must resist personal and collective injustice with unselfish courage and fearlessness." The misery of the continent "expresses itself as injustice which cries to the heavens."

The Medellin meeting in 1968 endorsed the priestly activism already widespread in Latin America and spurred more. One such activist was the Rev. Gustavo Gutierrez, a Peruvian theologian who had been influenced by Father Metz and the Christian-Marxist dialogue. In 1971 he published his book *Theology of Liberation*, which gave a movement its name.

From the book's first sentences, Gutierrez said his work was not simply an academic exercise but something that grew out of "the oppressed and exploited land of Latin America." Crediting Marxism with encouraging theologians to "reflect on the meaning of the transformation of the world," Father Gutierrez said, "To deny the fact of class struggle was really to put oneself on the side of the dominant sectors."

"It is not a question of admitting or denying a fact which confronts us," he went on. "Rather, it is a question of which side we are on." The Church, he said, must side definitively with the poor, for whom Christ had shown special love. To eliminate poverty "is to bring closer the moment of seeing God face to face, in union with other men."

Although liberation theology planted itself more deeply in some Latin American countries than others, Father Gutierrez's writings and those of his liberationist colleagues were clearly an instance in which ideas had consequences. This was evidenced most dramatically in the Sandinista revolution in Nicaragua. A large part of the church joined the opposition to the dictatorship of Anastasio Somoza Debayle, and many of the most important leaders of the revolution were priests who had linked Christian and Marxist concepts of liberation. The Vatican barred some of them from their priestly functions. The liberationists also spawned thousands of "base communities" of poor people that blended prayer with political reflection, organization, and action.

Within parts of the Latin American hierarchy, there was a sharp and immediate reaction to the theory and practice that grew out of Medellin. Led by Archbishop Alfonso Lopez Trujillo of Colombia—he was named a cardinal by John Paul in 1983—the more conservative bishops, with support in the Vatican, sought to blunt the revolutionary thrust.

John Paul found himself in the midst of this fierce infighting within three months of his election as pope. During a triumphal tour of Mexico in 1979, he opened a meeting of Latin American bishops in Puebla. He left no doubt about where he stood.

On the one hand, the pope spoke of the need to "humanize political and economic systems." He told the bishops that owners of private property carried the responsibility of a "social mortgage," and that Christ had shown that "in the last analysis he will identify himself with the disinherited."

But the bulk of his address was a clear warning. Besides scoffing at the idea of Christ as "a political figure," John Paul warned against the "mutilation" of the faith, the setting off of an "institutional" Church against a "people's" Church, and urged the bishops not to allow Catholicism to "be contaminated by other brands of humanism."

The idea of Marxism as fundamentally atheistic and of "class struggle" as being foreign to Christian ethics guided the Vatican's Congregation for the Doctrine of the Faith in its two documents on liberation theology issued in the 1980s. Their principal author was Cardinal Ratzinger. The first, issued in September 1984, warned of the "terrible contradictions" involved in integrating Marxism with Christianity, since "atheism and the denial of the human person, his liberty and his rights are at the core of Marxist theory."

In a passage that resonated with the pope's own experience with Communism in power in Poland, the document declared that revolutionary movements fighting in the name of freedom for the oppressed often betrayed those whom they claimed to be liberating.

The reaction among Latin American advocates of the theology was a mixture of caution and anger. Many asserted that they had never been Marxists and that the document could not be about them. The Rev. Leonardo Boff of Brazil, a leading liberation theologian, complained that the document betrayed "a peculiar outlook, one foreign to the milieu where the theology in question originated, flourishes and is being practiced." He added, "This massive attack on Marxism will reinforce, objectively, those who, in the name of anti-Marxism, persecute, torture and kill."

A few months later, Father Boff was officially silenced by Rome for nearly a year. Both Vatican officials and supporters of the Brazilian insisted that he had been singled out not for his social teaching but as an advocate of changes in the structure of the Church. Yet in their criticisms of Boff, Gutierrez, and other liberation theologians, John Paul and Ratzinger were clearly closing the door that John XXIII had opened to the Left.

But was the door closed all the way? Shortly after the silencing of Father Boff was lifted, Ratzinger issued his second document on liberation theology. While it contained many of the same warnings as the first document, it spoke repeatedly of the Church's obligations to the poor, of the right of the poor themselves to struggle for justice—and even, in extreme circumstances, to use "armed struggle" to overthrow unjust regimes.

If there appears to be a certain ambivalence in the Vatican's view on change and revolution at the theoretical level, this became clear at a practical level when Jaime Cardinal Sin, the archbishop of Manila, threw the Church into the movement to oust Ferdinand E. Marcos as president of the Philippines.

At first, the signals from the Vatican were favorable. But it became clear over time—confirmed later by Cardinal Sin himself—that the pope was decidedly uncomfortable with the overt political role that the Church had played, even though its actions were based throughout on a strategy of nonviolence. Still, the pope never criticized Cardinal Sin directly or in public.

As Sin's example suggested, restiveness and dissent were not confined to the Americas. The condemnation of Swiss-born theologian Hans Kung struck a blow against a liberal thinker of worldwide reputation. In 1985 the Roman Catholic bishops of England and Wales issued a statement warning against "a lack of tolerance and a certain new fundamentalism" in the Church. The statement called for greater local autonomy and argued against what the bishops saw as a habit of referring to Rome "decisions which could be made locally."

But the local churches themselves were profoundly changed by John Paul. The power to appoint is the power to control, and the pope literally outlasted his adversaries. As liberals in the Church leadership passed on, John Paul replaced them with loyalists, minimizing dissent at the top. Emblematic of these changes were the pope's appointments of John J. O'Connor as archbishop in New York City and Bernard F. Law as archbishop in Boston. (O'Connor has passed away, and Law left Boston for a Vatican post after he was widely criticized for his handling of the sex-abuse scandal.) The two were dubbed "Archbishops Law and Order" for their assigned roles of enforcing the pope's version of orthodoxy on the restive American Church. There are now many more bishops like them (and, in fairness to O'Connor, a fascinating man who retained a strong commitment to social justice, many are far more conservative than he ever was).

The pope's insistence on democracy outside the Church thus did not translate to democracy inside the Church. His skilled spokesman, Joaquin Navarro-Valls, once offered a pair of aphorisms to explain why. "Authority is a guarantee of unity," Navarro-Valls said. "Authority is also a guarantee of truth." It's also true that authority too readily invoked can spark dissent, and some of John Paul's "truths"—like the proposition that women may never, under any circumstances, become priests—were simply not accepted by many liberal Catholics, particularly in the United States.

There is, of course, something profoundly dissatisfying about creating dueling balance sheets—the Liberal List and the Conservative List—in judging John Paul's papacy. It reflects that temptation again: to reduce all religion and spirituality to politics. Doing so ignores what John Paul saw as the heart of his mission: the recovery of the sacred in an often profane world. If John Paul stood for one large thing, it was that the spiritual always took precedence over the material. Almost everyone has thus found something to praise and something to criticize about this man, because almost all Catholics—indeed, most religious people influenced by modernity—embrace some aspects of the modern world while worrying about modernity's spiritual black holes. We all agreed with John Paul some of the time.

Dislike the alienating aspects of modern capitalism? So did the pope. During a visit in the mid-1980s to Ciudad Guayana, an isolated industrial town in eastern Venezuela, the pope said workers should be protected from "dehumanizing" conditions. He attacked an "ideology of technology" that "imposed the primacy of matter over spirit, of things over the human person." That's why he could demand, as he did in Ecuador, that none could feel "tranquil" while "there is a child without school, a family without a home, a worker without a job, an ill or elderly person without adequate attention."

But John Paul equally opposed the "dialectical and historical materialism" at the heart of Marxism because it dismissed religion as "a kind of idealistic illusion." For him, materialism was the greatest of illusions. He thus opposed efforts to politicize the person of Christ, to depict him as "a political activist, as a fighter against Roman domination and the authorities, and even as someone involved in the class struggle." In his 1979 address to the Latin American bishops in Mexico, John Paul insisted that "the conception of Jesus as a political figure, a revolutionary, as the subversive from Nazareth, does not tally" with the Church's teaching.

At some level—and this genuinely troubled left-wing Catholics—the pope's politics were antipolitical since he always insisted on personal redemption above all else. This could be seen most clearly in his analysis of sin. Left-wing Christians have insisted on the idea of "sinful structures," that is, economic and social institutions which, by their nature, perpetrate evil.

John Paul accepted the idea of sinful structures. But he turned the emphasis around, worrying that the structural argument "leads more or less unconsciously to the watering down and almost abolition of personal sin." It became too easy, the pope said, to blame evil on "some vague entity or anonymous collectivity, such as the situation, the system, society, structures or institutions." Sin, the pope argued, "is always a personal act."

His Easter message of 1986 offered a classic John Paul formulation: "Man commits sin without calling by name what he does. But this is not the way of liberation. This is only the way of falsifying the truth."

At bottom, the Pope often said, he was calling not for revolution but individual conversion. "Change hearts," he asserted in a message to young people in the mid-1980s, "and you will change the world."

There were times during his travels when the pope seemed more at home with the deep spirituality of poor non-Christians in the Third World than with the affluent, modernized Christians of the West. During a 1986 visit, he spoke of India as "a religious nation generously committed to a spiritual pilgrimage," a place of "great simplicity, asceticism and renunciation" with the mission "to offer the world a spiritual vision of man." He said of India's ascetic hero: "Gandhi was much more Christian than many people who say they are Christians."

His sympathies extended to Africans who followed traditional beliefs about the divinity of nature. During a 1985 visit to Togo, he told a group of animist priests: "Nature, exuberant and splendid in this place of forests and lakes, impregnates spirits and hearts with its mystery and orients them spontaneously toward the mystery of He who is the author of life." John Paul, the doctrinal conservative, was not selling out his Christian faith or embracing New Age religion. But he did seem to be leading a worldwide popular alliance in rebellion against modernity's denial of the sacred.

In 1986 the pope declared that "Easter in the church means the passage to Eternal Life that comes from God and is life in God. No promised land on this earth can assure such a liberty, such a life."

Those of us still on "this earth," often struggling for the faith that so animated John Paul, will inevitably debate the meaning of his legacy in the secular terms that so dominate our times. We should try to remember that these were not the terms on which he lived his life.

So who was John Paul? In my experience, at least, he was both powerful and serene. He could be warm and stern, mystical and down-to-earth, immensely worldly and thoroughly committed to the world beyond this one. Yeah, I liked the guy.

But I have great anxieties about splits between left and right that deepened under John Paul. I worry about the declining number of priests and nuns and the dwindling ranks of clerics inspired by Vatican II. I worry about what my daughters will make of a Church that reserves so much power for men. I worry that the balance between free inquiry and doctrinal rigor has shifted too decisively in favor of a very particular definition of orthodoxy.

I have little doubt about how John Paul's impact on his times will be judged. In the world's large struggles—over human rights and democracy, poverty and social justice, war and peace, life and death—the pope, to use a quasi-Marxist phrase he would probably hate, put the Church on the right side of history. And yet his structural impact on the Church may well weaken the very liberal achievements that he embraced. He will remain a paradoxical figure in the historical accounts no less than he was during his papacy.

III

On the morning of November 24, 1985, some 165 bishops and archbishops from around the world gathered in St. Peter's Basilica for a papal mass inaugurating a solemn assembly that would alter the course of Roman Catholic history.

Shortly before noon, John Paul stood before Bernini's altar to open an Extraordinary Synod of Bishops, designed to assess the course the Church had taken during the two decades since the Second Vatican Council. Near the pope was a white-haired, quiet-spoken West German. On the street, Joseph Ratzinger could seem a shy and self-effacing man, easily mistaken for a visiting parish priest from his native Bavaria. Yet he emerged in those years as the second most powerful man in the Vatican. And it is not without cause that many dubbed that meeting "Ratzinger's Synod." Raising up Joseph Ratzinger to a paramount position in the Church that helped him to become Pope Benedict XVI was one of John Paul's most important legacies.

No man, other than John Paul himself, was so identified with the changes in the Church during the 1980s and 1990s. And no one, including John Paul, came under such bitter attack over what many saw as an attempt to roll back the changes wrought by Vatican II.

It is perhaps a sign of just how much the Roman Catholic Church has changed since Vatican II that as cardinal, Ratzinger became the center of attention not only because of his job as the guardian and promoter of Catholic orthodoxy but also for an interview in the 1980s with an Italian journalist, first published in *Jesus*, a Catholic magazine.

In astonishingly clear language, unencumbered by diplomatic hedges, the cardinal declared the postconciliar years as "decidedly unfavorable for the Catholic Church."

Public statements to reporters are not the way the mysterious Roman curia used to work its will. Yet merely by agreeing to a reporter's request for a long interview, Ratzinger became nearly everyone's reference point in the 1980s and beyond. To be for or against Ratzinger—that, among many Catholics, became the question. Vatican II had declared the Church to be "the people of God." But how were the people of God faring on their pilgrim journey through a most confused era?

Ratzinger offered a clear answer. "What the Popes and the Council Fathers were expecting was a new Catholic unity," Ratzinger told Vittorio Messori during the *Jesus* magazine interview. "Instead," he continued, "one has encountered a dissension which seems to have passed over from self-criticism to self-destruction."

If Vatican II was about anything, it was about optimism. Its documents rang out with the words "freedom" and "liberty." Vatican II, it should be stressed again, shattered a tradition within Catholicism that saw the modern world as an enemy to be fought and resisted. The message many drew from Vatican II was that modernity had a lot to be said for it; at the very least, it had to be assimilated.

Symbolically, the council marked change in another way: theologians who only a decade or so before had been condemned as unorthodox or regarded with suspicion suddenly emerged as the council's experts and intellectual heroes. There was no more powerful symbol of freedom and openness. Yet the council's efforts to assimilate modernity and still be true to a two-thousand-year tradition also created the potential for vast misunderstanding. The council called upon the Church to uphold, simultaneously, freedom and orthodoxy, cultural openness and identity, change and continuity, modernity and tradition, hierarchy and participation. That was a tall order.

Ratzinger was not at all sure that if the Church kept all these commitments, the center could hold. By misusing the intentions of Vatican II, he said, rebels in the Church created a situation in which "truly every type of heretical aberration seems to be pressing on the doors of the authentic faith."

Joseph Ratzinger was born in Marktl am Inn in Bavaria on April 16, 1927, the son of a policeman and a hotel cook. The Germany he grew up in was Nazi Germany, and he argues that it was Catholicism—"a citadel of truth and righteousness against the realm of atheism and deceit"—that immunized him against Nazism, even if he was forced to join the Hitler Youth.

He invoked the experience of Nazi Germany in his arguments against the growing influence of national bishops' conferences. Where liberals saw the power of the bishops' conferences in the 1980s as a progressive force against the power of a centralizing Vatican, Ratzinger saw them as diminishing the responsibility of individual bishops. In so doing, he also implicitly criticized the Church's stand in Germany at the time.

"The really powerful documents against National Socialism were those that came from individual courageous bishops," he said in the famous interview. "The documents of the Conference, on the contrary, were often rather wan and too weak with respect to what the tragedy called for."

Joseph Ratzinger was ordained a priest at age twenty-four, in 1951. In a written interview he granted me in 1985 for the *New York Times*, Ratzinger described his attraction to the priesthood in mystical terms. "I was convinced—I myself don't know how—that God wanted something from me, something which could be accomplished only by becoming a priest," he said.

As a young man, he said, he was drawn by the beauty and the mystery of the Roman Catholic liturgy. "The aesthetic aspect was so stunning, as it was the real meeting between God and me."

But his interest quickly moved to the academic. "When I started studying theology I became interested also in the intellectual problems; and this, once again, because they revealed the drama of my life and particularly the secret of truth," he said. "What interested me was thus neither purely 'esthetic' nor purely 'intellectual.' In fact it was, if we want to use a fashionable word, 'existential'."

The movement to writing was natural. "From the very beginning, I had a big need to communicate; I wasn't able to keep for myself the knowledge which seemed to be so important to me. The beautiful thing in it was the possibility of giving it to others."

It is one of the many ironies of the postconciliar period that Ratzinger's first major public role came as a progressive theological expert at Vatican II. Caught up with the then-Father Ratzinger in the spirit of freedom and hope was a young Polish Bishop named Karol Wojtyla, later John Paul II.

A further irony is that the young Father Ratzinger served as a theological adviser to Joseph Cardinal Frings, who could display independence from Rome and during Vatican II spoke of the Congregation Ratzinger later came to head as a place "whose methods and behavior do not conform to the modern era and are a source of scandal to the world."

Central to Ratzinger's disillusionment with the progressive cast of mind was the student revolt of the 1960s, which in turn is critical to understanding his reaction to Marxism in Latin American liberation theology in the 1980s.

"For so many years," he said in his interview with the *Times*,

the 1968 revolution and the terror created—in the name of Marxist ideas—a radical attack on human freedom and dignity, a deep threat to all that is human.

At the time, I was dean of the faculty of theology at Tubingen, and in all the university assemblies in which I participated, I could notice all kinds of terror, from subtle psycho-terror up to violence.

This was accomplished in the name of freedom, with theories that were so hypocritical, if one only compared them with the praxis. Up to then, I had known Marxism and neo-Marxism only from books and thought it was good to discuss; I even thought at the beginning that this could be a corrective of Bultmann's existentialism that was dominating Tubingen. [He was referring here to the great liberal theologian, Rudolph Bultmann.] However, I learned that it is impossible to discuss with terror and on terror, as there are no premises for a discussion— and such a discussion becomes collaboration with terror.

I think that in those years, I learned where discussion must stop because it is turning into a lie and resistance must begin in order to maintain freedom.

Ratzinger first met the future John Paul, a man who shared his skepticism of Marxism, during the Bishops' Synod of 1977. "I was particularly impressed by his human warmth and the deep inner rooting in God which appeared so clearly," Ratzinger said of John Paul in the *Times* interview. "And then, of course, I was also impressed by his philosophical education, his acuteness as a thinker and his ability to communicate his knowledge."

And so was formed a new, critical alliance in the Roman Catholic Church, between the Polish and West German hierarchies. Divided in history, the two churches were united now by many things, notably an attitude toward Communism.

IV

In choosing Ratzinger to be the head of the Congregation for the Doctrine of the Faith, Pope John Paul made what his spokesman, Joaquin Navarro-Valls, called "one the most personal choices of his Pontificate." On other appointments, the pope consulted widely, making bows to various constituencies; Ratzinger, Navarro said, was very much the pope's personal preference.

There can be little doubt that the pope knew exactly the sort of man he was getting: brilliant, quietly thoughtful, and on a collision course with Catholic liberalism and the Left. According to Navarro and others, Ratzinger did not, at first, want the job, perhaps the toughest in the Vatican. The department was once known as the Holy Office, and before that, the Congregation of the Roman and Universal Inquisition—not, the cardinal's friends were quick to point out, to be confused with the Spanish Inquisition. The task of its prefect is to insure that the church's "deposit of faith," handed down through the centuries, remains intact, unsullied by heresy, deviation, intellectual corruption. (The very phrase "deposit of faith" is inherently controversial because of its lack of dynamism; a "deposit" is not to be stolen or trifled with in any way. For traditionalists, that is precisely the point. For progressives, such a static view gets in the way of the development of doctrine.)

It is not a popular job; some in the Church say it is dangerous that it exists at all. And holding the job was not generally conducive to becoming pope. The fact that the Congregation under Ratzinger showed an increased willingness to take action against liberals and leftists led to fears among progressives that "a new Inquisition" was beginning. The progressives, and some who might be cast as "moderates," argued that the Church was abandoning the commitment to freedom and openness it made at Vatican II. What had become known as "the spirit of the Council," the liberals argued, was being cast aside. In its place, a spirit of "Catholic Restoration" was at work, reasserting old certitudes that Vatican II itself called into question.

In the 1980s the Rev. Richard A. McCormick of Georgetown University's Kennedy Institute of Ethics referred to a tendency toward "magisterial maximalism," wherein little or no distinction is made between religious truths that must be "definitively held" by the church, and others that "are more provisional and reformable." McCormick, who died in 2000, was famous for his warning against a static view of orthodoxy which he said amounted to "faith in formaldehyde." He offered a classic formulation of the progressives' view: "One of theology's most important roles is a critical one, a distancing from past formulations and the proposal of new ones more adequate to the circumstances and insights of the time."

In 1985 *La Civilta Cattolica*, a Jesuit magazine with close Vatican ties, shocked many in Rome by publishing an article questioning overly broad invocations of papal infallibility. It was interpreted by some as a criticism of Ratzinger.

Ratzinger, on the other hand, used the term "Restoration" himself in a generally positive light. And he directly challenged the liberals' use of the phrase "the spirit of the Council," arguing that it was really an "anti-spirit" intent on distorting the council's real meaning.

The liberals struck back. "Joseph Ratzinger is afraid," Hans Kung declared in a seven-thousand-word commentary on the state of the church published in September 1985. "And just like Dostoyevsky's Grand Inquisitor, he fears nothing more than freedom."

Nicholas Lash, a professor of divinity at Cambridge University, argued in *New Blackfriars*, the British Dominican monthly magazine: "It is not Catholicism that is 'decomposing' or 'collapsing,' but a particular citadel which we once erected."

Mary Gordon, the novelist whose *Final Payments* reflected her own experience in the church, declared in *Commonweal*: "What is at issue, what is not defined, what is, in fact, ignored, is the bias against women that quickly becomes a bias against sexuality as well."

For supporters of Ratzinger and John Paul, the Church cannot be seen simply as a human creation that can be changed at will. It is divinely inspired. And this has certain implications. Even Vatican II, after all, affirmed the hierarchical nature of the Church.

"If one is blind to this mysterious sacramental vision of the Church," Ratzinger said, "one will find the arbitrariness of its essentially hierarchical order incomprehensible."

Indeed. For too many liberals, Ratzinger's "mystery" was in fact "mystification," a way of sanctifying what is essentially the worldly power of the Vatican hierarchy. It is the Church as "the people of God," also asserted by Vatican II, that is sacred.

There is, finally, the fundamental difference that underlies all the other disputes: the struggle over the meaning of the modern world.

"The 'world' is not entirely inhabited by hedonistic bourgeois materialists, any more than it is by abortionists, pornographers or concentration camp commandants," Eamon Duffy, a member of Cambridge University's divinity faculty and historian of Catholicism, wrote in *New Blackfriars.* "The 'world' is the place where ordinary men and women live and must find their salvation."

And the "world" had undergone much change since the 1950s, transformations that were at once sociological and theological. "The major problem the hierarchy faces may be that Catholics simply don't believe in hell and eternal punishment the way they used to," said Monika Hellwig, a leading liberal theologian who served as president of the Catholic Theological Society of America in the 1980s. "The American laity, especially the college-educated, is well aware that the hierarchy doesn't have many sanctions against them. It's harder to frighten them."

That loss of fear in the modern world was reflected in one of the most widely quoted conciliar phrases drawn from John XXIII: that the Church needed to be open to "the signs of the times." Not surprisingly, those words enraged traditionalists who felt they were deployed to justify every conceivable capitulation by Catholicism to modernity and secularism. On this point, too, Ratzinger made himself clear: "You know neither the Church nor the world if you think that they could meet without conflict or that they could even coincide."

The task of the Christian, Ratzinger concluded, "is to recover the capacity for nonconformism" and "to rethink that euphoric vision of the post-Conciliar period."

And in the *Times* interview, he made clear that he understood the costs of the nonconformism he was endorsing. When asked to explain the difference between his stern public image and the amiable intellectual his friends describe, the cardinal replied: "If it is true that a Christian faith taken seriously means nonconformity with a not inconsiderable number of contemporary social standards, then a more-or-less negative image is unavoidable. Nonconformists, after all, who enjoy general applause, are somewhat ridiculous figures, or at the least unconvincing."

For Ratzinger, the very terms "preconciliar" and "postconciliar" were distortions, "tantamount to accepting a rupture in the history of the Church." In Ratzinger's view, "there are no leaps in this history, there are no fractures and there is no break in continuity." That is, when you think about it, a deeply conservative view, in the best and most profound sense of that term.

On the contrary, the progressives replied, conservatives such as Ratzinger were seeking to so narrow the Church's understanding of the Second Vatican Council as to render it almost meaningless in the broad flow of Church history. "The appeal to literalism is only meant to obstruct or impede a reading of the Council documents which is sensitive to their history," said Giuseppe Alberigo, a Catholic theologian at Bologna's Institute for Religious Sciences. Contemporary conservatives, he argued, were seeking to use phrases inserted in compromise council texts by yesterday's conservatives to win battles their side lost twenty years ago.

As for Joseph Ratzinger, he was destined to defy history. His unlikely base at the Congregation for the Doctrine of the Faith vaulted him into a leadership role in the Church. As Pope John Paul's health failed him, the cardinal became an increasingly important figure in the Vatican. And in the face of criticism, he maintained the sort of serenity that comes to those convinced they will be vindicated in the long run.

He expressed his views on the matter in an address to a 1984 Catholic bishops' workshop in Dallas, quoting a passage from the First Epistle of St. Peter that might apply equally well to himself and to his adversaries: "Do not fear their intimidation and do not be troubled. . . . Sanctify Christ as Lord in your hearts, *always being ready to make a defense to everyone who asks you to give an account for the hope that is in you.*" It was a yearning within the College of Cardinals for this confident sense of orthodoxy that, twenty-one years later, propelled Joseph Ratzinger to the papacy.

V

The words broke like a thunderclap inside St. Peter's Basilica. Cardinal Joseph Ratzinger, addressing the world's cardinals just hours before they sequestered themselves to choose the next leader of the world's one billion Catholics, decided to define the conclave gathered to select the next pope after John Paul's death. He spoke on April 18, 2005, two decades after that Extraordinary Synod in which he had played such a central role.

"We are moving," Cardinal Ratzinger declared, toward "a dictatorship of relativism . . . that recognizes nothing definite and leaves only one's own ego and one's own desires as the final measure."

The modern world, Ratzinger insisted, had jumped "from one extreme to the other: from Marxism to liberalism, up to libertinism; from collectivism to radical individualism; from atheism to a vague religious mysticism; from agnosticism to syncretism and on and on."

Those were fighting words. They guaranteed that Ratzinger would either set the Church's course or offer his fellow cardinals the ideas they would choose to react against in selecting their next leader. At that moment, Ratzinger made himself the central figure in the conclave. In the end, those words helped make him pope.

What made Ratzinger's election as Pope Benedict XVI so significant and unusual was not simply that he had a longer and clearer record—a "paper trail," if you will—on every significant issue before the Church. (He also wrote well and clearly, much more so than John Paul, so there were few ambiguities.) It was not just his necessarily controversial history as head of the Congregation for the Doctrine of the Faith. There was also this: the cardinals gathered in 2005 disagreed fundamentally over what the election itself was really about, in part because they differed in their judgments over what the most important issues confronting the Church were.

Ratzinger spoke for the conservative side of a cultural and intellectual argument that was of particular interest to Europeans and North Americans. When Ratzinger said in that opening address that "to have a clear faith according to the church's creed is today often labeled fundamentalism," his words were undoubtedly welcomed by religious conservatives far outside the ranks of the Catholic Church—including, it should be said, many outside the traditionally Christian West. One could also imagine that liberals of various stripes shuddered.

But for the many cardinals from the Third World—20 of the 115 voting were from Latin America, 11 from Africa, 10 from Asia—the battle over relativism was less important than the poverty that afflicted so many of their flock. Some of these cardinals shared points in common with Ratzinger on doctrine. But for them, the struggle against suffering and social injustice was a daily part of their lives.

Many of these same cardinals, and many elsewhere, placed a higher priority on Christianity's rekindled competition with Islam and the urgency of Muslim-Christian dialogue.

Ratzinger, in other words, became central to two very different dynamics inside the conclave. Cardinals were asked to decide whether Ratzinger's theological approach was right, and they were asked to judge whether his priorities were the right ones. They settled both questions in his favor.

The simple political truth is that Ratzinger won election because he had a base. He was supported from the outset by a substantial cadre of traditionalist cardinals who shared his commitment to presenting an uncompromising alternative to modern secularism. His election also reflected the slow erosion of the progressive hopes created by the Second Vatican Council. It was a wakeup call for liberal Catholics and many moderates, a sign of how urgent it was for those in progressive ranks to revive, and make credible, Vatican II's hopeful vision of a Church that has much to teach the modern world, and much to learn from it.

Shortly before noon on the day of Ratzinger's election, I found myself in St. Peter's Square with a smart young Carmelite priest from Ireland. We were watching black smoke pour out of what, for a few days at least, was the most famous chimney in the world. By chance, or perhaps thanks to the Holy Spirit's intervention, Father Simon Nolan was the kind of Catholic who could strengthen one's faith in the Church's future. A philosopher who studies medieval topics, he was at once orthodox, warm, and open. We talked about Ratzinger's attack on the "dictatorship of relativism," and Father Nolan said he sympathized with what Ratzinger said because relativism meant that there were no truths that mattered. That meant there could be "no real arguments." If parties in a discussion believed that truth existed, he said, they would care passionately about what the other was claiming. No truth, no serious arguments—a good Catholic position that has much to say to the world.

But Father Nolan also expressed his worries about those who would back away from engaging the world as it exists and from joining those arguments. He did not like the idea of a Church that closed itself off intellectually. He thought the Church could be firm in insisting on what was right and still learn things from its interlocutors outside. He believed that the most likely outcome of the conclave would be a compromise pope, and he thought this would be good for the Church. We learned otherwise in the early evening.

As I wrote at the time, my reaction to Ratzinger's election was decidedly impure. As a journalist, I had written about Ratzinger's importance to the future of the Church early on. I had been thinking about and reading Ratzinger for more than two decades. The morning of his election, a wise editor headlined the column I had written about his dictatorship of relativism speech "Cardinal Ratzinger's Challenge." Most of my readers on the East Coast of the United States saw the column shortly before or shortly after his election, enhancing (unjustly) my reputation as a pundit and political tout.

Yet as a liberal American Catholic, I was petrified. I worried that the man who took the name Benedict XVI saw liberal Catholics primarily as products of the worst excesses of the 1960s and not as people genuinely grateful for the Catholic tradition and the Church's efforts since Pope John to interpret it anew for our times. Many of us know that modernity urgently needs criticism, agree that it is urgent to insist that truth exists, and remain Catholic precisely because we think that the Church's emphasis on the sacramental and the communal provides a corrective to a culture that overemphasizes the material and lifts up the narrowest forms of individualism.

But we also think that not all that is new is bad. Our Church was soft on slavery. It was terribly slow to embrace democracy. It still does not seem to understand that the desire of women for power in the Church reflects legitimate—and, yes, Christian—claims to justice, not weird ideological enthusiasms. Those who say that change in the Church is simply capitulation to a flawed culture must explain whether they really think the Church would be better off if it had not come to oppose slavery, endorse democracy, and resist anti-Semitism and other forms of religious intolerance.

As soon as Pope Benedict was elected, leaders and spokesmen for the American Church understood they had a problem with liberal and even moderate sections of their flock. They quickly went into damage control, insisting that the pope's critics should give him a chance, and suggested he could be a Nixon-to-China sort, exceptionally sensitive to the range of Catholic opinion. I had too much respect for Benedict's intellectual integrity to believe that *he* believed fully in this p.r. campaign. Yet I did hope that this very intelligent man understood the struggles within the American Church that I was part of. For the agony of the liberal Catholic is now a central feature of our nation's political life—more so than in Europe, given the long history of fruitful interaction between liberalism and Catholicism in the United States. It is to that struggle we turn next.

6. What Happened to the Seamless Garment?

THE AGONY OF LIBERAL CATHOLICISM

Al Smith, under vicious attack from the nativist and anti-Catholic press in 1928 as the first Roman Catholic to be nominated for president by a major party, found himself having to answer for the contents of various papal encyclicals that were deemed to be quite inconsistent with American ideals. Smith is reported by Reinhold Niebuhr to have looked at his aides and declared: "Will someone tell me what the hell a papal encyclical is?"

The relationship between American Catholic politicians and Rome has long been vexed, not simply because of particular conflicts (as in the case of John Kerry and the abortion issue in 2004), and not simply because the politics of the Vatican have not always been in sync with the American variety. It is also true that many American Catholics, quite faithful in their practice and loyal in their commitment, have not always found it necessary to be fully knowledgeable about Rome's pronouncements—and have sometimes found it convenient not to know more than is absolutely necessary.

And Smith might be seen to have been operating in simpler times. The American Catholic story has always been complicated by demographics and geography, as we'll see shortly. But the recent Catholic story must be understood in light of sweeping social changes since the 1960s.

The transformations wrought by the Second Vatican Council produced ferment all over the world, but the American Church may have been affected more than most because Vatican II coincided with an upheaval in the United States that affected Catholics no less than others. The coincidence of the election of John F. Kennedy as president and Pope John

XXIII's presence in the Vatican was seen as a "providential coincidence" by Father Greeley. Garry Wills, in his classic 1972 book *Bare Ruined Choirs*, offered a more acerbic view in discussing "The Two Johns":

> Under one John, professors went to Washington and created The New Frontier. Under another, enlightened young theologians went to Rome and created Vatican II. Vigor in the White House. "Updating" (*aggiornamento*) in the Vatican. Stuffy officials pushed into swimming pools. Gothic windows, long sealed, now thrown open. The liberal era had dawned.

And then came the later 1960s, with their attacks on authority, tradition, the old norms of sexual behavior, family life, patriarchy, and, at times, religion itself. American Catholicism was thus shaken by several revolutions within a decade.

Yet while church attendance and affiliation rates dropped among American Catholics during the 1960s, these drops were not as precipitous as declines over the decades in other Western nations. Where many Catholics worldwide, particularly liberals, had left the Church, large numbers of American Catholics remained inside, bound by a complex set of religious, family, ethnic, and class loyalties.

Lisa Sowle Cahill, a Christian ethicist at Boston College and a powerful voice for the liberal wing of the Church, perfectly captured the depth of the Catholic connection. "Being a Catholic is like being a member of a family," she said. "You have to be pushed out in order to break with it. It's not like any other voluntary organization." If Catholic conservatives thought the liberals should leave, the liberals were not about to accept the invitation.

There is a large body of evidence to support Cahill's insight. In their detailed 2007 study *American Catholics Today*, William V. D'Antonio and his colleagues concluded that "the big picture is that most Catholics remain Catholic." They continue:

> Even if they are unhappy with Church leadership or Church moral teachings and even if they are disgusted with the way the bishops handled sexual abuse cases, they stay Catholic. They may attend Mass less frequently or give less to diocesan appeals, but they stay Catholic. Someone has said that with respect to maintaining their Catholic identity, Catholics are more like Jews than like Protestants. It seems true.

D'Antonio and his coauthors also explain why so many American Catholics saw the 1960s as such a transformative decade. Simply put, the 1960s came after the 1950s—and the 1950s were actually the unique decade. The 1950s, they write, were

> a period of unusually high participation in the sacraments. It was a period unlike anything earlier or later. For example, Mass attendance was lower in the early 1900s. And it was lower again in the 1980s and 1990s. The same inverted U-shaped pattern describes the trend for other sacraments as well, such as Confession and Holy Orders. Rather than seeing the high participation levels of the 1950s as normal and other periods as unusual (as many Catholics do), it is more accurate to see the 1950s as unusual and other periods (including the present) as more typical of the American Catholic experience.

As we saw earlier in the broader culture-war debate, seeing the 1950s as representing the permanent condition of humanity before the rise of the 1960s' counterculture both overrates the importance of the '60s and underrates the extent to which the '50s were atypical. Catholic liberals and Catholic conservatives alike are prone to both errors—and thus inclined to reach conclusions that are flawed, though in quite different ways. The 1960s seemed even more revolutionary than they were because they came on the heels of the peculiar 1950s.

Nonetheless, it is undeniable that the forces buffeting the American Catholic Church during the 1960s were vast. As the old ethnic enclaves slowly broke up, millions of American Catholics were shorn from their roots. Parochial schools tied to the ethnic parishes declined. The educational levels of American Catholics rose dramatically, leading to a more inquisitive and often more skeptical flock.

The cultural and sexual revolutions of the 1960s coincided with the council and had a large effect of their own. The late Rev. Thomas Herron of Philadelphia, a conservative and an aide to Cardinal Ratzinger in the 1980s, argued then that the Vatican Council's liberalizing effects were often confused with the far broader upheaval in American society. "People tend to blame the council for many things that had far more to do with the counterculture," he said. "We are still dealing with the effects of an enormous revolution that we still do not fully understand."

"What is clear," he said, "is that the 1960s involved a revolt against authority, and few institutions had such a powerful sense of authority as the Catholic Church. So the rebellion in the church may have been much stronger than against almost any other institution."

Even before the 1960s and Vatican II, American Catholics had often been at the forefront of liberal struggles in the Church—even as there was always a strong conservative strain in the American Church fighting this tendency. In the 1890s controversy broke out over what came to be known as the "Americanist" heresy. Foes of Archbishop John Ireland of St. Paul, Minnesota, saw him as a dangerous liberal (he would not be viewed that way now) because of his sympathy for American ideas about church-state separation and his general approval of American political forms. Ireland ran into fierce opposition not only in the Vatican, but also from conservative enemies in the U.S. hierarchy who looked to Rome to take strong action against him. (Yes, the story has a familiar ring.)

Action came in the form of *Testem benevolentiae nostrae* (Witness to Our Good Will), Leo XIII's 1899 encyclical. Leo described it as "Concerning New Opinions, Virtue, Nature and Grace, with Regard to Americanism." The pope condemned ideas that "would give rise to the suspicion that there are among you some who conceive and would have the Church in America to be different from what it is in the rest of the world." In particular, Leo argued that

> the confounding of license with liberty, the passion for discussing and pouring contempt upon any possible subject, the assumed right to hold whatever opinions one pleases upon any subject and to set them forth in print to the world, have so wrapped minds in darkness that there is now a greater need of the Church's teaching office than ever before, lest people become unmindful both of conscience and of duty.

American conservatives in the Church welcomed the document. The liberals reacted with great shrewdness, arguing, in effect, that whatever it was the pope condemned was not anything they had believed in the first place. The entire controversy, they insisted, was based on a large misunderstanding of the American Church. The contention was quickly diffused, but it led to a certain prudence (an excessive prudence, in the minds of many liberals) in the American hierarchy.

Yet the core commitment to the idea of religious freedom remained strong in the American Church. Steeped no less in the democratic tradition than other Americans, Catholics in the United States had a special devotion to minority rights as a minority in a predominantly Protestant nation. For American Catholics, the idea of "freedom of conscience" was not only worthy for its own sake; it was an absolute necessity. The Second Vatican Council's "Declaration on Religious Liberty" thus bore a heavy American imprint, notably that of the Jesuit theologian John Courtney Murray, who before the council had been virtually silenced under Pope Pius XII.

In the 1980s, in a mild but still serious replay of the Americanist controversy, more liberal American bishops—notably Bishop James W. Malone of Youngstown, Ohio, then president of the National Conference of Catholic Bishops—were at the forefront of the battle for "collegiality." The idea, again a very American one, called for a diffusion of responsibility to the bishops and the national churches. It was this initiative that drew Cardinal Ratzinger's skepticism and opposition.

He and conservative Catholics in the United States saw the American liberals as intent on undercutting the Vatican's power and watering down the church's more unpopular teachings. "The problem in the American church is a problem about the structure of the church and where authority comes from," Joaquin Navarro-Valls, the Vatican spokesman, said at the time. "The Catholic Church says the bishops get their power as successors to the Apostles and the Pope as successor to St. Peter. That is the central issue."

Rocco Buttiglione, later a prominent center-right Italian politician and a strong ally of John Paul's, similarly argued that many Americans often confuse political structures of the democratic state with the governing structures of a hierarchical church. "Democracy is a wonderful formula for political society, but the church is not a democracy," he said. "Sometimes the church simply has to say unpopular things."

Among American Catholics, those "unpopular things" included the Church's views on sexuality, birth control, and the role of women. Many American Catholic women could not understand why the foundations of the Church would shake if the male hierarchy shared more power. Nor could American Catholics accept that the birth control pill—invented, as it happened, by a Roman Catholic—should necessarily undermine the entire structure of Catholic moral teaching on marriage and sexuality. Many quite orthodox theologians, including members of a papal commission on the subject, agreed.

The question of women's rights has special resonance in the United States, not only because of the strength of its women's movement but also because women—particularly the nuns who staffed the schools, ran the hospitals, and oversaw so much social service work undertaken by the Church—have played an unusually large role in building American Catholicism. The American bishops regularly encountered difficulties in drafting statements on women's rights not only because of their own divisions but also because of conflicting worries about appearing to move beyond Vatican teaching and offending Catholic women-in-the-pews restive over their role in the Church.

The sexual revolution may have jolted the Catholic Church more than it did most other American institutions because the church's members cleaved so faithfully—and for so long—to traditional morality, especially on birth control.

In a study published in 1963, the Rev. Andrew M. Greeley, the American author and sociologist, found substantial acceptance among Catholics of the Church's birth control teaching. But between 1963 and 1974, astonishing changes took place: opposition to birth control fell from 52 percent to 13 percent; to divorce, from 46 to 25 percent.

The revolt against the church's sexual teaching was paralleled by a decline in church attendance, and Father Greeley argues that the church's ban on contraception was the major cause of this disaffection. Some in the hierarchy accepted his finding. In a carefully worded speech at a 1980 Bishops' Synod in Rome, the then-archbishop of San Francisco, John R. Quinn, said he supported the church's teaching on birth control but added a pointed reference to dissent among the faithful. "Unless one is willing to dismiss the attitude of all these people as obduracy, ignorance or bad will," he said, "this widespread opposition must give rise to serious concern."

The battles over women and sexuality and the rise of culture-war politics inside the Church often obscured a broad continuity in Catholic social teaching over the entire period of controversy. Simply put, the American Catholic Church—with many conservative dissenters in its ranks—proved to be a powerful ally of movements for social justice and labor rights throughout the twentieth century. This had sociological roots: in many working-class areas, allegiance to the Church, the Democratic party, and the union blended seamlessly. It also had theological roots: Leo XIII may have condemned "Americanism," but his 1891 social encyclical *Rerum novarum* was a kind of Magna Carta for the modern labor movement and the welfare state. It unleashed intellectual creativity and social activism around the world, and particularly in the United States. John A. Ryan, a young Catholic priest influenced by the Populist movement, used *Rerum novarum*'s mandate to develop what became an inspiring social doctrine. His first book, *A Living Wage*, published in 1906, sparked one of the central demands of the American labor movement.

In a seminal article in *Boston Review* highlighting "the Catholic roots of American liberalism," Lew Daly argued that the view offered in *A Living Wage* was rooted in a simple but powerful theological concept: "the moral worth of the person as measured by his intrinsic and equally given (God-given) faculties of reason, self-improvement, and love of God." Daly, who has done genuinely innovative work on Christianity and social policy, summarized the argument this way:

> Ryan regarded the wage system skeptically—even despairingly—for its separation of workers from the productive resources that could best secure prosperity for themselves and their families. . . . [B]oth Ryan and Pope Pius XI, Leo's great intellectual successor, strongly supported strategies to give workers a stake in the appreciating wealth of industry. But they did not draw a line against wage labor in principle. Instead they argued, as Ryan put it, that "human needs constitute the primary ethical title or claim to material goods." This standard cannot be applied "to all possible human needs," but to those basic needs the satisfaction of which safeguards a reasonable life as measured by the faculties of self-improvement that all human beings share (making them equal in their right of basic sustenance). So defined, "the validity of needs as a partial rule of wage justice" rests ultimately on the foundational principle that "God created the earth for the sustenance of *all* His children; therefore, that all persons are equal in their inherent claims upon the bounty of nature." The subsistence wage of modern business theory did not meet this standard. Only a living wage met this standard, supporting the person, not just the labor; supporting the person in his faculties of self-development, not just in his service to capital.

Ryan's theories laid the basis for the Catholic bishops' "Program of Social Reconstruction" issued on February 12, 1919—appropriately, as Daly points out, Abraham Lincoln's birthday. As Daly noted, the "program contained a set of immediate reforms, including the establishment of a legal minimum wage, public housing for workers, labor participation in industrial management, and social insurance for illness, disability, unemployment, and old age, funded by a levy on industry." It also urged more "fundamental" reforms for the future, including "worker ownership of capital, universal living wages, and abolition and control of monopolies." The document closed on this powerful note about "the capitalist":

> He needs to learn the long-forgotten truth that wealth is stewardship, that profit-making is not the basic justification of business enterprise, and that there are such things as fair profits, fair interest and fair prices. Above and before all, he must cultivate and strengthen within his mind the truth which many of his class have begun to grasp for the first time during the present war [World War I]; namely, that the laborer is a human being, not merely an instrument of production; and that the laborer's right to a decent livelihood is the first moral charge upon industry. The employer has a right to get a reasonable living out of his business, but he has no right to interest on his investment until his employees have obtained at least living wages. This is the human and Christian, in contrast to the purely commercial and pagan, ethics of industry.

It is probably too much to argue that the bishops' program became the blueprint for Franklin Roosevelt's New Deal. The New Deal, in its breadth and occasional incoherence, had multiple inspirations. The bishops themselves were clearly reflecting contemporary currents in a social justice shaped as well by Protestant, Jewish, and secular thought. Yet it's clear that the Catholic social thought developed by Ryan and the Catholic bishops was essential to New Deal liberalism, reflecting Roosevelt's broad view that capitalism could be preserved only if it were reformed with an eye toward distributive justice and the rights of labor. Roosevelt himself honored Ryan with a message to a banquet on the priest's seventieth birthday. "With voice and pen," FDR declared, "you have pleaded the cause of social justice and the right of the individual to happiness through economic security, a living wage, and an opportunity to share in the things that enrich and ennoble human life." With these words, as Daly pointed out, Roosevelt was offering "a rough draft of the famous 'Second Bill of Rights' he would propose five years later in his State of the Union Address."

And if the progressive tendencies within American Catholicism were the product of an older social teaching and the new rebellions of the 1960s, they were augmented by the rise of Catholic radicalism and pacifism in the movement against the Vietnam War. This strain of Catholicism long predated the war and has survived to this day in the Catholic Worker movement. Founded by Dorothy Day and Peter Maurin in 1933, the Catholic Worker's commitment was to "nonviolence, voluntary poverty, prayer, and hospitality for the homeless, exiled, hungry, and forsaken." It directed its energies against "injustice, war, racism, and violence of all forms." The Worker's following grew in the 1960s, as did pacifism's influence on rank-and-file Catholics. The Revs. Daniel and Philip Berrigan— both made the FBI's Ten Most Wanted list for their antiwar activities— inspired Catholics and others to nonviolent but dramatic resistance to the draft, the war, and the military. Their successors and followers were deeply engaged against President Reagan's policies in Latin America in the 1980s, including priests and nuns who served in Nicaragua, El Salvador, and elsewhere. Their ranks included three Americans nuns killed in El Salvador in 1980. The murders of Catholic clerics and sisters by right-wing death squads became a major source of tension in the Central American debate throughout the 1980s. This branch of the American Catholic Left was greatly influenced by the theology of liberation that later met with the Vatican's disapproval.

Thus, while Rome moved slowly in a more conservative direction, significant parts of the American Church were moving in a progressive direction—building on a significant progressive history. In the John Paul era, Catholic liberals often welcomed the Vatican's social teachings, its initiatives on war and peace, and the pope's strong declarations against the death penalty. They pushed back against Vatican centralization, its teaching on birth control and the role of women, and its condemnations of theologians. But as John Paul's papacy continued, the progressives found themselves losing ground in the hierarchy and facing increasing hostility among conservatives mobilized around opposition to abortion and unease about the decline of traditional family life. Eventually, these forces began to be felt in electoral politics.

II

The political loyalties of American Catholics have always been a rich amalgam of religion and sensibility, ethnicity and class, family, neighborhood, and region. Irish, Italian, German, Polish, and French Canadian Catholics often voted differently—depending upon their time of arrival in the country, the relative needs of Republicans and Democrats for new allies at any given time, the saliency of foreign policy questions involving their native lands, and sometimes, quite simply, who disliked whom more in a given place. These differences had little to do with doctrine, theology, or competing interpretations of the faith.

Class divides Catholics as it divides most Americans. That's true even though Catholics, including white Catholics, tend to be somewhat more Democratic across income groups than white Protestants. Moreover, the class position of Catholics has improved with time, making them more Republican than they once were. Upward mobility has not had the same effect on Jews and African Americans. The wealthy among them defy their class positions. Catholics merely resist theirs.

As a result, the political scientist David Leege has shown, Catholics were never quite so uniformly Democratic as popular memory (reflected in Mrs. O'Reilly's story at the beginning of this book) often suggests. We remember the outpouring of Catholic votes for John F. Kennedy in 1960—he won close to 80 percent of their ballots. We forget that just four years earlier, Dwight D. Eisenhower carried roughly half of the Catholic vote. Before the Kennedy election, and especially before the New Deal, the Catholic vote was split by competition among ethnic groups. Italians, Germans, and French Canadians often feuded with the Irish—inside and outside the Church—and many of them gravitated toward the Republicans.

Large regional differences affect the voting behavior and political allegiances of Catholics. Those who live in the Northeast and Midwest have, for some time, been more Democratic than Catholics who live in the South. On the whole, white Catholics who remained in the original areas of immigrant settlement maintained their Democratic loyalties longer than those who moved away. Given racial polarization in the South, southern white Catholics—Louisiana, with its large Cajun community, is a partial exception—voted like other white southerners.

Young Catholics live in a more complicated social and moral space. They are, on the whole, more traditional than their non-Catholic peers and more modernist than formal Church teaching. Leege has found that they are divided quite sharply by gender: younger Catholic women are more Democratic, younger Catholic men more Republican. Here, one sees a gender gap rooted more in contemporary politics than in anything specifically Catholic, since this split mirrors the overall gender gap.

Differences are also visible even across state lines. The case of Massachusetts and New York Catholics, explored in the past by Douglas Schoen and Milton Gwirtzman, is particularly instructive. In separate studies written some two decades apart, Schoen and Gwirtzman found that over a series of elections, New York Catholics were roughly 20 points more Republican than Massachusetts Catholics. The differences are not explained by the habit of rooting for the Yankees instead of the Red Sox. Both Schoen and Gwirtzman found that the key lay in the different ethnic and racial rivalries that characterized politics in the two states.

In Massachusetts, political competition came to be defined for decades as a straightforward contest between Yankee Protestants and Catholics. The Protestants were Republicans so the Catholics were Democrats. In New York, competition was more complex, pitting Catholics, Protestants, and Jews—and, later, African Americans and Hispanics—against each other in a complex struggle for power. Jews and Catholics were often engaged in a robust competition for influence in New York's Democratic party, with Catholics tending to favor moderate-to-conservative factions close to the older political organizations, and Jews supporting more liberal factions, including, in many cases, the reform movements that took root in the 1950s. As a result, one group would defect when the other gained dominance: Catholics to the Republicans when more liberal forces dominated the party, Jews to either progressive Republicans or third parties when the more conservative forces triumphed. Racial politics further confused the battle lines.

Catholic defections from New York Democrats grew with the establishment of a Conservative party in New York's unique multiparty system. The Conservatives were an especially powerful symbol of a shift rightward in a large part of the Irish Catholic community. The party was founded by men named O'Doherty and Mahoney who went on to run William F. Buckley Jr. for mayor of New York City in 1965.

By contrast, most conservative Catholics in Massachusetts remain Democrats to this day. When George McGovern carried Massachusetts and—other than the District of Columbia—Massachusetts alone in 1972, his victory was often attributed to Massachusetts' unusual role as the home to so much of the liberal academy: Harvard and MIT, Smith and Mount Holyoke, Amherst and Williams, Brandeis, Boston College, and Holy Cross. In fact, McGovern won in significant part because of the enduring loyalties of working-class Democrats in the old mill towns and cities, places where many Catholics were still voting for the party of Al Smith and John F. Kennedy. Needless to say, Richard Nixon carried New York in 1972 with strong support from Catholics.

Divisions over race drove many white Catholics toward the Republicans in the 1960s and 1970s. Jonathan Rieder's book *Canarsie*—it is subtitled *Catholics and Jews in New York against Liberalism*—is a brilliant and fair look at racial reaction in the 1960s and 1970s. There was racism and there was also the fact of competition in the cities between white Catholics on the one side and African Americans and Latinos on the other. Catholic communalism, a loyalty to neighborhood and parish, also came into play, as Gerald Gamm dramatized in his book *Urban Exodus: Why the Jews Left Boston and Catholics Stayed*.

And there can be no adequate understanding of American Catholicism absent an awareness that it is increasingly defined by its fastest-growing group, Latinos—and that Latinos themselves cannot be thought of as a single bloc, either. Ethnicity matters among Latinos, as it did among the Irish, Italians, and Poles. Cuban Americans are predominantly Republican; Puerto Ricans, Democratic. Mexican Americans in Texas are Democrats, but there are, as we saw earlier, more willing to vote Republican than Mexican Americans in California. Florida has become a competitive state because of the immigration of non-Cuban Hispanic groups, and Latino immigration is also changing the face of politics and the Catholic Church in Colorado, Nevada, California—and, with the dispersion of Latinos, many other states as well.

Finally, it is almost always forgotten that roughly 10 percent of African Americans are Catholic, including roughly a third of African Americans in Louisiana.

III

It can thus be said that there is no Catholic vote—*and* that the Catholic vote is important. Catholics are the largest single religious group in the United States, they vote in large numbers, and whoever wins the Catholic vote in a presidential election has a very high probability of winning election. That's because Catholics, as we saw earlier, have become a classic swing group: perhaps 40 percent of Catholics are reliably Democratic. A comparable group is reliably Republican. The rest move around.

"Catholics may be the most maddening electoral group in American politics," says Steve Wagner, a shrewd Republican consultant who specializes in Catholic voting, "the demographic bloc that drives pollsters, pundits and politicians of all stripes to distraction." Leege put it this way: "Despite a veritable cottage industry of scholars who have studied religion and politics among American Catholics, a single theory that explains the dynamics of Catholic political behavior has eluded their grasp."

Just contemplate these names: Ted Kennedy, Mario Cuomo, Sam Brownback, Richard Neuhaus, Peter and Peggy Steinfels, Pat Buchanan, Rick Santorum, Bob Casey, Bill Bennett, Rosa DeLauro, Peter King, Joe Biden. All are Catholics. The disagreements among members of this group alone could fill hours, even weeks, of time on contentious talk shows.

Argument among Catholics is normal because, as is clear by now, the Church's formal political positions have never mapped neatly with those of our political parties or our conventional ideologies. To summarize: the Catholic Church is strongly opposed to abortion, stem-cell research, assisted suicide, and gay marriage. It is also opposed to the death penalty, skeptical of an interventionist foreign policy, committed to a substantial government role in fighting poverty, and has been wary since at least John Ryan's time of unregulated capitalism.

These pressures and ambivalences make Catholics potentially disruptive for both parties. Catholics who are liberal Democrats are more inclined to oppose abortion than other sorts of liberals. Catholics who are conservative Republicans value tradition and community and not just the free market. Catholics who support the death penalty know how strongly their bishops and their pope oppose it. A poll by the Pew Forum on Religion and Public Life and the Pew Research Center suggested that opposition to the death penalty was often religiously motivated: opponents of the death penalty were far more likely than its supporters to say their position was primarily motivated by their religious convictions.

Tensions between Catholics who emphasize the "life issues" and those who lay heavy stress on social justice have been a central component of Catholic life since the *Roe v. Wade* decision in 1973. The late Cardinal Joseph Bernardin sought in the 1980s to bring the entirety of Catholic social teaching together under the rubric of the "seamless garment." Support for life included opposition to abortion but also opposition to the death penalty, skepticism about war, and help for the poor. The 1980s saw the high point of Catholic progressivism as the nation's Catholic bishops issued two pastoral letters, the economic statement discussed earlier and another on war and peace. Both were seen, rightly, as critiques of Reagan administration policies. More conservative Catholics were critical of both letters and of the seamless garment framework, which they saw as subordinating opposition to abortion to a more progressive agenda.

On so many of the issues in American politics, being a Catholic liberal or a Catholic conservative inevitably meant having a bad conscience about some issue—often many. All this makes Catholic political and electoral behavior confounding. Consider the difficulty of categorizing two prominent Catholics, the late Robert Casey (or, for that matter, his son who carries on his name and advances his worldview as a Democratic senator from Pennsylvania) and Bill Bennett, the prominent Republican author and talk show host.

As governor of Pennsylvania from 1987 to 1995, Casey was as liberal as any Democrat on social welfare and union issues. But he was seen by many as "conservative" solely because of his staunch opposition to abortion. Bennett, a solid conservative, has nonetheless said that "unbridled capitalism is a problem . . . for the whole dimension of things we call the realm of values and human relationships."

Bennett was getting at something a senior White House adviser during the Clinton administration, Sidney Blumenthal, noticed in 1997: why had so many Democrats who had been more or less in favor of free trade in the past declined to give the president "fast-track" authority to negotiate new trade agreements? They were insisting that the agreements include social and labor protections, and that the government do more to assist those who lost jobs or income because of free trade. Blumenthal stared at the list of House members who had turned against the president's position and suddenly noticed that most of the defectors were Catholic. "This was not simple protectionism," Blumenthal says. "It involved a deeply rooted tradition of Catholic social reform and solidarity." Even after a long period of upward mobility, the tradition of John Ryan and the 1919 bishops' program never fully left the Catholic soul.

Nonetheless, between the 1980s and the dawn of the new century, the leadership of the American Church became steadily more conservative as the late Pope John Paul II's bishops gradually replaced the bishops named by Pope Paul VI. There has been a renaissance of conservative Catholic thinking led by such figures as Father Neuhaus, Michael Novak, George Weigel, and Princeton University's Robert George. The formal positions of the Church remain relatively unchanged. While the Church continued to take broadly liberal positions on many questions—welfare reform, the war in Iraq, the death penalty, and immigration reform—the public voice of Catholicism is decidedly more conservative than it was in the New Deal or civil rights eras.

Against this backdrop, the battle for the votes of American Catholics raged.

IV

After the surge of support to the Democrats in 1960 and 1964 (Lyndon B. Johnson's advantage against Barry Goldwater was almost as high as John Kennedy's), the Catholic vote became significantly more competitive. Hubert Humphrey's share fell below 60 percent as Richard Nixon, pursuing what came to be known as the "peripheral urban ethnic" strategy, substantially expanded on his Catholic vote of eight years earlier. George Wallace, appealing to racial resentments, also won a slice of the Catholic vote. Nixon narrowly won Catholics in 1972, a historically significant achievement. His victory reflected an effective—if, some might say, unfair—campaign against George McGovern as an "ultraliberal." Again, racial politics also played a role. Jimmy Carter recaptured Catholics for Democrats in 1976 against Gerald Ford, but narrowly. The fact that Carter was a born-again Southern Baptist almost certainly made some Catholics nervous.

Ronald Reagan's 1980 triumph was built in part on Catholic votes. Along with southerners, Catholics formed the heart of the "Reagan Democrats" who became a force through the decade. Many blue-collar and lower-middle-class Catholics were tugged toward the Democrats on issues of social justice and workers' rights. But on issues related to family and cultural values—including abortion—they leaned toward the Republicans. Ronald Reagan's trinity of "family, work, and neighborhood" (linked to "peace and freedom") had enormous power in the old Catholic neighborhoods. The Peter Berger and Richard John Neuhaus volume *To Empower People* emphasized the very mediating structures Reagan loved to describe. Their book might well be seen as the manifesto for the Reagan Democrat, especially the Catholic Reagan Democrat.

Bill Clinton's ability to regain Catholic votes was a building block of his victories in the 1990s. "It's the economy, stupid" helped a great deal in 1992. But Clinton's strategic corrections in Democratic policy were aimed quite clearly at Reagan Democrats, white southerners, to be sure, but also—and perhaps especially—Catholics.

The Democratic Leadership Council slogan that Clinton helped coin and then adopted, "Community, Opportunity, Responsibility," could have been used as a headline on any number of bishops' statements. Clinton married toughness on crime and prowork welfare reform with a general defense of a compassionate state. Even on abortion, Clinton's use of the phrase "safe, legal, and *rare*" to describe his approach gave Catholics a chance to latch onto the last word—to the later frustration of some who thought it was lost somewhere along the way. Reading Clinton speeches on voluntary national service, on the positive role of churches, on the importance of rebuilding neighborhoods, one could even imagine that he, too, had read Berger and Neuhaus. And in 1996, when Clinton was appealing to the soccer moms who became so famous that year, he spoke often of school uniforms and school discipline. Catholics were familiar with both.

In 2000 there was little reason to believe that Al Gore—as faith-friendly as Clinton had been, even if he lacked Clinton's preacher's cadences—would suffer losses among Catholics. But few Republicans have been as shrewd in their approach to Catholics as George W. Bush and Karl Rove. In both of his campaigns, Bush invested heavily in moving the middle fifth of the Catholic vote in the Republicans' direction, and in turning out the most conservative Catholics.

Bush did so not only by emphasizing his support for a "culture of life," but, particularly in the 2000 election, by his calls for "compassionate conservatism." This was made to order for wavering Catholics who were uneasy with what they perceived as Republican indifference to the poor, but who were also socially conservative and disenchanted with the old welfare state. Compassionate conservatism acknowledged an obligation to the poor while insisting that one-on-one, local and church-based initiatives were the best way to meet it.

Bush was not shy about using the classic Catholic word "subsidiarity." He regularly cited John Paul II, whose work his chief speechwriter Michael Gerson had closely studied. Joining John Paul in calling for a "society of free work, of enterprise, of participation," Bush emphasized the link between individual and social responsibility. He also campaigned hard for the votes of Latinos, particularly among those who were evangelical Protestants, but also among religiously devout and prolife Latino Catholics. Bush lost Catholics narrowly in 2000 but carried their votes, narrowly, in 2004.

The Bush strategy was crafted in part by Steve Wagner, who has argued that the old "social justice" orientation of Catholics is giving way to an emphasis on "social renewal." Partisans of social renewal, he says, are "Mass-attending Catholics" who see the country in "moral decline," are suspicious of popular culture, and worry that the federal government is "inflicting harm on the nation's moral character." The future of the Catholic vote may depend in part on the ability of liberal and Democratic Catholics to link social justice themes with those of social renewal.

But until 2004, the shifts within the Catholic vote were seen as the product of a largely autonomous Catholic electorate responding to national issues and the sometimes shrewd signaling of party nominees. Since Church teaching was an amalgam of liberal and conservative themes, the Catholic hierarchy was not on the whole seen as pushing the Catholic vote in a particular direction, despite the Church's strong stand against abortion which occasionally looked like a tilt in the Republicans' direction. In 2004 a slight push toward the Republicans became a shove—or so it seemed, at least to liberal Catholics.

V

During the 2004 presidential campaign pitting George W. Bush against John Kerry, conservative voices in the hierarchy were dominant, fearless, relentless—in brief, overwhelming. Progressive voices in the Church leadership were, to be charitable, conflicted. It might be said that progressive Church leaders had qualms because of the abortion and stem-cell issues. But the issues of poverty, social justice, and war did not seem to detain the conservative leaders in the Catholic Church from speaking out strongly in a way that left little doubt that they supported the reelection of George W. Bush.

The conservative bishops gave power to the views of leaflets that suddenly appeared in the reading racks at the back of Catholic churches all over the country. Political pamphlets disguised as religious tracts issued by a mysterious group calling itself "Catholic Answers" declared that there were just five "nonnegotiable" issues for Catholics in the coming election: abortion, stem-cell research, euthanasia, gay marriage, and cloning. Not social justice. Not war and peace. Not the death penalty. It was not an accident that each of these issues pushed voters in the direction of President Bush. The leaflet might as well have said that voting for Bush was itself a nonnegotiable position for Catholics. Indeed, there was a strong suspicion that the tracts were created by the Republican campaign, though the financing and background of "Catholic Answers" was to remain obscure—no doubt in line with the wishes of the effort's organizers. It was a sign of the deep political divisions in the Church over the election that more conservative pastors tended to leave the leaflets in the racks with the authentic religious tracts; more liberal pastors kept trying to remove them.

A signal moment in the campaign came on October 12, 2004, with the appearance of a story on the front page of the *New York Times* under the headline "Group of Bishops Using Influence to Oppose Kerry." The story, by David D. Kirkpatrick and Laurie Goodstein, began this way: "For Archbishop Charles J. Chaput, the highest-ranking Roman Catholic prelate in Colorado, there is only one way for a faithful Catholic to vote in this presidential election, for President Bush and against Senator John Kerry." It went on:

> "The church says abortion is a foundational issue," the archbishop explained to a group of Catholic college students gathered in a sports bar here in this swing state on Friday night. He stopped short of telling them whom to vote for, but he reminded them of Mr. Kerry's support for abortion rights. And he pointed out the potential impact his reelection could have on Roe v. Wade. "Supreme Court cases can be overturned, right?" he asked. Archbishop Chaput, who has never explicitly endorsed a candidate, is part of a group of bishops intent on throwing the weight of the church into the elections. . . . In an interview in his residence here, Archbishop Chaput said a vote for a candidate like Mr. Kerry who supports abortion rights or embryonic stem cell research would be a sin that must be confessed before receiving Communion. "If you vote this way, are you cooperating in evil?" he asked. "And if you know you are cooperating in evil, should you go to confession? The answer is yes."

The story proved highly controversial. Some liberal Catholics argued that the press was paying attention only to the more conservative bishops.

Chaput himself said the interview had been a distortion and put out the entire transcript on the Denver Archdiocesan website. And it is true that in the course of the interview—in a comment with some significance for the future—the archbishop predicted that if the prochoice Rudy Giuliani were the 2008 Republican nominee, "you're going to see the Republicans screaming at the church for making such a big issue of a pro-life matter." In the fall of 2007, some Catholic leaders, including Bishop Raymond Burke, did indeed speak out against Giuliani's position on abortion.

Yet Chaput's was not an isolated voice in 2004, and anti-abortion bishops who believed that this issue mattered more than all others made clear that Catholics who chose to vote on other questions—poverty, the death penalty, the war in Iraq—were in danger of losing their souls. And so, of course, was John Kerry.

In West Virginia, for example, Bishop Bernard W. Schmitt proclaimed abortion "the greatest moral evil of our age" and declared that voting for candidates who favored abortion rights amounted to "formal cooperation in grave evil." Newark archbishop John Myers went to the *Wall Street Journal* op-ed page to make the anti-Kerry case. Myers cited a memorandum by then-cardinal Ratzinger declaring that Catholics could support a candidate favoring abortion rights only "in the presence of proportionate reasons." Then Myers said flatly, "Certainly policies on issues such as welfare, national security, the war in Iraq, Social Security or taxes, taken singly or in any combination, do not provide a 'proportionate reason' to vote for a pro-abortion candidate."

The right to life, wrote Colorado Springs Bishop Michael Sheridan in a pastoral letter, is the "right that grounds all other human rights. This is the issue that trumps all other issues."

Forty-four years before Kerry ran for president, John F. Kennedy became the nation's first Roman Catholic president by repeating over and over that his faith would have no effect on how he would govern. In 1960 Kennedy said things about Catholic bishops that might, in today's climate, be condemned as insolence toward church authority. "I believe in an America where the separation of church and state is absolute—where no Catholic prelate would tell the president, should he be Catholic, how to act," Kennedy told the Greater Houston Ministerial Association in September 1960. "I do not speak for my church on public matters—and the church does not speak for me."

Kennedy, of course, spoke those words in an effort to fight anti-Catholic bigotry. That was long before the 2004 campaign in which Kerry, only the third Roman Catholic in American history to be nominated for the presidency by a major party, found himself fending off conservative bishops intent on denying the Democratic nominee Communion—and the votes of the Catholic faithful.

Unfortunately for Kerry, it was the perfect storm. There was, first, the frustration of many bishops who lean Democratic on most public issues over how hard it was for even mildly anti-abortion Democrats to gain traction or much respect within their party. That began to change in 2006, particularly with the active support the prolife Bob Casey won from the Democratic establishment in his successful Pennsylvania Senate campaign. But such moves came too late to save Kerry.

Second, Kerry's approach to questions of religion and politics, particularly early in the campaign, was awkward and uncertain. His reference in early April 2004 to a nonexistent pope, "Pius XXIII," was not especially helpful in courting the devout or attentive (though the wry Mark Shields argued that perhaps Kerry should be seen as "a visionary" for anticipating a future papacy). Kerry became more comfortable discussing his faith by the end of the campaign and continued to develop his views after the election was over. But here again, the adjustments did not come in time.

But a third factor was decisive: an active campaign on the part of conservative Catholic Republicans to make abortion the one true litmus test for Catholic politicians. These conservatives were strongly committed to President Bush's reelection and were quite pleased to see Kerry squirm over whether he might be denied Communion. Interestingly, many of the conservatives who cheered bishops when they argued for voting against Kerry because of his support for abortion rights denied the bishops any standing to oppose President Bush on the Iraq War.

During the abortion controversy of 2004, George Weigel—a leading Catholic conservative who had written a well-respected biography of Pope John Paul II—echoed the conservative bishops in a column: "What would possibly be the 'proportionate reasons' that would cause a Catholic to vote, with a clear and well-formed conscience, for a candidate who is terribly wrong-sided on the great civil rights issue of the day?" He was referring to abortion. Weigel then mocked the possible reasons: "Because you agree with that candidate on the minimum wage? On the appropriate level of Medicare premiums? On whether the highest federal tax rate should be

36 percent or 38 percent or 40 percent?" Weigel's conclusion: "The 'proportionate reasons' for pro-life Catholics to support pro-abortion candidates must be very, very weighty indeed. Catholics considering a vote for pro-abortion candidates . . . must define what those reasons would be. Theirs is a difficult task."

Yet in the run-up to the Iraq War, Weigel challenged the authority of bishops, priests, and other religious leaders to lecture the constituted authorities—in this case President Bush—on whether the war was just. Deploying the term "charism," a gift usually associated with the saints, Weigel argued in the magazine *First Things*:

> If the just war tradition is indeed a tradition of statecraft, then the proper role of religious leaders and public intellectuals is to do everything possible to clarify the moral issues at stake in a time of war, while recognizing that what we might call the "charism of responsibility" lies elsewhere—with duly constituted public authorities, who are more fully informed about the relevant facts and who must bear the weight of responsible decision-making and governance. It is simply clericalism to suggest that religious leaders and public intellectuals "own" the just war tradition in a singular way. . . .
>
> There is a charism of political discernment that is unique to the vocation of public service. That charism is not shared by bishops, stated clerks, rabbis, imams, or ecumenical and interreligious agencies. Moral clarity in a time of war demands moral seriousness from public officials. It also demands a measure of political modesty from religious leaders and public intellectuals, in the give-and-take of democratic deliberation.

Given the disaster that unfolded in Iraq, it is easy to question Weigel's confidence that the "duly constituted public authorities" were "more fully informed about the relevant facts." The bishops who opposed the war seemed, in retrospect, to have a better sense of statecraft and a firmer hold on "the charism of political discernment." And for Catholic liberals, there was also something suspicious about the tendency of conservatives to encourage political outspokenness from bishops when such boldness favored conservative causes, but to insist on "political modesty" when bishops opposed conservative ends or the policies of conservative politicians.

During the 2004 campaign, there were certainly moderates and liberals in the Church—and even some conservatives who disliked politicizing the

Church's message—who were uneasy about the controversy over Kerry's right to receive Communion. "The political reality is that it will be interpreted as favoring Bush over Kerry," said the Rev. Joseph Komonchak, one of the Church's most distinguished theologians and historians. The bishops, he said, were aware of the "danger of a backlash."

There was also the theological question. "I don't myself think it a good thing to use the Eucharist as an instrument of public disciplining," Komonchak said. "It is not a bad thing to have officeholders and candidates reminded of certain duties and commitments that flow out of basic Christian convictions about human life." This "obviously should not be done solely with reference to a single issue such as abortion, but just as obviously neither should any issue, such as abortion, be excluded as a matter of merely private choice."

Moderate bishops partly diffused the controversy through an artful interpretation of Cardinal Ratzinger's statement and a general agreement to let local bishops decide. Key to protecting Kerry's right to receive the Body of Christ was Cardinal Theodore McCarrick, then the archbishop of Washington, DC, who met with Kerry and signaled his opposition to using the withholding of Communion as a political sanction. Yet even the most liberal bishops were concerned over the severity of what they saw as the imposition of an abortion rights litmus test on Democrats. "There's a frustration that the Democratic Party doesn't have much room for anyone who dissents from the most unrestricted access to abortion," Komonchak said. Conservatives with a powerful interest in Bush's reelection played on this frustration.

Indeed, Catholics, with their profound awareness of the power of original sin, should have known better than most the difficulty of achieving what Peter Steinfels called "moral purity in politics." Writing in the *New York Times*, Steinfels cited the case of Senator Rick Santorum, the conservative Pennsylvania Republican who was to lose his seat to Bob Casey in 2006. A strong foe of abortion, Santorum campaigned hard in Pennsylvania's Republican primary earlier in 2004 for Senator Arlen Specter, a supporter of abortion rights. Specter prevailed narrowly over Representative Pat Toomey, a staunch abortion opponent.

Steinfels asked the essential question: Why was it acceptable for a committed Catholic foe of abortion like Santorum to support Specter over an antiabortion candidate, but not acceptable for others to support Kerry over Bush? Might Specter's party label have had something to do with it? That was a suspicion that haunted Catholic liberals and Democrats. "In other words," Steinfels wrote, suggesting but not drawing a conclusion, "relating religion, morality and politics can be a complex business, full of ambiguities—as demonstrated by Mr. Santorum's unstinting support for a colleague with radically different views on the protection owed early life."

The Communion issue was not simply a theoretical question. For some Catholic Democrats, it came to affect their faith and worship life. Representative David Obey, a Wisconsin Democrat and one of the most respected members of the House, was denied Communion in 2003 by a hard-line bishop because of his mixed voting record on abortion. There was irony in this because Obey's record was too prolife for advocates of choice on abortion—he had cast more than sixty votes limiting abortion rights. But Obey had the misfortune of finding himself in the diocese of Bishop Raymond L. Burke, who later became the archbishop of St. Louis and continued moving aggressively against Catholic politicians who broke with the Church's view on abortion, stem-cell research, and other issues.

Obey insisted that his bishop did not have the right to "dictate how I vote on any public matter," echoing what John F. Kennedy had said. He has not sought Communion since Burke's ruling because he doesn't want to put a sympathetic priest who would administer it in an awkward position. It might be thought of as the act of an authentic Christian.

Obey has long struggled to balance the demands of his faith with the obligations of pluralism. In 2005 he spoke of offering an amendment to increase funding for child care, job training, and domestic abuse programs as a way of "taking some of the pressure off women to have abortions." The idea, he said, was to challenge those "whose concern for life ends at the checkbook's edge."

Obey recalls that a member of his staff was later berated by a family-planning lobbyist who said, "How dare he imply that women would succumb to pressure?" Such are the rewards for those who seek common ground on the most difficult moral issues.

The frustration of Catholic liberals and Democrats boiled over after the 2004 election, feeding a new sense of energy and urgency among those who remained true to the broad vision of Catholic social thought pioneered by Ryan and to Cardinal Bernardin's view that common ground could be found around the common good. New organizations—among them Catholics in Alliance for the Common Good, an important group with a meaningful name—arose to provide a counterweight to the influence of conservative lay organizations and activists within the Church.

Catholic Democratic politicians also began speaking out openly against what they saw as the growing alliance between factions in the Church and the Republican party. February 2006 saw the release of a remarkable document, "Statement of Principles by Fifty-Five Catholic Democrats in the U.S. House of Representatives." It was an unprecedented attempt by a large number of Catholic elected officials to explain the relationship between their religious faith and their public commitments.

"As Catholic Democrats in Congress," the statement began,

> we are proud to be part of the living Catholic tradition—a tradition that promotes the common good, expresses a consistent moral framework for life and highlights the need to provide a collective safety net to those individuals in society who are most in need. As legislators, in the U.S. House of Representatives, we work every day to advance respect for life and the dignity of every human being. We believe that government has moral purpose.

The six-paragraph statement included an expression of loyalty to Catholic social teaching about the obligations to "the poor and disadvantaged." On abortion, the signers declared that "each of us is committed to reducing the number of unwanted pregnancies and creating an environment with policies that encourage pregnancies to be carried to term."

This was significant because the statement was not an attempt by pro-choice Catholics to "reframe" the abortion question. The signatories included some of the staunchest opponents of abortion in the House, including representatives Bart Stupak, Dale Kildee, Tim Holden, James Oberstar, and James Langevin.

Rather, it reflected the worries of Democrats on both sides of the abortion question that the issue was crowding out all other concerns. In very polite language, the Catholic Democrats suggested that their bishops allow them some room to disagree. "In all these issues, we seek the church's guidance and assistance but believe also in the primacy of conscience," they wrote (it was yet another echo of Kennedy). "In recognizing the church's role in providing moral leadership, we acknowledge and accept the tension that comes from being in disagreement with the church in some areas."

Representative Rosa De Lauro, a Connecticut Democrat who was a prime mover behind the statement, was candid in describing it as a direct response not only to bishops who seemed to direct most of their ire toward Democrats and liberals, but also to politicians who seemed ready to use the Church in partisan battles. "People felt their faith was being questioned, and they were angry that ideologues were using the church for their own purpose," she said. "Our faith does and should affect how we deal with issues, but we're rebelling against the idea of a one-issue church."

She added, "We were silent for too long."

VI

Silence is certainly no longer the rule in the Catholic struggle over politics and partisanship. What was true across so many dimensions of American public life during the Bush years was true of the Catholic Church: a period of aggressive conservative assertion and ideological belligerence called forth both a progressive reaction and a rejection of ideology and partisanship. If the evangelical world was engaged in ferment and reformation, and if progressive impulses within both mainline and evangelical Protestantism were on the rise again, so too were new forces at work in the Catholic Church. The hierarchy might have become, on the whole, more conservative than it had been two decades earlier, but this, in turn, led many moderate and progressive Catholics to act.

They rebelled against the fact that the outspokenness of the conservative Church leaders—and the reticence of so many liberals and moderates in the hierarchy—created the impression that the Church as a whole had enlisted on one side of the 2004 campaign. Democrats who favored abortion rights were routinely and roundly condemned. Republicans who broke with the Church on all manner of other questions from social justice to the death penalty were left largely undisturbed. Many progressive politicians who had worked closely with the Church over the years on issues related to social welfare, international social justice, and peace asked how they should respond when Catholic representatives approached them for help again. Year after year, on issue after issue, progressives worked with the Church on these questions while conservatives often opposed the Church's view. Yet at election time, it seemed, only the progressives faced ecclesiastical punishment. This is a practical problem. And for progressive Catholics, it is a source of genuine anguish.

Speaking now personally as one of those progressive Catholics, our anguish grows from our own affection for the Church, the debt we feel we carry for its moral guidance, for its opening up the possibility of faith, and for its passing along the inspiration of Christian hope.

Over the years, the disdain that some liberals showed toward the Catholic Church and other churches bothered us—*especially* because so many of us came to what are seen as liberal views largely because of, *not* in spite of, Christianity and the church. As Pope John Paul II said over and over, it's impossible to be a Christian and to remain indifferent to the suffering created by unjust social structures. A few months before his death, John Paul called upon us "to advance a radical commitment to justice and a more attentive and determined display of solidarity." This call to solidarity is precisely what progressive Catholics—and progressives in all traditions—have responded to in their approaches to political and civic action.

Progressive Catholics who reject the idea of the Church joining a Republican political machine do not see the alternative as turning it over to a liberal or Democratic machine. In questioning certain elements of liberal orthodoxy, the Catholic Church has done a valuable service.

As we've seen, there *is* a powerful link between the moral behavior of individuals and the kind of society we create. Family breakdown has, indeed, caused serious problems for children and has contributed to economic inequality. Those who believe in "family values" must believe in social justice—and those who believe in social justice must concern themselves with family values.

Of course we'd rather have teenagers use condoms than not. But it is hardly irrational to ask if it's really possible to have much impact on high school students if we separate what we teach teenagers about sex from broader lessons about responsibility, marriage, and child rearing. And yes, our culture needs to show greater respect for life. That's why it is heartening that many prolife and prochoice progressives have joined in efforts to reduce the number of abortions.

Ideally, the Catholic Church's role in politics is to cause discomfort, to encourage questions, to challenge narrowly ideological views. Oddly, a Church that is seen as dogmatic has often had a moderating effect on politics. Conservative Catholics who cheer the Church's stance on abortion are affected by what it says about peace and justice. They are pushed away from a narrowly ideological conservatism. Liberal Catholics who cheer what the Church says about social justice and just war are affected by what it says about abortion and family life and assisted suicide. They are pushed away from a narrowly ideological liberalism.

Think of what this means for each of our political parties. Catholic Democrats are, or should be, a moderating force within their party on litmus-test values issues. Catholic Republicans are, or should be, a moderating force in resisting a sink-or-swim free market and in insisting that our leaders exercise moral caution before marching us off to war. Catholic Democrats and Republicans alike call attention to the importance of mediating structures, of solidarity and subsidiarity, of the importance of both social and individual responsibility.

It is also important to be honest in seeing that the political differences among Catholics—and this applies to those associated with other religious traditions—are often rooted in ideas and impulses only marginally connected to our faith commitments. This does not mean that faith is irrelevant. It simply accepts Peter Berger's point that modernity subjects individuals to a variety of forces and ideas, and that the modern person assimilates these as best he or she can. A Catholic trade unionist and a Catholic investment banker who disagree on, say, national health insurance or repealing the capital gains tax are not, I suspect, thinking too much about Catholic social thought when they take their respective stands. I would side with the trade unionist but would not deny the investment banker Communion.

In my ideal world, the Church would not endorse my own political choices, but neither would it become part of the other side's political organization. The Church's proper role is to be a ginger group, to borrow a British term, a kind of leaven in each coalition. On the whole, Catholics are, as William Bole argued in *Commonweal,* "soft communitarians." We are likely to find ourselves quite loyally, but not always comfortably, supporting our respective parties. Discomfort is not a bad thing. A bit of discomfort may be exactly what contemporary politics needs.

But if the Church causes discomfort only to one side in the debate when both sides are in need of repentance, it is not being the Church. It is not good enough for Catholic leaders to point to the long list of issues on which the Church's stand is, by any rational measure, progressive. If at election time all those progressive issues are ignored by the Church's most powerful spokespeople, or are spoken of in only a soft voice, then by the default of some and the intention of others, the Church will inevitably be seen as taking a partisan stand. If the only "nonnegotiable" issues happen to be in only one party's platform, what conclusion are Catholics expected to draw? What conclusion is the public expected to draw? And if Catholic candidates who do not agree with all of the Church's positions are subjected to far more criticism and denunciation than non-Catholic candidates, if some bishops would choose to deny them Communion, what message is the Church sending about Catholic participation in American political life?

Yes, as Steinfels suggested, this is a complex business. I devoutly believe that one can be a conservative and be a good Christian, and that one can be a progressive and be a good Christian. We know our obligation, as political scientist Glenn Tinder has put it, both to give and to receive help on the road to truth. I understand the frustrations of so many prolifers with progressives and liberals. I understand the commitment of political conservatives to finding a path to compassion and love. I understand that many good people in the Church speak out about the problems with *both* parties.

But yes, I am worried. The 2004 election, more than any other in recent memory, left progressive Catholics wondering if the institutional Church was taking sides in a partisan fight. If this is a misunderstanding, the Church has the urgent task of clearing it up. I do not presume to know how God would vote—and I don't think anyone else should, either.

During the 2004 election, in a reaction against the message that abortion should trump all other issues, the Catholic peace organization Pax Christi ran advertisements arguing against single-issue voting. Pax Christi insisted that political candidates "must understand that the Church stands against any policy or course of action which diminishes life, dignity or the rights of the human person: abortion, capital punishment, war, scandalous poverty, denial of healthcare, mistreatment of immigrants and racism." The headline on its ads read: "Life Does Not End At Birth."

VII

At the outset, I noted that I write as a Christian and a Catholic. The commitments to subsidiarity, solidarity, and community that underlie this book have specifically Catholic roots. My notion of the common good is shaped by my own reading of the scriptures in light of Catholic social thought. My moral and political commitments have been shaped by many sources—not just Catholic, but also Jewish and Protestant, liberal and social democratic, even by the kind of conservatism identified with Edmund Burke and Robert A. Nisbet. Yet my starting points on many issues were, more than I often realized, set by Catholic ideas and assumptions.

For a Catholic of my sort, the last decade has been discouraging. There was, first, the pedophilia scandal in which so many Church leaders behaved with an unconscionable irresponsibility. The contradiction between what the Church preached about sexuality and compassion toward the young and how its leaders reacted to the flagrant violation of those norms by priests moved Catholics of all ideologies to anger, and led many to fall away from the Church. The profound failures shook not merely allegiances to a particular institution, but faith itself.

This was followed by the spectacle of the 2004 campaign, in which important parts of the Church seemed to side with the conservative party and the conservative candidate, even if so many of his views were at odds with Catholic social teaching. As I've made clear, this struck me as a terrible mistake—not only because it contradicted my own political views, but, more importantly, because it diminished the richness of a Catholic tradition that has always grappled with the essential political questions: How should a just society be organized? How and when should wars be fought? How can government serve the common good? A great tradition should not turn itself into a political faction.

Yet the Church's history is long. Its membership is blessedly varied. Its positions on political questions are not immutable. Its teachings can still inspire. As a personal matter, a large group of priests, nuns, and lay people—including those to whom this book is dedicated—have continued to provoke awe by doing the practical work of justice and mercy. Many of them have continued to make public arguments for a broad view of Catholic social thought. I think here especially of my friends among priests, notably the late Phil Murnion, J. Bryan Hehir, and Ray Kemp, and those model lay Catholic intellectuals, Peter and Peggy Steinfels. All have been devoted to serving individuals and not just to justice in the abstract. Others who have offered passion and love in serving the day-to-day spiritual and corporal needs of their congregations include my long-time pastor Msgr. Tom Duffy, Father Percival DaSilva, Msgr. John Enzler, and my friend and occasional political sparring partner, Msgr. Peter Vaghi.

Pope Benedict XVI played a good-natured trick on people like me with his first encyclical, *Deus caritas est,* "God Is Love," by largely avoiding every issue that has created controversy, and concentrating on the essence of faith. The idea of a loving God, a God who is Love, was revolutionary in human history. And the notion, as Benedict put it, that "[o]nly if I serve my neighbor can my eyes be opened to what God does" is both a demanding and liberating standard. It declares that "if in my life I fail completely to heed others, solely out of a desire to be 'devout' and to perform my 'religious duties'"—note that Benedict himself put those phrases in quotation marks—"then my relationship with God will also grow arid." Benedict, of course, is not urging us to ignore those "religious duties," but he is putting them in their proper perspective. A God whose primary demand is that we love others is rather different from other gods that have been known in history.

Battles over whether abortion should or should not be a "nonnegotiable issue" for Catholics seem inevitable—and Benedict has come close to arguing that it is. Yet in his encyclical, Benedict did not ignore the developments in Catholic social thought over the last century. "Building a just social and civil order, wherein each person receives what is his or her due, is an essential task which every generation must take up anew," he writes. At another point he says, "A just society must be the achievement of politics, not of the Church. Yet the promotion of justice through efforts to bring about openness of mind and will to the demands of the common good is something which concerns the Church deeply." And so it should.

My own hope is not that the Church give up its concern for the right to life, but that it will embrace—or re-embrace—its larger mission to promote the common good and advance a communitarian alternative to radical individualism.

In October 2002 *Commonweal* published a manifesto on behalf of this idea by Michael Lacey, a historian, and William Shea, a theologian.

"Communitarians," Lacey and Shea argue,

stress the importance of doing whatever is possible to maintain a thriving civil sector, meaning the whole kit and caboodle of nongovernmental human associations, from families and bowling leagues, to churches, unions, and corporations. But they don't accept perspectives that pit government and civil society against one another as natural enemies, the way conservatives like to do. They are the same at the source: people like us. Thus liberal communitarians seek a certain kind of competence in the public sector. They look for responsiveness, cooperation, and the closer integration of government and society, not their separation.

Lacey and Shea offer new twists on the old Catholic concepts of subsidiarity and solidarity. They argue that

Subsidiarity is a way of thinking about the ideal of responsiveness in the social order. It speaks to the morality of giving and receiving help. It points to . . . the need to provide help without harm up and down the line—to furnish welfare support for those who need it, for example, without financing a caste system and undermining fulfillment of the obligation to look after ourselves and our own. Finding and holding that line can be difficult, and subsidiarity asks a lot from each of us. It can be understood minimally to say: Ask for help when you need it, give when asked, but don't spoil yourself (or anyone else), take care of your own business, and don't be an intrusive busybody.

Solidarity, on the other hand, cautions against complacency and getting lost in your own business. Pope John Paul II speaks of it as a virtue to be cultivated through reflective participation in society and politics. He describes solidarity as an overriding will to community in keeping with our intuitions of the divine will. "It is not," he says, "a feeling of vague compassion or shallow distress at the misfortunes of so many people, both near and far. On the contrary, it is a firm and persevering determination to commit oneself to the common good." Thus understood, solidarity is an open ended sense of moral obligation that helps us to see the "other" as one of us, and works to prevent communities, including religious communities, from closing in on themselves. The post–Vatican II papacy has carefully championed the sacred dignity of all human persons, not just Catholics in good standing. The new tone and the cautious apologies evident in the Vatican's attempts to repair rifts with the world's Jewish communities, to reopen talks with other Christian groups and with secularists, to dispel some of the old biases against science—these are public exercises of the virtue of solidarity.

I wrote earlier that the new concern about religion in public life reflects anxieties over the loss of a civic glue once provided by mainline Protestantism. A public argument over the meaning of subsidiarity and solidarity is a precondition for mixing a new civic glue. Doing so would enrich a political discussion of morality that has been defined so narrowly. It would call upon our religious traditions to speak to the most important questions of public life.

Catholics and mainline Protestants are two key swing groups in American politics—Catholics because they are less Democratic than they once were, mainline Protestants because they are less Republican. Both communities are, at heart, moderate in their orientation, and each has over the decades developed a powerful set of arguments on behalf of the public interest. Their commitments have come to coincide with those of an American Jewish community long devoted to social justice, personal tolerance, and freedom, and also with the concerns of many evangelicals disappointed with the fruits of divisive ideological politics. As a Catholic, I hope the Church finds its way toward a revival of its commitment to a public theology of the seamless garment—an emphasis on community and equality, liberty, justice, and life, all rooted in an insistence upon the imperatives of personal, social, and political responsibility. A church called Catholic should not shrink from this expansive vocation.

7. Solidarity, Liberty, and Religion's True Calling

Many Americans, and not just atheists, would like religious voices to shut up and clear out of the public square. We have had enough, they say, of policies based on faith, not fact; compassion based on words, not deeds; and wars based on dreams, not prudent analysis. We are tired of sentimental moralism passing as serious thinking, religion transformed into narrow, ideological politics, and prejudice cloaked in the scriptures. This is not an implausible view, and it holds that religion entered the public square and was found wanting. Better to leave religion to its potentially beneficial, or at least relatively harmless, role in the private lives of individuals.

The irony here is that the rise of such sentiments is a direct response to the aggressiveness of those who insisted a few decades ago that a rampant secularism was coming to dominate the United States. The loudest and most militant in demanding a strong public role for religion have called forth an unprecedented reaction against religion's place in public life because so many in their ranks did more than simply defend the prerogatives and rights of religious people. They insisted that only those who subscribed to a very particular conservative agenda and supported a particular political party could claim to be faithful. After an initial round of success in legitimizing religion's public role, this movement's partisans threaten to discredit religious voices—including their own.

But it would be a great loss to democratic life if the response to the religious Right is reduced to a demand that religion confine itself to the private sphere. This is impossible in any event. All traditions have a right to defend themselves in public. In our history, Catholics have battled anti-Catholicism, Jews have organized against anti-Semitism, and, more recently, Muslims have defended their religious and civil rights at a moment when they seemed threatened. For many evangelical Christians, their recent forms of self-assertion were aimed primarily at pushing back against their sense of exclusion from the dominant culture and grew from their belief that an elite held strong prejudices against them and their worldview.

Religion is also necessarily public because those who hold to particular religious traditions and ideas have a right to advance those propositions in public and to win new allies, and new souls. And it is in the nature of our great traditions to have a public as well as a private face, to call political, economic, and cultural systems to account in the name of standards of morality and justice.

It is also the right of all citizens in a democracy—including religious citizens and, yes, including those whose views I have criticized in these pages—to join our public deliberations, to organize in pursuit of their definition of the public good, to reach political conclusions on the basis of their faith commitments. Denying them that right only courts the backlash we have experienced in recent decades. "Secularism," as Jeffrey Stout, a professor of religion at Princeton University has said, "comes across to believers as a mixture of insult and exclusion. Believers who feel that they have been written off as irrational or deprived of an opportunity to express their deepest concerns when important issues come up for discussion are apt also to feel alienated and resentful." Indeed.

It's true, as Stout says, that democracy "is threatened in a religiously plural society not only by theocratic attempts to impose religious unity on the public, but also by religious factionalism—that is, by religiously motivated unfriendliness." But he adds, "The answer is not . . . to exclude religious reasons from public discussion. Religious people are unlikely to go along with such a policy in any event, so the secularists are wasting their breath in proposing it."

We do not need, and should not want, to end religion's public role. We *do* need a more capacious understanding of what that role is. We need a more demanding standard whereby religious people live up to their obligations to religious pluralism and religious liberty by making public arguments that are accessible to those who do not share their assumptions or their deepest commitments. And we need to understand that religion offers its greatest gift to public life not when it promotes certainty, but when it encourages reflection, self-criticism, and doubt.

II

To assert that encouraging doubt is one of faith's tasks may seem paradoxical. But that is the case only if faith is defined solely as a demand that everyone assent without reservation to a long and particular list of propositions. This is an inadequate understanding of religious faith. The Christian and Jewish traditions in particular will always call us to a form of moral doubt that the political theorist William Galston has argued "questions our motivations and pretensions to special virtue."

Galston, quite naturally, turns to Reinhold Niebuhr as the great exponent of this faithful form of doubt. Niebuhr reminded us that "no virtuous act is quite as virtuous from the standpoint of our friend or foe as it is from our standpoint." He argued that "[s]ome of the greatest perils to democracy arise from the fanaticism of moral idealists who are not conscious of the corruption of self-interest." In an assertion that might usefully have guided us before our country went to war in Iraq, Niebuhr warned: "A nation with an inordinate degree of political power is doubly tempted to exceed the bounds of historical possibilities, if it is informed by an idealism which does not understand the limits of man's wisdom and volition." As Galston concludes, "The absence of moral doubt makes it far too difficult to recognize and rectify our mistakes. The cure, Niebuhr teaches, is the humility that comes from the acceptance of limits to human striving."

In invoking Niebuhr, Galston is describing what has been through the ages religious faith's great contribution to liberty. By insisting on ultimate standards, religious faith calls human power to account. By arguing that perfection is not given to humankind, religious faith questions promises of worldly utopias and insists that we must place limits on our own will to power. It is not surprising that Niebuhr wrote and gained a wide following during and after the struggles against Nazism and Stalinism, ideologies that justified despotic pretensions in the name of creating new human beings and perfect societies. This is religion's essential *conservative* role, a form of conservatism far removed from ideology and from any claims that religion—and Christian faith in particular—can be used as a detailed textbook for creating the perfect society here on earth. Even the old battle cry of the religious Left, of our obligation to "build the Kingdom" of God's justice and fairness on earth, emphasizes a constant act of creation—*building*—not a final outcome that human beings can achieve on their own. And there have been times when the religious Left itself needed Niebuhr's correction to limit its claims. Niebuhr's recovery of the ideas of St. Augustine and the importance of original sin was a reaction against what he saw as a potentially dangerous naiveté in the Social Gospel movement that arose in tandem with the Progressive era. As the political philosopher Jean Bethke Elshtain has noted, Augustine taught both the limits and the possibilities of politics. "If Augustine is a thorn in the side of those who would cure the universe once and for all," she writes, "he similarly torments critics who disdain any project of human community, or justice, or possibility." Wisdom, Elshtain says, "comes from experiencing fully the ambivalence and the ambiguity that is the human condition."

David Price, a Democratic member of Congress from North Carolina, notes Niebuhr's admiration of Abraham Lincoln's second inaugural address, perhaps the finest expression of religious humility by an American politician. Speaking after almost four years of civil war, Lincoln declared:

> Both [sides] read the same Bible, and pray to the same God; and each invokes His aid against the other. It may seem strange that any men should dare to ask a just God's assistance in wringing their bread from the sweat of other men's faces; but let us judge not, that we not be judged. The prayers of both could not be answered—that of neither has been answered fully.

Price cites Niebuhr's view that this passage "puts the relation of our moral commitments in history to our religious reservations about the partiality of our own moral commitments more precisely than, I think, any statesman or theologian has put them." Lincoln, Price notes, "expresses the moral commitment against slavery in uncompromising terms, along with the determination to 'finish the work we are in.' But there follows the religious reservation, the recognition that ultimate judgment belongs to God alone, *the refusal, even in this extreme instance, to presume an absolute identification between his own cause and God's will.*" (Emphasis added)

The doubt and humility promoted by religion is not a form of weakness, but rather represents faith's greatest potential contribution to public life. The forms of religious engagement in public life that are rooted in doubt and humility are far more likely to be effective—and far more apt to be just—than approaches rooted in utter assurance and arrogance, in the total identification of a human political agenda with the cause of God. Lincoln demonstrated as clearly as any statesman that it is possible to undertake great tasks in politics with firmness, commitment, principle, and courage and still not pretend to absolute certainty about one's course, one's intentions, or the purity of one's motives. It is a style of public religion that badly needs to be rediscovered and put into practice. It's especially urgent to do so if we are to preserve the advances religious voices have made in what I have called the third stage of our national conservation about religion and public life.

III

This third stage is worth building on, not scrapping, because what makes the American situation so distinctive is our combination of a high degree of religious public commitment with a strongly secular, durable, and democratic government. Many democracies have religious parties (Christian in Europe and South America, Jewish in Israel, Muslim in parts of the Middle East and Asia). In the United States, on the other hand, religion plays a large public role without dominating any political party. Paradoxically, this seems to have strengthened religion's role in American society. European nations with explicitly religious parties seem far more secular than the United States. There are many reasons for this, but it is clear that the presence of religiously inspired political groupings provides no guarantee that religion itself will thrive in their societies. And highly sectarian religious parties can marginalize religion's role even as they might advance particular religious interests.

American-style church-state separation, as Paul Starr noted in his 2007 book *Freedom's Power*, "helps protect religious life from political control, and government from entanglement in religious passions." Starr explicitly contrasts the European habit of granting government support to churches with the American refusal to do so and notices that by most measures, including church attendance, American religious institutions are stronger. "Inasmuch as churches in a free, pluralistic religious economy depend on voluntary contributions rather than government subsidies," Starr writes, "they tend to be more innovative and entrepreneurial than tax-supported churches in developing and marketing services that attract and keep members." Some religious people might legitimately bridle at the use of words such as "marketing" and "services," but Starr's is a view that Rick Warren would certainly understand.

Yet I do not want to pretend that my own interest is simply in the preservation of a public role for religion. My argument is rooted in a passion for democracy, a belief that democratic forms and democratic ideas are more likely than other forms and other ideas to promote justice, liberty, and community—and are also more likely to check the concentrations of power that naturally arise from the imperfections in human nature to which Niebuhr constantly called our attention.

As a Christian and a democrat, I believe the two ideas are more than compatible. I would argue that Christianity contained at least some of the seeds that gave life to democratic ideas and democratic practice, a point made by Tod Lindberg in *The Political Teachings of Jesus.*

But is this just wishful thinking? Is it merely a sentimental effort to marry two incompatible systems of thought toward which one happens to feel affection?

As it happens, H. Richard Niebuhr grappled with this question at a moment when democracy was imperiled. He began a lecture on "Religion and the Democratic Tradition" at Berkeley Divinity School in October 1940 with these words: "To speak again of the relations of Christianity and democracy is to venture on ground well-trodden by angels and fools."

Niebuhr explained the desire of so many of us to find links between democracy and our own traditions—in his case and mine, Christianity— this way: "We tend to become so devoted to Christianity that we do not inquire too diligently into its character; we love democracy so dearly that we do not ask it too many questions about its heredity, its religion, its virtues and its vices. We find beauty in both because we love them, as well as love them because they are beautiful. Defensiveness increases confusion in this realm."

As was always true of both Niebuhrs, Richard was acutely aware of the paradoxes and contradictions involved in his inquiry. On the one hand, he saw the danger of pretending that democracy was divinely ordained. "When the divine absolute is acknowledged," he wrote, "all human absolutes appear as dangerous usurpers of the Kingdom of God." He noted that if Lincoln's phrase "of the people, by the people and for the people" were taken literally—as Lincoln himself did not take it—"then Christian faith must question it as an adequate definition of government."

Niebuhr went on: "No people can live in the world of God who live for themselves, who consult only their own desires in making laws, who are their own last court of appeal, their own beginning and their own end." I'll have more to say about this in a moment.

Yet in the end, perhaps reflecting the fact that he, like many of us, perceived beauty in both Christianity and democracy, Niebuhr concluded that "[d]emocracy is a gift which is added to men who seek first the King-dom and its righteousness."

Here's how he reached that conclusion: "The positive relation between Christian faith and democracy," he wrote,

> is more a moral than intellectual one. Whenever confidence in the rule of God is vital in a society it leads to the limitation of all human power, to increased participation by the people in government, to the willing-ness to grant liberty to men, and to the political recognition of human equality. Whether or not these are the marks of true democracy, they are the features of the political organization of nations which have been influenced by Jewish and Christian faith.

Now I agree with Niebuhr on this, and yet I do so bearing in mind his own admonition: that perhaps I do not want to see any conflict between the traditions of Christianity and Judaism and the tradition of democracy because I love both so fervently. Christians and Jews certainly did not always revere democracy as most Christians and Jews do today. At the very time Niebuhr spoke, a significant wing of German Christianity was defending dictatorial rule that led to genocide. My own Catholic Church was far more open to democracy after Vatican II and the papacy of Pope John XXIII than it was before.

It's thus fair for critics of religion to ask how successful and permanent the reconciliation of Christianity to democracy, toleration, and pluralism really is. But let us assume from the evidence at least of the last sixty years that a powerful link has been forged, that there is now a durable logic in favor of democracy within both the Christian and Jewish traditions. What are we to make of the present and possible future connections between democracy and the orientation of the other great monotheistic religion, Islam? And what are the obligations of Christians and Jews, through their own behavior and their own arguments, to assist Muslim democrats? I speak here not of waging wars, but of creating models.

We already know that Islam *can* be compatible with democracy. Muslims play a vital role in democracies in which they find themselves a minority—India notably, but also the United States, Canada, and Great Britain, among other places. We also know that Indonesia, the largest Muslim country in the world, has enjoyed some real successes in its strug-gle toward democracy and that Pakistan, with the world's second largest

Muslim population, has had moments of democracy. Turkey's Muslim society, despite past and current problems, has also made democracy work.

Yet there is a great debate about how successfully Islam can accommodate itself to modernity and democracy as a theoretical and theological matter. Consider the 1986 essay by Fouad Ajami about what he called the "impossible life" of Muslim liberalism. I cite him here not because I am certain he is right, but because he describes the challenge well. It is striking how similar in texture this passage is to so much of what has been written about Catholicism's failed encounter with liberalism in the nineteenth century. Ajami wrote:

> A whole literature of Moslem apologetics had stressed the compatibility between Islam and democracy, Islam and tolerance, and so on. All of that literature was part of a long intellectual dialogue that these modernists had carried on with Western intellectuals and critics. They were busy debating with the foreigner; they looked past the popular sensibilities of the masses, past the intolerance of religion and the obscurantism of the religious institutions. And thus they were not ready when Islam refused to take a bow, to deliver its exit lines.

The task that both Niebuhrs and John Courtney Murray, among others, took on in the 1940s and 1950s—to develop what might be called a theology of democracy—is once again urgent. It will require work across traditions and within traditions. And it is work that should be undertaken with hope, though not with false optimism. Roman Catholic democrats, after all, drew on their own tradition but also on the Reformation and the Enlightenment. They encountered many setbacks and were often accused by their enemies of unfaithfulness and of trying to twist the tradition to a secular purpose. But over the course of a century—and partly because of the failure of the authoritarian alternatives—the Catholic democrats won.

I am not, I hope, naive about this, and I do not pretend that Islam will automatically reproduce the same outcome in the struggle for democracy that has largely taken hold within Christianity and Judaism. Moreover, the achievements of liberal theology are tenuous. Mark Lilla, a shrewd and tough-minded critic of liberal theology, has argued that "the liberal deity turned out to be a stillborn God, unable to inspire genuine conviction among a younger generation seeking ultimate truth." Lilla was speaking of the time after World War I. "The liberal house was tottering," he writes, "and after the First World War it collapsed."

Lilla makes a rigorous and sophisticated case, but it is worth asking if he is too pessimistic about the achievement of liberalism within the theological realm—and, in particular, if he understates the staying power of democratic ideas among orthodox Christian and Jewish believers. If the experience of World War I caused disillusionment among religious democrats and liberals, the struggles against fascism during World War II gave modernity a new lease on intellectual life and created a new urgency for theologies of democracy and liberty.

Lilla is certainly right to argue that the West cannot by itself expect to transform Islam, that it must be changed from within, and that those he calls "renovators," rather than liberal or leftist revolutionaries, will be the key to reform. "If liberalizers are apologists for religion at the court of modern life," he writes, "renovators stand firmly within their faith and reinterpret political theology so believers can adapt without feeling themselves to be apostates." Lilla has a point, but, again, he may be underestimating the role of renovators within Christianity and Judaism. Surely figures such as the Niebuhr brothers, Jacques Maritain, John Courtney Murray, Martin Buber, and Pope John XXIII were more than apologists for religion in modern life; they also mobilized their faith to offer productive critiques of modernity itself. Isn't it possible to imagine comparable developments within Islam?

I raise these issues in a book devoted almost entirely to the American experience to underscore responsibility to make our model of religious liberty work. The United States and the democratic West as a whole must develop approaches that grapple seriously with the issues raised for pluralism and liberty when religious diversity explodes within free societies. Will Herberg's classic about American pluralism from the 1950s, *Protestant, Catholic, Jew,* would now have to be called *Protestant, Catholic, Jew, Muslim, Hindu, Buddhist, Sikh, Jain, Confucian, Baha'i.* And even this ungainly title is incomplete.

Perhaps understandably, the issues raised by the new pluralism were missing from the American religious agenda a generation ago when the Christian Right came to prominence. These questions must be central to the next agenda.

IV

So, too, must be the challenge from the new atheists. At their best, today's neo-atheists are engaged in a providential call, a demand not unlike St. Peter's who enjoined Christians: "Always be ready to give an account of the faith that is in you." The very fact that neo-atheists are reviving arguments offered in the nineteenth century is a sign of religion's persistence, of the limits of secularization, of the power of the spiritual calling. By challenging the very basis of religious faith, the new atheists force believers back to the essential questions. Religion at root is not primarily about politics, or ethics, or community. It does, in the end, come down to God. "God is either of no importance or of supreme importance," wrote Abraham Joshua Heschel. "God is He whose regard for me is more precious than life. Otherwise, he is not God. God is the meaning beyond mystery."

"Faith is both certainty and trial demanding strain, sacrifice, wrestling," Heschel continued. "For certainty without trial becomes complacency, lethargy, while trial without certainty is chaos, presumption, as if God had never reached us, as if history were always a monologue."

It is not the purpose of this book to engage in metaphysical argument with my neo-atheist friends. They have already called forth many creative responses, and also a reengagement with the older responses by earlier generations of believers to earlier generations of doubters. But two core propositions that provide the neo-atheists with their energy are relevant here: that religion, as Christopher Hitchens has put it, "poisons everything," and that religious faith is, finally, built on unreason and weakness.

This view depends for sustenance on calling attention to all of religion's manifest sins, and none of its virtues; to religion's crimes, and none of its achievements; to the times when religion encouraged arrogance, unquestioning loyalty, and violent self-assertion, not when it promoted humility, self-questioning, and the reach for transcendent standards of conduct and morality. To the extent that believers, through their words and actions, confirm the neo-atheists' worst charges and harshest judgments, they cannot be doing the work of God.

Yet even more devastating is the argument that believers must finally lose themselves in irrationality, that the very act of "hoping against hope" is rooted in false promises and flimsy premises. Hitchens refers to the "contempt for the intellect" that religion can inspire and the danger to those who "put their reason to sleep." He makes this argument in a chapter discussing the manipulation of Buddhism in imperial Japan, but it is representative of his broader critique of religion.

The consequences of what Hitchens describes are certainly nasty: "One of two things may happen," Hitchens writes. "[T]hose who are innocently credulous may become easy prey for those who are less scrupulous and who seek to 'lead' and 'inspire' them. Or those whose credulity has led their own society into stagnation may seek a solution, not in true self-examination, but in blaming others for their backwardness."

No rational person can disagree with Hitchens's warnings against the sleep of reason and a contempt for the intellect. No moral person can approve of the manipulation of religion by ruling groups to aggrandize their own power and to lead others to violence. And no honest person of faith can deny that many religious traditions, including his or her own, have been misused in these ways—and probably will, at some point, be misused again.

What must be challenged is the assumption that religion depends on anaesthetizing reason, holding the intellect in contempt, waging war on science, denying the possibility of progress, or supposedly manipulating the "innocently credulous"—the last a rather less than democratic view of humankind. Faith in God does not lead ineluctably to contempt for *this* life and *this* world, to the loss of faith in human possibility, or to the death of human self-respect.

The radical challenge of the neo-atheists should remind believers, whatever their politics, that they live under the obligation to fight the assertion that "religion poisons everything"—and to do so *through their actions even more than through their words.* The new atheism did not arise spontaneously. It is a direct response to abuses committed in God's name. The believer is thus obligated to embrace the mission described in the title of Rabbi Jonathan Sacks's powerful call to "the ethics of responsibility," *To Heal a Fractured World.* "I am troubled by the face that religion often shows the postmodern world," writes Sacks, the chief rabbi of Great Britain. "Too often, it appears on the news and lodges in the mind as extremism, violence and aggression."

Coining a word, Sacks warns that when "political conflict is religionized, it is absolutized." He continues: "What in politics are virtues—compromise, the willingness to listen to both sides and settle for less than one would wish in an ideal world—are, in religion, vices. Religion can therefore act not as a form of conflict resolution, but, rather, conflict intensification."

And Sacks offers a call to a religious humanism that is surely not limited to his own tradition: "The message of the Hebrew Bible," he writes, "is that serving God and serving our fellow human beings are inseparably linked, and the split between the two impoverishes both. Unless the holy leads us out toward the good, and the good leads us back, for renewal, to the holy, the creative energies of faith have run dry."

Nearly sixty years before Sacks wrote, Karl Barth, the neo-orthodox giant of twentieth-century Protestant theology, had offered a strikingly parallel definition of Christian ethics. "According to Christian ethics," Barth wrote, "man as such, every man, has a legitimate claim to be seen, affirmed and accepted. Christian ethics is not neutral. It is not interested in some mighty It, no matter how lofty. Rather, it is concerned wholly and solely with I and Thou."

"For Christian ethics," Barth continues, with a bow to Kant, "man can never be a means to an end. He is the end himself, the final end. Because he is a man, he is honorable, more important than the most glorious thing. Why? Because man is such a good and glorious being? No, but rather because God so honored and dignified him by becoming Himself one of his kind."

And what Sacks asserted about Judaism's relationship with the good and the holy, Barth asserted about prayer and work. Christian ethics, he wrote, "allows no talk of prayer which does not of itself lead into work, and no talk of work which is not grounded in prayer."

With Sacks, people of faith should beware of absolutizing politics. With Barth, they should be wary of any form of politics that treats human beings as means, not ends. With both Niebuhrs and Augustine, they should not expect too much of politics, but neither should they accept too little. There is, finally, only one genuinely persuasive response to the neo-atheists from believers: by our works shall you know us—and to act accordingly.

V

In early June 2007 the three leading Democratic candidates for president participated in an event more in keeping with the party of William Jennings Bryan than with our perceptions of the contemporary party of

Hillary Clinton, Barack Obama, and John Edwards. The three candidates split an hour of time on CNN to talk about not Iraq or taxes or budgets or health care (though these subjects did come up, directly or indirectly), but their religious faith and its implications for their political views. The gathering was sponsored by *Sojourners*, the progressive Christian group and magazine led by Jim Wallis. This, too, was part of something new: while a Christian Left has existed, in one form or another, for well over a century, it was hard to remember a time when religious progressives had chosen to play such a large role, so early, in the process of nominating and electing a president. It was difficult to find any precedent for the media attention showered on an event that focused on questions posed to politicians from a point of view that was simultaneously religious *and* progressive.

That the three front-running Democrats were more at ease with religious questions than their Republican counterparts was also something new—or seemed new, given the popular assumptions of just a few years earlier. Rudy Giuliani's prochoice views on abortion earned him, as we have seen, attacks from parts of the Christian Right and some Catholic bishops. John McCain had lambasted the religious Right during the 2000 campaign and tried unsuccessfully afterward to make peace. Mitt Romney's allegiance to Mormonism, a faith much mistrusted in evangelical circles, made him stick to rather general comments about his religious commitments, at least in the early part of the campaign. Of that period's front-runners, only Romney had led a personal and family life that could meet the exacting standards traditionalists, in theory at least, set for political leaders. And the two Republicans most publicly engaged in their faith, former governor Mike Huckabee of Arkansas, a Baptist minister, and Senator Sam Brownback of Kansas, a Catholic convert from evangelicalism, trailed badly at the time. Brownback eventually dropped out of the race, but Huckabee emerged as a genuine alternative to the front-runners. The close links Huckabee drew between his own Christianity and such issues as health care and education made his invocations of religion more similar in spirit to those of the top Democrats than of his Republican rivals.

If nothing else, the sharp turn in the political situation a mere two and a half years after the 2004 election suggested how so many sweeping statements about religion in politics had been based on the experience of one politician, George W. Bush, and the temporary electoral alignment he built. No wonder that in July 2007, *Time* magazine ran a cover story about the new engagement between Democrats and religious faith that included the headline: "Leveling the Praying Field."

The fact that many of the best moments of the *Sojourners* discussion were deeply personal—Edwards discussed how religious faith helped him through the death of his teenage child, Clinton spoke movingly of the role of prayer in grappling with her husband's infidelity—suggests how difficult it is to separate religion's public role from its importance to the private lives of individuals and to the intuitive judgments voters make about candidates and their character. One of the most striking developments of our time, as the sociologist Jose Casanova has argued, is the resurrection of "public religion," the "deprivatization" of religion in contemporary life. Yet religion is and always will be both public and private. It is the drama of the interaction between these two spheres that makes public religion so contested, even if religion's power makes it an inescapable part of public life. Our democracy must learn to live with this interaction better than it has in the recent past—to accept it while subjecting its expressions to legitimate skepticism. Voters will never base their decisions solely on criteria proposed by a learned committee of rationalists, nor should they.

American politics is at a turning point. Evangelical Christians are an increasingly diverse group. Many in their ranks are broadening their tradition's agenda to include a commitment to the poor, an engagement with international human and religious rights, opposition to genocide in Darfur, a passionate commitment to relieving the burden of AIDS on the African poor, and a deepening belief in the obligation of stewardship toward the environment. Mainline Protestants are battling through the moral approaches of their churches toward homosexuality even as they maintain powerful and long-standing commitments to peace, social justice, and a strong version of the common good. Catholics, as we have already seen in some detail, have a rich history of social concern that is not about to disappear. Consider the tens of thousands of Catholics in groups such as Just Faith, Pax Christi, Catholics in Alliance for the Common Good, and Call to Action. Consider also the diocesan social action directors, the activists in the Catholic Campaign for Human Development, and the aid workers and organizers at Catholic Relief Services. These engaged believers are not about to allow their church to fall short on its commitment to justice. African American and Latino church leaders are dedicated to working on behalf of equality not only as a moral matter, but also because of their concern for the survival and success of their own congregations, neighborhoods, and communities. American Jews have been unwavering in their devotion to justice, equality, and the common good. And our country's growing Muslim community has a vital interest in equal justice and in religious liberty and pluralism. There is very good reason to believe that in the coming years, America's religious communities will no longer be seen as the natural allies of political conservatism.

But this view accepts the fact that religious groups will necessarily be engaged in public life. It is based on the idea that those who repaired to political activism on behalf of conservatism were by no means wrong about everything. The Christian Right had reason to rebel against the marginalization of religion's public role, but it was wrong to identify faith with an agenda so narrow that Jesus's commands to lift up the poor were lost in polemics against permissiveness and "the liberals." It was right to remind us of the importance of family life, but wrong to suggest that family breakdown was the fault of gays and not the primary responsibility of married heterosexuals. It was right to tell us that intact families promoted social justice, but wrong to forget that social justice and a degree of economic security are necessary for healthy family lives. It was right for Christian conservatives to worry about the dysfunctions of popular culture, but wrong to ignore the extent to which this culture is rooted in the very materialism that many of their political allies celebrate. Above all, it was wrong to see righteousness as the exclusive possession of one political party or one ideological movement.

A concern for human life from the moment of conception must be carried through all of life—and even fetal life might be better advanced through means other than the criminalization of abortion. "The old ways of encouraging the reduction of abortions, the strident ways, are not productive," says the Rev. Joel Hunter. The number of abortions cannot be attributed solely to moral or cultural breakdown. Other forces—poverty, notably—are, and always have been, at work in the incidence of abortion. And a respect for life is demonstrated not only by our attitude toward abortion, but also by our concern for those who are imprisoned, our views on the death penalty, the help we give those suffering from AIDS, the compassion we show impoverished children whose mothers, in bringing them into the world, have chosen life.

Insisting that science is not the only valid form of human knowledge is both rational and necessary—but this view must not be turned into an attack on science itself. New scientific discoveries must be subjected to moral questioning and can be legitimately regulated. The fantastic new possibilities of genetic manipulation have the potential of curing many diseases—but they could also radically alter how we define what is human. We dare not advance in this research without attending to the views of philosophers, ethicists, and theologians, and, yes, religious people.

As the philosopher Michael Sandel has argued, those who worry about "the pursuit of perfection" in human beings through science should not be marked out as know-nothings or enemies of scientific discovery. Sandel (who, incidentally, favors stem-cell research), puts it this way:

> To acknowledge the giftedness of life is to recognize that our talents and powers are not wholly our own doing, despite the efforts we expend to develop and to exercise them. Appreciating the gifted quality of life constrains the Promethean and conduces to a certain humility. This sense of giftedness is in part a religious sensibility, but its resonance reaches beyond religion, and there are ways of understanding this idea, this ethic, that don't depend on religious notions.

Sandel is particularly wary of the temptation parents might experience to create "perfect" children with science's help:

> This helps us see that the deepest moral objection to enhancement or to the pursuit of designer children lies not in the perfection that it seeks, but in the human disposition that it expresses and promotes. The problem is not that parents usurp the autonomy of the child whose sex they choose or whose traits they design, because the child wouldn't otherwise choose her genetic traits for herself. Autonomy is not what's at issue. The problem lies in the hubris of the designing parents in their drive to master the mystery of birth. Even if this disposition doesn't make parents tyrants to their children, still it disfigures the relation of parent and child and deprives the parent of the humility and of the enlarged human sympathies that an openness to the unbidden can cultivate.

I quote Sandel at length here because he provides a particularly powerful example of how communitarian sensibilities might create common ground for an ethical conversation across the religious and ideological divides. Sandel is neither a Christian nor a conservative, yet he understands why Christians and conservatives are uneasy about certain developments in science. We are much more likely to have the moral conversations Christian conservatives seek if these discussions are carried out in a spirit of intellectual solidarity, not sectarianism. Liberals, in turn, are far more likely to win the battles they wage on behalf of science if they acknowledge that ethical and moral concerns about the new capacities of science and medicine are not confined to the right-wing fringe. "Americans have a deep faith in science," Robert P. Jones and Rachel Laser wrote in an important 2007 report for the group Third Way, "but also worry that scientific advances are outrunning our best moral thinking."

The United States has always moved back and forth between libertarian and communitarian poles, between a concern for solidarity and a concern for freedom. At our best, Americans understand the need to keep a balance between the two. Community and solidarity require liberty, while liberty is best preserved in societies where community is strong and where solidarity encourages all of us to come to the defense of each other's freedom. We have been reasonably perceptive in recognizing when the balance has shifted too far in one direction or the other, and we can see in the commotion over religion a concern with community's realm.

Capturing what Americans "really" believe about community and its requirements is a major academic and commercial industry. Applebee's restaurants built their success on understanding how community works in the suburbs and exurbs, and so have the megachurches. The link between the two is made explicitly in *Applebee's America*, the book by Democrat Douglas Sosnik, Bush's former pollster Matthew Dowd, and Associated Press writer Ron Fournier. The power of their volume comes from its insight that the next stages in American social and personal life will be defined in significant part in the new neighborhoods, not the old ones, in the growing parts of the country, and among young families. As I argued early on, these developments also work against the narrowly ideological politics of the past. They decidedly work against a narrowly ideological view of religion.

VI

Yet not everything is new. There is also, as Catholic University's John White has said, a new politics of old values. For a very long time, I have believed that many of the old values that a new politics would seek to advance can be found in Frank Capra's sturdy old Christmas movie, *It's a*

Wonderful Life. Indeed I would make a large claim for this dear, schmaltzy movie: it tells politicians and religious leaders almost everything they need to know about how Americans think and feel about "moral values." Watching it is a lot cheaper than paying for focus groups.

As I suspect many readers will know, *It's a Wonderful Life* is the story of George Bailey, played by Jimmy Stewart. Bailey is a small-town guy desperate to leave and see the world. He never makes it. He stays in Bedford Falls and runs the family's savings and loan while his brother wins glory in World War II. George marries his sweetheart (played by Donna Reed) and has a bunch of kids. Managing the S&L entails lending money to the town's working people so they get to own their own tidy homes. In so doing, George faces down the town's evil "big" banker, Mr. Potter, who doesn't care a whit about working stiffs. At the end of the movie, George is close to killing himself when his bank is threatened with bankruptcy because his absent-minded uncle loses a deposit. His bank's failure would give Mr. Potter a local monopoly.

Enter George's guardian angel, Clarence. He shows George how much poorer the world would have been without him. George is convinced his life is wonderful. Call me a sap: I always get a tear in my eye at the closing scene, when George bursts into the Christmas celebration at his home, where all his neighbors have gathered to help him out of his jam.

Now, why is this 1946 film still so popular? It is easy to dismiss *It's a Wonderful Life* as a nostalgic celebration of small-town life—as a flight from complexity, from racial, ethnic, and religious diversity, from changing gender roles and sexual mores, from the achievements of twenty-first-century capitalism and the new technologies it has created. Perhaps there is something to such a critique, but I believe it misses what endows this film with its power into our own time. It remains popular, finally, because Capra understood commitments that still run deep in the American character. So consider the following as a focus group report based on an unusually perceptive movie:

1. Americans are deeply egalitarian but also believe in upward mobility and the value of owning property. Mr. Potter is a cad because he doesn't believe in the town's "ordinary" people, who are worthy of respect. George respects them enough to help them become property owners.

2. Capitalists can be good, but only if they recognize moral limits—the "social mortgage" on their wealth. Americans believe in capitalism, but of a certain kind. As Chuck Collins and Mary Wright argue in their 2007 book, *The Moral Measure of the Economy*, there is good reason to oppose "the stifling of individual initiative and enterprise," but also to mistrust "market capitalism" unless it is "balanced with the common good and concerns for justice." George Bailey is a capitalist who understands both halves of this commitment. He makes a good living and is a leader of his community. He's a smart capitalist, too, saving his bank during the Great Depression, a fact grudgingly admired by Mr. Potter. But George is loved because he has put his bank's money to work for others, letting them share capitalism's bounty. Mr. Potter, the parody of the selfish miser so popular in Christmas stories, is loathed because all he cares about is cash. He has no friends, no concern for Bedford Falls.

3. These commitments—to egalitarianism, upward mobility, property ownership, capitalism within moral limits—are important because they underwrite a set of values. When Clarence shows George what life would have been without him, he shows him a Bedford Falls (renamed Pottersville) that has been turned into a honky-tonk gambling town. Rackets, drunkenness, prostitution, and meanness have replaced the quiet warmth of a real community. The proud working people George knew have become sullen, angry, and resentful, robbed of the chance to rise and to own their own stake. By showing life with and without George Bailey, Capra shows us two alternative social systems and makes clear which one works.

4. Americans love "family values" but dislike harsh condemnations of those who may fail in their efforts to live up to them. George is the classic model of the loving "family man." But he risks scandal by lending money to an old friend who has become, in the parlance of the time, a "bad girl." The movie celebrates George's behavior and paints blue-nosed scandalmongers as cheap and tawdry.

At its heart, this movie points to a past that lives on. It puts forward a balanced set of commitments that still inspire most Americans. It is a classic attempt to describe what a society that seeks both liberty and community looks like—and it also shows what happens when this balance is lost. Those who would move forward from the religious wars of the last quarter century would do well to understand and embrace George Bailey Politics.

VII

The work of justice in a free society is, as Pope Benedict says, the work of politics. In our country, that means democratic politics, which, in turn, means broad coalitions of believers and nonbelievers who would work together for justice. Here is where we must abandon the sectarian and ideological divisions of recent decades and pursue something very different. Jeffrey Stout points us in a promising direction by reminding us of what happened in John Paul's native land. "Justice would be better served," Stout argues, "by something like the coalition of religious groups and secular intellectuals that came together in Poland in the 1980s under the name of Solidarity. If that coalition was able to weaken the grip of Soviet oppression, simply by refusing to kneel in its presence, there is no telling what could happen if we wiped the crust of complacency from our eyes and demanded justice from our governmental and corporate elites."

"Our situation," Stout insists, "calls for a new democratic solidarity, appropriate to our time and place." Such solidarity could transform the nation, and there are many signs that it is busy being born.

The "Christian Right" is, finally, an abstraction. Millions of committed Christians who may well have responded to the appeals of a political movement at a particular moment are rethinking not so much their politics as the public implications of their faith. They are growing impatient with narrow agendas as they reach out to the poor in Africa and in their own communities, as they worry about the obligation to stewardship of the earth, as they grapple with practical ways to reduce the number of abortions, and as they struggle to approach gay friends and relatives in a spirit that is consistent with being Christian.

Liberals are changing, too. They are remembering things they had forgotten about the spiritual sources of their own dreams. They are recalling that one of the great successes of the last half century was a civil rights movement led by a Christian preacher inspired by the Declaration of Independence *and* by scripture. They are realizing that bigotry against people of faith is still bigotry. They are accepting that if religion can sometimes promote prejudice, it often promotes justice. They are coming to understand that their central goals—to lift up the poor, feed the hungry, shelter the homeless, care for the sick, and challenge injustice—have biblical roots and religious sanction.

To end the religious and cultural wars and to allow religion to flower in public life, we need passion and we need humility. These two virtues do not always come together, but they must. We need a passion for moving our nation out of a period in which public problems went unsolved and the possibilities of broad alliances were lost because narrow political imperatives triumphed over the idea of a common good. And we need humility to understand how prejudices—of believers against unbelievers, and unbelievers against believers—have obstructed our path and blurred our vision.

"The final enigma of history," Reinhold Niebuhr wrote, "is therefore not how the righteous will gain victory over the unrighteous, but how the evil in every good and the unrighteous in the righteous is to be overcome."

We must realize that self-righteousness is the enemy of righteousness, and that hope is the virtue on which faith and love depend.

Notes

A note on sources: I have tried to provide a reference to all published sources, including books, magazine and newspaper articles, and major speeches. However, this book is also based on extensive interviews and conversations. I have not created notes for interviews I conducted myself, to save the reader from a list of self-referential citations.

Introduction. Is God's Work Our Work?

2 Harvey Cox, "Afterword," in *The Secular City Debate*, ed. Daniel Callahan (New York: Macmillan, 1966), 179.

2 Harvey Cox, "Appendix: Beyond Bonhoeffer: The Future of Religionless Christianity," in ibid., 214.

2 Edmund Burke, *Reflections on the Revolution in France*, ed. L. G. Mitchell (Oxford: Oxford University Press, 1999), 77.

4 Rick Warren, *The Purpose Driven Life: What on Earth Am I Here For?* (Grand Rapids, MI: Zondervan Publishing Company, 2002).

4 Stephen McGinty, "Flock'n'Roll as Churches Turn to Bono," *Scotsman*, 3 April 2006.

4 Harvey Cox, *The Secular City: Secularization and Urbanization in Theological Perspective* (New York: Macmillan, 1965).

5 Alan Wolfe, *One Nation, After All: What Middle-Class Americans Really Think about God, Country, Family, Racism, Welfare, Immigration, Homosexuality, Work, the Right, the Left and Each Other* (New York: Viking, 1998).

5 Alan Wolfe, *Moral Freedom: The Search for Virtue in a World of Choice* (New York: Norton, 2001), 203.

5 Alan Wolfe, "The Final Freedom," *New York Times*, 18 March 2001.

5 David Brooks, *Bobos in Paradise: The New Upper Class and How They Got There* (New York: Touchstone, 2000), 224.

5 Robert Wuthnow, *American Mythos: Why Our Best Efforts to Be a Better Nation Fall Short* (Princeton: Princeton University Press, 2006), 146.

6 Robert Wuthnow, *After Heaven: Spirituality in America since the 1950s* (Berkeley: University of California Press, 1998), 3.

6 Ibid., 15.

7 Rick Warren, "Myths of the Modern Mega-Church," Pew Forum Faith Angle conference, Key West, FL, 23 May 2005.

8 Sam Harris, *The End of Faith: Religion, Terror, and the Future of Reason* (New York: Norton, 2005), 13; Christopher Hitchens, *god Is Not Great: How Religion Poisons Everything* (New York: Twelve, 2007); Richard Dawkins, *The God Delusion* (Boston: Houghton Mifflin, 2006).

8 Ronald Aronson, "The New Atheists," *Nation*, 25 June 2007.

8 Michael Novak, *Belief and Unbelief: A Philosophy of Self-Knowledge* (New York: Macmillan, 1965), 21.

9 Leon Wieseltier, "Under God and Over," *New Republic*, 12 April 2004.

9 David Hollenbach, "Afterword: A Community of Freedom," in *Catholicism and Liberalism: Contributions to American Public Philosophy*, ed. R. Bruce Douglass and David Hollenbach (Cambridge: Cambridge University Press, 1994), 334.

9 Ibid., 336–37.

9 David Hollenbach, *The Common Good and Christian Ethics* (Cambridge: Cambridge University Press, 2002), 113.

9 Wieseltier, "Under God and Over."

9 Harris, *End of Faith*, 14–15.

10 Michael Novak, "Lonely Atheists of the Global Village," *National Review*, 19 March 2007.

10 Dom Aelred Graham, *Zen Catholicism* (New York: Crossroad Publishing Co., 1994).

11 Dom Aelred Graham, *The End of Religion* (New York: Harcourt Brace Jovanovich, 1971).

11 Martin Luther King Jr., *Strength to Love* (Philadelphia: Fortress Press, 1981).

15 Jesusland refers to a cartoon map of North America that spread across the Internet after the 2004 presidential election. It depicts the continent as divided into "Jesusland" (consisting of the American Midwest, South, and Alaska) depicted in red, and the "United States of Canada" (consisting of Canada, Hawaii, the West Coast, and the North East) depicted in blue.

16 Hebrews 11:1, New English Bible.

16 Jaroslav Pelikan, *The Melody of Theology: A Philosophical Dictionary* (Cambridge: Harvard University Press, 1988), 86–89.

17 Jürgen Moltmann, *Theology of Hope: On the Ground and the Implications of a Christian Eschatology*, trans. James W. Leitch (Minneapolis: Fortress Press, 1993), 35.

17 Michael Walzer, *Exodus and Revolution* (New York: Basic Books, 1985).

18 Jacques Ellul, *What I Believe*, trans. Geoffrey W. Bromiley (Grand Rapids, MI: Eerdmans, 1989), 171.

18 Peter Berger, *A Far Glory: The Quest for Faith in an Age of Credulity* (New York: Free Press, 1992), 17. Subsequent quotes are from pp. 46 and 218.

18 H. Richard Niebuhr, *Radical Monotheism and Western Culture: With Supplementary Essays* (Louisville: Westminster/John Knox Press, 1993), 37.

19 George F. Will, Forward to *Conservatism in America* by Clinton Rossiter (Cambridge: Harvard University Press, 1982), v.

23 Reinhold Niebuhr quoted in Arthur Schlesinger Jr., "Forgetting Reinhold Niebuhr," *New York Times Book Review*, 18 September 2005.

23 C. S. Lewis, *Mere Christianity* (San Francisco: HarperSanFrancisco, 2001), 87.

24 Abraham Joshua Heschel, *Man Is Not Alone: A Philosophy of Religion* (New York: Farrar, Straus and Giroux, 1951), 11, 13–14.

1. Is Religion Conservative or Progressive?

25 Kaine television ad, quoted by Tyler Whitley in "Differing on Death Penalty; Both are Catholic, but Kaine opposes capital punishment while McDonnell supports it," *Richmond Times Dispatch*, 15 October 2005.

25 Jerry Falwell, *Strength for the Journey: An Autobiography* (New York: Simon & Schuster, 1987), 290.

25 King quoted in Taylor Branch, *Parting the Waters: America in the King Years, 1954–63* (New York: Simon & Schuster, 1988), 140–41.

26 *The Letters of William Lloyd Garrison.* Vol. 5: *Let the Oppressed Go Free, 1861–1867*, ed. Walter M. Merrill (Cambridge: Belknap Press of Harvard University Press, 1979).

26 John F. Kennedy, Inaugural Address, 20 January 1961.

26 Dr. Martin Luther King Jr., "I Have a Dream" speech, Washington, DC, 28 August 1963. An excellent collection of King's work is *A Testament of Hope: The Essential Writings and Speeches of Martin Luther King Jr.*, ed. James Melvin

Washington (San Francisco: HarperSanFrancisco, 1991). The "I Have a Dream" speech is on pp. 217–20.

26 Michael Kazin, "The Fate of the Christian Left," in *One Electorate under God?*, ed. E. J. Dionne Jr., Jean Bethke Elshtain, and Kayla M. Drogosz (Washington, DC: Brookings Institution Press, 2004), 133.

27 Tod Lindberg, *The Political Teachings of Jesus* (New York: HarperCollins, 2007).

27 Peter Steinfels, "The Failed Encounter: The Catholic Church and Liberalism in the Nineteenth Century," in *Catholicism and Liberalism*, ed. Douglass and Hollenbach.

27 Quoted in ibid., 39.

27 Quoted in ibid., 40, 41.

28 H. Richard Niebuhr, *The Kingdom of God in America* (Middletown, CT: Wesleyan University Press, 1988), 193.

28 Russell Kirk, *The Conservative Mind*, 2d rev. ed. (Chicago: Regnery, 1987), 8–9.

29 "Cultural Conservatism: Toward a New National Agenda" (Lanham, MD: Institute for Cultural Conservatism/Free Congress Research and Education Foundation, 1987).

29 Jaroslav Pelikan, *The Christian Tradition: A History of the Development of Doctrine* (Chicago: University of Chicago Press, 1971).

30 Michael Kazin, "The Fate of the Christian Left," 130.

30 Garry Wills, *Under God: Religion and American Politics* (New York: Touch-stone, 1990), 99.

30 Theodore Roosevelt's speech to the Progressive Party Convention, Chicago, IL, August 1912.

31 The Catholic Bishops' Program of Social Reconstruction can be found at http://www.osjspm.org.

31 Reinhold Niebuhr, *The Children of Light and the Children of Darkness* (New York: Charles Scribner's Sons, 1944), xi.

32 Abraham Joshua Heschel, *Moral Grandeur and Spiritual Audacity: Essays*, ed. Susannah Heschel (New York: Farrar, Straus and Giroux, 1996), 301.

32 Leo P. Ribuffo, *The Old Christian Right: The Protestant Far Right from the Great Depression to the Cold War* (Philadelphia: Temple University Press, 1983).

32 Reinhold Niebuhr, letter to the editor, *New Republic*, 31 October 1960.

33 Peter Steinfels, "Reinventing Liberal Catholicism: Between Powerful Enemies and Dubious Allies," *Commonweal*, 19 November 1999.

33 Elisabeth Sifton, *The Serenity Prayer: Faith and Politics in Times of Peace and War* (New York: Norton, 2003).

36 Stephen L. Carter, *The Culture of Disbelief* (New York: Anchor Books, 1994).

36 Terry Eastland, "In Defense of Religious America," *Commentary* 71, 6 (June 1981): 42.

37 Richard John Neuhaus, *The Naked Public Square: Religion and Democracy in America* (Grand Rapids, MI: Eerdmans, 1984), 9.

37 Nathan Glazer, *We Are All Multiculturalists Now* (Cambridge: Harvard University Press, 1997).

37 Ralph Reed, *Active Faith: How Christians Are Changing the Soul of American Politics* (New York: Free Press, 1966).

38 Senator Joseph Lieberman's address at the launch of the Pew Forum on Religion and Public Life, National Press Club, Washington, DC, 1 March 2001. Available at http://pewforum.org/events/?EventID=5.

39 John McGreevy, *Catholicism and American Freedom: A History* (New York: Norton, 2003).

39 Bill Clinton quoted in John F. Harris, "Clinton Says Schools Can't Bar Religion; Statement Ordered Sent to All Districts," *Washington Post*, 13 July 1995.

40 Hamid Reza Asefi quoted in Agence France Presse, "Tehran Criticizes France's 'Extremist' Decision to Ban Headscarves," 21 December 2003.

40 Elaine Ganley, "Private Catholic Schools Could Be Next Step for Muslim Girls Who Refuse to Remove Head Scarves," Associated Press, 18 December 2003.

40 Christopher Marquis, "U.S. Chides France on Effort to Bar Religious Garb in Schools," *New York Times*, 19 December 2003.

40 Ibid.

40 Chirac quoted in Keith B. Richburg, "French President Urges Ban on Head Scarves in Schools; Chirac confronts spread of Islam," *Washington Post*, 18 December 2003.

41 Ian Buruma, *Murder in Amsterdam: The Death of Theo van Gogh and the Limits of Tolerance* (New York: Penguin Press, 2006).

41 Wilfred M. McClay, "Two Concepts of Secularism," in *Religion Returns to the Public Square: Faith and Policy in America*, ed. Hugh Heclo and Wilfred M. McClay (Washington, DC: Woodrow Wilson Center Press, 2003), 46, 33, 52.

42 Editorial, "We're Prime Time, Baby!" *Christianity Today*, June 2005, 23.

42 Michael J. Sandel, *Public Philosophy: Essays on Morality in Politics* (Cambridge: Harvard University Press, 2005), 246.

43 Richard Wightman Fox, "The Niebuhr Brothers and the Liberal Protestant Heritage," in *Religion and Twentieth-Century American Intellectual Life*, ed. Michael J. Lacey (New York: Cambridge University Press, 1989), 115.

43 Berger, *A Far Glory,* 77.

43 John F. Kennedy, Inaugural Address, 20 January 1961.

44 Pope Benedict XVI, address at the University of Regensburg, Germany, 2006.

44 David Hollenbach, "The Life of the Human Community," *America* 187, 14 (4 November 2002).

2. Why the Culture War Is the Wrong War

45 William Jennings Bryan, Cross of Gold speech at the National Democratic Convention, Chicago, IL, 9 July 1896.

46 Jack Kerouac, *On the Road* (New York: Viking Press, 1957).

46 Norman Podhoretz, "The Know-nothing Bohemians," *Partisan Review* (Spring 1958): 25.

47 2004 National Election Pool exit poll. Unless otherwise noted, all subsequent exit poll references are to this survey.

48 Morris P. Fiorina, *Culture War? The Myth of a Polarized America* (New York: Pearson Longman, 2006), 8.

49 William Galston and Elaine Kamarck, "The Politics of Polarization" (Washington, DC: Third Way, 2005).

49 Michael Barone, "American Politics in the Networking Era," *National Journal,* 26 February 2005.

49 James Davison Hunter, *Culture Wars: The Struggle to Define America* (New York: Basic Books, 1991), 44.

53 Andrew Greeley and Michael Hout, *The Truth about Conservative Christians: What They Think and What They Believe* (Chicago: University of Chicago Press, 2006), 180. The subsequent quote is from p. 102.

53 William C. Velasquez Institute, "2004 WCVI National Exit Poll of Latino Voters" (8 March 2005).

53 Annenberg Public Policy Center, "Bush 2004 Gains among Hispanics Strongest with Men, and in South and Northeast, Annenberg Data Show," 21 December 2004.

54 Survey conducted by the Pew Research Center for the People and the Press, and the Pew Forum on Religion and Public Life, July 2006. Full questionnaire and dataset available at http://people-press.org/dataarchive/.

55 Albert J. Menendez, *Religion at the Polls* (Philadelphia: Westminister Press, 1977), 188–98.

55 Thomas Frank, *What's the Matter with Kansas? How Conservatives Won the Heart of America* (New York: Metropolitan Books, 2004).

55 Thomas Byrne Edsall and Mary D. Edsall, *Chain Reaction: The Impact of Race, Rights, and Taxes on American Politics* (New York: Norton, 1991).

55 Jonathan Rieder, *Canarsie: The Jews and Italians of Brooklyn against Liberalism* (Cambridge: Harvard University Press, 1985).

55 For an excellent history of the McGovern campaign, see Bruce Miroff, *The Liberals' Moment: The McGovern Insurgency and the Identity Crisis of the Democratic Party* (Lawrence: University Press of Kansas, 2007), esp. pp. 137–39. Miroff rightly notes that the "acid, amnesty and abortion" charge was unfair to McGovern but effective.

55 Kevin P. Phillips, *The Emerging Republican Majority* (New Rochelle, NY: Arlington House, 1969).

56 Quoted in John B. Judis, *William F. Buckley, Jr.: Patron Saint of the Conservatives* (New York: Simon & Schuster, 1988), 378.

56 Chilton Williamson Jr., "Country and Western Marxism: To the Nashville Station," *National Review* 30, 23 (9 June 1978): 711–17.

56 Everett C. Ladd Jr. and Charles D. Hadley, *Transformations of the American Party System: Political Coalitions from the New Deal to the 1970s* (New York: Norton, 1975).

56 Nathan Glazer, "Fundamentalism: A Defensive Offensive," in *Piety and Politics: Evangelicals and Fundamentalists Confront the World*, ed. Richard John Neuhaus and Michael Cromartie (Washington, DC: Ethics and Public Policy Center, 1987), 245–58.

57 Larry M. Bartels, "What's the Matter with *What's the Matter with Kansas?*" *Quarterly Journal of Political Science*, 1 (2006): 201–26.

59 Pew Research Center, "Changing Faiths: Latinos and the Transformation of American Religion," 25 April 2007.

61 Thomas Fitzgerald, "The 'God Gap' Lessened in Last Election," *Philadelphia Inquirer*, 26 November 2006, A01.

61 Scott Keeter, "Election '06: Big Changes in Some Key Groups," Pew Research Center, 16 November 2006.

64 John C. Green, *The Faith Factor: How Religion Influences American Elections* (Westport, CT: Praeger Publishers, 2007), 45.

65 2006 Ohio exit polls.

65 2006 Pennsylvania exit polls.

66   Andrew M. Greeley, *Why Can't They Be Like Us? America's White Ethnic Groups* (New York: E. P. Dutton, 1971).

67   Wolfe, *One Nation, After All.*

68   Allan David Bloom, *The Closing of the American Mind: How Higher Education Has Failed Democracy and Impoverished the Souls of Today's Students* (New York: Simon & Schuster, 1987); Robert H. Bork, *Slouching Towards Gomorrah: Modern Liberalism and American Decline* (New York: ReganBooks, 2003); Robert D. Putnam, *Bowling Alone: The Collapse and Revival of American Community* (New York: Simon & Schuster, 2000); John Miller, *Egotopia: Narcissism and the New American Landscape* (Tuscaloosa: University of Alabama Press, 1997).

68   Francis Fukuyama, *The Great Disruption: Human Nature and the Reconstitution of Social Order* (New York: Free Press, 1999).

68   Richard Sennett, *The Corrosion of Character: The Personal Consequences of Work in the New Capitalism* (New York: Norton, 1998), 10.

68   William Bennett, *The Death of Outrage: Bill Clinton and the Assault on American Ideals* (New York: Free Press, 1998).

68   Gertrude Himmelfarb, *The De-Moralization of Society: From Victorian Virtues to Modern Values* (New York: Knopf, 1995).

69   Robert N. Bellah, Richard Madsen, William M. Sullivan, Ann Swidler, and Steven M. Tipton, *Habits of the Heart: Individualism and Commitment in American Life* (Berkeley: University of California Press, 1996).

69   Benjamin R. Barber, *Consumed: How Markets Corrupt Children, Infantilize Adults, and Swallow Citizens Whole* (New York: Norton, 2007).

3. What Are the "Values" Issues?

71   Alan Wolfe, "Myths and Realities of Religion and Politics," in *Red and Blue Nation?* ed. Pietro S. Nivola and David W. Brady (Washington, DC: Brookings Institution Press, 2006), 210.

72   Jim Wallis, *God's Politics: Why the Right Gets It Wrong and the Left Doesn't Get It* (San Francisco: HarperSanFrancisco, 2005), 4.

73   George W. Bush, First Inaugural Address, 20 January 2001.

74   Hillary Rodham Clinton, *It Takes a Village: And Other Lessons Children Teach Us* (New York: Simon & Schuster, 1996).

74   Michael Kelly, "Saint Hillary," *New York Times Magazine,* 23 May 1993.

75   Peter Berger and Richard John Neuhaus, *To Empower People: The Role of*

Mediating Structures in Public Policy (Washington, DC: American Enterprise Institute for Public Policy Research, 1977).

75   Hillary Clinton quotations, and Steinfels comments, are from Peter Steinfels, "Beliefs," *New York Times*, 29 May 1993.

75   Robert Moses, *Radical Equations: Math Literacy and Civil Rights* (Boston: Beacon Press, 2001), 125.

76   Bane and Mead quotations from Mary Jo Bane and Lawrence M. Mead, in *Lifting Up the Poor: A Dialogue on Religion, Poverty & Welfare Reform*, ed. E. J. Dionne Jr., Jean Bethke Elshtain, and Kayla Drogosz (Washington, DC: Brookings Institution Press, 2003). Bane's comments are drawn from pp. 14 and 114; Mead's appear on pp. 71 and 67.

78   Barack Obama, Call to Renewal Conference Keynote Address, 28 June 2006. The address is available at http://obama.senate.gov/podcast/060628-call _to_renewal_1/.

78   David Espo, "Obama: Democrats Must Court Evangelicals," Associated Press, 28 June 2006.

78   Stephen Holmes, *Passions and Constraint: On the Theory of Liberal Democracy* (Chicago: University of Chicago Press, 1995), 23.

79   William Bennett and John DiIulio, "What Good Is Government" *Commentary* 4, 5 (November 1997): 25.

79   Michael Walzer, *Spheres of Justice: A Defense of Pluralism and Equality* (New York: Basic Books, 1983), 4.

80   Holmes, *Passions and Constraint*, 12.

80   Father Philip Murnion shared this with me in a conversation, and I later heard it in a number of his public speeches and sermons.

81   Pope John Paul, Encyclical *Centesimus annus*, 1991.

82   Richard Neuhaus, "The Pope Affirms the 'New Capitalism'," *Wall Street Journal*, 2 May 1991, A16.

82   National Conference of Catholic Bishops, "Economic Justice for All: Pastoral Letter on Catholic Social Teaching and the U.S. Economy," U.S. Catholic Conference, 1986.

82   Richard Neuhaus, *Doing Well and Doing Good: The Challenge to the Christian Capitalist* (New York: Doubleday, 1992).

84   William Simon and Michael Novak, *Toward the Future: Catholic Social Thought and the U.S. Economy: A Lay Letter* (New York: Lay Commission on Catholic Social Teaching and the U.S. Economy, 1984). This fascinating document was distributed through the American Enterprise Institute in Washington.

84   Michael Novak, *The Catholic Ethic and the Spirit of Capitalism* (New York: Free Press, 1993), 138. Subsequent quotations are from pp. 216, 135, 147, 190–91, and 137.

86   J. Bryan Hehir, "Reordering the World; John Paul II's 'Centesimus annus,'" *Commonweal* 118, 12 (14 June 1991): 393.

86   Shirley Robin Letwin, "An Encyclical in Conflict with Itself," in *A New Worldly Order: John Paul II and Human Freedom*, ed. George Weigel (Washington, DC: Ethics and Public Policy Center, 1992), 109.

86   Milton Friedman, "Goods in Conflict?" in ibid., 76.

86   Novak, *The Catholic Ethic and the Spirit of Capitalism*, 67.

87   Michael Novak, *The Spirit of Democratic Capitalism* (Lanham, MD: Madison Books, 2000), 166.

90   Rebecca M. Blank and William McGurn, *Is the Market Moral? A Dialogue on Religion, Economics, and Justice*, ed. E. J. Dionne Jr., Jean Bethke Elshtain, and Kayla Drogosz (Washington, DC: Brookings Institution Press, 2004), 23.

90   Calvin Skaggs and David Van Taylor, *With God on Our Side: George W. Bush and the Rise of the Religious Right* (Lumiere Productions, 2004).

90   David von Drehle and Thomas B. Edsall, "Life of the Grand Old Party; Energized coalition enters another political phase," *Washington Post*, 14 August 1994.

90   Jeffrey Bell, "What Falwell Wrought: Just the biggest voter realignment in modern history," *Weekly Standard* 12, 35 (28 May 2007).

4. Selling Religion Short

92   Remarks by Bill Clinton at the Metropolitan Baptist Church, Washington, DC, 7 December 1997.

93   George W. Bush, State of the Union Address, 28 January 2003.

93   John F. Kennedy, Inaugural Address, 20 January 1961.

93   Diane Francis, "Mighty U.S. Takes Care of No. 1 First: Address will backfire in its bid to seize moral high ground," *National Post* (Canada), 30 January 2003.

94   See Morton M. Kondracke, "Religion, Politics Do Mix—But They Deserve Explanation," *Roll Call*, 20 December 1999.

95   See Nicholas Riccardi, "Christian Coalition Chief Out," *Los Angeles Times*, 29 November 2006. I also interviewed Hunter on 8 October 2007.

95 Joel Hunter, *Right Wing, Wrong Bird: Why the Tactics of the Religious Right Won't Fly with Most Conservative Christians* (Longwood, FL: Distributed Church Press, 2006).

95 Joel C. Hunter quoted in Mark I. Pinsky, "Who Speaks for America's Evangelicals?" *USA Today,* 6 August 2007. See also Mark I. Pinsky, "The New Breed on the Right," *Orlando Sentinel,* 2 July 2007.

95 Rick Warren's comments during an interview on Fox News Network's *Hannity & Colmes,* 1 December 2006.

96 George W. Bush: This quote and those following are from an interview with the author in September 1999. The interview was conducted for a long profile I wrote for the *Washington Post Magazine,* "In Search of George W," 19 September 1999.

98 Laura Stuart, "New Deal Has Old Roots: Sociologist Omar McRoberts Traces Presidential Overtures toward Black Churches," *University of Chicago Magazine* 98, 6 (August 2006).

98 See Scott Shepard, "Gore Takes Broad Leap for Faith," *Atlanta Journal-Constitution,* 25 May 1999, 1A.

99 Joe Lieberman on ABC's *Nightline,* 14 February 2000.

100 Rev. Jim Wallis et al., Open Letter from Call to Renewal, 9 June 2003.

100 David Kuo, "Poverty 101: What Liberals and Conservatives Can Learn from Each Other," in *Community Works: The Revival of Civil Society in America,* ed. E. J. Dionne Jr. (Washington, DC: Brookings Institution Press, 1998).

100 David Kuo, "Please, Keep Faith," Beliefnet, 14 February 2005.

100 David Kuo, *Tempting Faith: An Inside Story of Political Seduction* (New York: Free Press, 2006).

101 David Kuo on CBS News's *60 Minutes,* 15 October 2006.

102 Jeffrey Rosen, "The Day after Roe," *Atlantic Monthly,* June 2006.

103 Mitt Romney quoted in Marc Ambinder, "Journey to the Right," *National Journal,* 10 February 2007.

103 Rudy Giuliani, Republican Primary Debate at the Ronald Reagan Library, Simi Valley, CA, 3 May 2007.

105 Judie Brown, "Why Did Pro-Lifers Lose in Mo. and S.D.?" *Human Events,* 13 November 2006.

105 "West River Conservatives Show Libertarian Side," Associated Press, 12 November 2006.

105 Combined/consolidated cases: *Gonzales v. Carhart et al.* and *Gonzales v. Planned Parenthood Federation of America.* See Robert Barnes, "High Court

Upholds Curb on Abortion: 5–4 vote affirms ban on 'partial-birth' procedure," *Washington Post*, 19 April 2007.

106 Judy Peres, "Abortion Battle Far from Over; Ban supporters, opponents vow to not give up," *Aberdeen American News* (South Dakota), 9 November 2006, A1.

107 Thomas R. Suozzi, speech at Adelphi University, 11 May 2005.

107 William Murphy quoted in Bruce Lambert, "Suozzi Calls for 'Common Ground' on Reducing Abortions," *New York Times*, 11 May 2005.

108 Christopher Trenholm et al., *Impacts of Four Title V, Section 510 Abstinence Education Programs* (Princeton: Mathematica Policy Research, 2007).

109 "Teen Birth Rates in the United States, 1940–2005," National Campaign to Prevent Teen and Unplanned Pregnancy, 21 November 2006.

109 "U.S. Teenage Pregnancy Statistics: National and State Trends and Trends by Race and Ethnicity," Guttmacher Institute, September 2006.

109 "Facts on Induced Abortion in the United States," Guttmacher Institute, May 2006.

110 Rachel Laser, "Winning the Abortion Grays: A strategy to win the battle of reasonableness and appeal to moderates," Third Way message memo, January 2006.

111 Sridhar Pappu, "Music to His Ears; Mike Huckabee hit a chord in Iowa and is off and running," *Washington Post*, 31 August 2007.

111 Rudy Giuliani's remarks during the Republican Presidential Primary Debate sponsored by the South Carolina Republican Party and Fox News Channel, University of South Carolina, 15 May 2007.

111 Andrew Sullivan, *Virtually Normal: An Argument about Homosexuality* (New York: Knopf, 1995). Quotations are from pp. 160, 95, and 179.

113 See E. J. Dionne Jr., "A Matter of Respect," *Washington Post*, 29 August 1995.

113 David Brooks, "The Power of Marriage," *New York Times*, 22 November 2003.

114 Jonathan Rauch, "Power of Two," *New York Times*, 7 March 2004.

115 Scott Helman, "Romney Places Focus on Family: Candidate showcases wife, children in race," *Boston Globe*, 11 March 2007.

115 David Boaz, "Don't Forget the Kids," *New York Times*, 10 September 1994.

116 See John Leo, "Tolerant on Gay Issue, GOP Analyzes Divorce," *South Bend Tribune*, 27 September 1994.

116 William G. Mayer, *The Changing American Mind: How and Why American Public Opinion Changed between 1960 and 1988* (Ann Arbor: University of Michigan Press, 1992). Also, conversations with author.

118 George W. Bush quoted in Charles Babington and Mike Allen, "Congress Passes Schiavo Measure; Bush signs bill giving U.S. courts jurisdiction in case of Fla. woman," *Washington Post*, 21 March 2005.

118 Barney Frank quoted in ibid.

119 Charles Babington and Michael A. Fletcher, "Analysts: GOP May Be Out of Step with Public," *Washington Post*, 22 March 2005.

119 George W. Bush quoted in Abby Goodnough and Adam Liptak, "Court Blocks Bid: New Schiavo tack by Governor Bush," *New York Times*, 24 March 2005, A1.

120 Dan Allen quoted in Jonathan Weisman and Ceci Connolly, "Schiavo Case Puts Face on Rising Medical Costs; GOP leaders try to cut spending as they fight to save one of program's patients," *Washington Post*, 23 March 2005, A13.

121 David Brown and Shailagh Murray, "Schiavo Autopsy Released; Brain damage 'was irreversible,'" *Washington Post*, 16 June 2005, A1.

121 Senator Bill Frist, Terri Schiavo, 109th Congress, Senate, 17 March 2005. *Congressional Record*.

121 Senator Bill Frist on ABC News's *Good Morning America*, 16 June 2005.

122 Tom DeLay, statement issued 20 March 2005.

122 Douglas W. Kmiec quoted in Adam Liptak, "Small Law, Big Implications," *New York Times*, 22 March 2005.

124 See Jim Wallis, "A Conversation on Moral Issues," *Sojourners* 36, 5 (1 May 2007).

124 The letter to the chairman of the National Evangelical Association board is available in Jim Wallis, "Dobson Gets Personal on Global Warming" on the Huffington Post website at http://www.huffingtonpost.com/jim-wallis/dobson-gets-personal-on-g_b_42656.html, posted 5 March 2007.

5. John Paul, Benedict, and the Catholic Future

126 This chapter is based in large part on my own reporting at the Vatican, in the United States, and also during John Paul II's journeys to India and Canada, and to various nations in Africa, South America, and Europe. I draw on work done when I was fortunate to be assigned to Rome by the *New York Times*, from 1984 to 1986, and later when I wrote for the *New Republic* on the death of John Paul and the election of Benedict. Material for which I have not provided notes comes from interviews and conversations with the

author; or, in the case of short quotations from Benedict or John Paul, from coverage of events that I attended myself.

For more extended versions of my take on John Paul and Benedict back in the 1980s—I draw upon these pieces in this chapter—see E. J. Dionne Jr., "Determined to Lead," *New York Times Magazine*, 12 May 1985; E. J. Dionne Jr., "The Pope's Guardian of Orthodoxy," *New York Times Magazine*, 24 November 1985; and a three-part series on the future of the Catholic Church published in the *New York Times* on 23, 24, and 25 December 1986. My articles in the *New Republic* were E. J. Dionne Jr., "Papal Paradox," *New Republic*, 18 April 2005; and E. J. Dionne Jr., "Benedictus," *New Republic*, 2–9 May 2005.

I refer to a number of papal encyclicals and other papal statements in this chapter. Again, to make it easier for the reader and not to clutter these notes, I offer web addresses for the relevant documents:

Centesimus annus,
http://www.vatican.va/holy_father/john_paul_ii/encyclicals/documents/hf_jp-ii_enc_01051991_centesimus-annus_en.html.

Laborem exercens,
http://www.vatican.va/holy_father/john_paul_ii/encyclicals/documents/hf_jp-ii_enc_14091981_laborem-exercens_en.html

Pacem in terris,
http://www.vatican.va/holy_father/john_xxiii/encyclicals/documents/hf_j-xxiii_enc_11041963_pacem_en.html

Mater et magistra,
http://www.vatican.va/holy_father/john_xxiii/encyclicals/documents/hf_j-xxiii_enc_15051961_mater_en.html

126 My story on the pope and angels ran in the *New York Times* on 18 July 1986.

130 Pope John Paul II, *Sign of Contradiction* (New York: Seabury Press, 1979).

131 See Steinfels, "The Failed Encounter," 19–44.

131 Quoted in Joseph A. Komonchak, "Remembering Good Pope John," *Commonweal*, 11 August 2000. Komonchak's observation is from the same article.

131 Speech of Pope John Paul II during a visit to the Yad Vashem Museum in Jerusalem, 23 March 2000. Available at http://www.vatican.va/holy_father/john_paul_ii/travels/documents/hf_jp-ii_spe_20000323_yad-vashem-mausoleum_en.html.

132 Address by Pope John Paul II on the Occasion of the Meeting with the Exponents of Non-Christian Religions in Madras, 5 February 1986. Available at http://www.vatican.va/holy_father/john_paul_ii/speeches/1986/february/documents/hf_jp-ii_spe_19860205_religioni-non-cristiane_en.html.

132 On Rev. Charles E. Curran's critique of the Church, see Charles E. Curran, *Loyal Dissent: Memoir of a Catholic Theologian* (Washington, DC: Georgetown University Press, 2006).

133 David E. Anderson, "Priest Chastized by Church Wins Support from Bishop," United Press International, 13 March 1986.

133 T. M. Pasca, "The Bishops' Synod; the three churches of Catholicism," *Nation*, 1 February 1986.

133 "Mater Si, Magistra, No," *National Review*, 21 August 1961.

133 Metz wrote many volumes. See, for example, Johannes B. Metz, *Theology of the World*, trans. William Glen-Doepel (New York: Herder and Herder, 1978), 107.

133 Medellín Conference, 1968, available at http://www.providence.edu/las/documents.htm#Medellin%20Conference.

134 Gustavo Gutiérrez, *A Theology of Liberation: History, Politics, and Salvation*, trans. and ed. Sister Caridad Inda and John Eagleson (Maryknoll, NY: Orbis Books, 1973).

135 Pope John Paul II, opening address at Puebla Conference in Seminario Palafoxiano, Puebla de los Angeles, Mexico, 28 January 1979. Available at http://www.ewtn.com/library/PAPALDOC/JP791228.htm.

135 The classic Ratzinger documents from the Congregation for the Doctrine of the Faith can be found at http://www.vatican.va/roman_curia/congregations/cfaith/documents/rc_con_cfaith_doc_19860322_freedom-liberation_en.html.

135 The Congregations Notification to Boff can be found at http://www.ewtn.com/library/CURIA/CDFBOFF.htm. A sympathetic view of Boff is offered in Harvey Cox, *The Silencing of Leonardo Boff: The Vatican and the Future of World Christianity* (Oak Park, IL: Meyer-Stone Books, 1988).

136 Pope John Paul II, opening address at Puebla Conference, 28 January 1979.

138 Pope John Paul II's Apostolic Pilgrimage to India, Mass at Indira Gandhi Stadium of Delhi. Homily of His Holiness John Paul II, 1 February 1986. Available at http://www.vatican.va/holy_father/john_paul_ii/homilies/1986/documents/hf_jp-ii_hom_19860201_stadio-delhi_en.html.

140 The text refers to two interviews with Cardinal Ratzinger. One was conducted by the journalist Vittorio Messori and published as *The Ratzinger*

Report, trans. Salvator Attanasio and Graham Harrison (San Francisco: Igna-tius Press, 1985). The quotations are from pp. 29, 105, 166, 61, and 34. The other was my own written interview with Ratzinger for the *New York Times Magazine* article cited at the beginning of the notes for this chapter.

144 Richard A. McCormick, S.J., *Corrective Vision: Explorations in Moral Theo-logy* (Kansas City, MO: Sheed and Ward, 1994), 74–76.

144 Nicholas Lash, "II: Catholic Theology and the Crisis of Classicism," *New Blackfriars* 66, 780 (1985): 279–87.

144 Mary Gordon, "Coming to Terms with Mary: Meditations on Innocence, Grief, and Glory," *Commonweal*, 15 January 1982.

145 Eamon Duffy, "I: Urbi, but not Orbi . . . the Cardinal, the Church, and the World," *New Blackfriars* 66, 780 (1985): 272–78.

147 Ratzinger's address to the conclave that included his criticism of the "dicta-torship of relativism" is available at http://www.oecumene.radiovaticana.org/en1/Articolo.asp?id=33987.

6. What Happened to the Seamless Garment?

151 Al Smith quoted in Reinhold Niebuhr, "Catholics and the State," *New Republic*, 17 October 1960.

152 Rev. Andrew Greeley quoted in Garry Wills, *Bare Ruined Choirs: Doubt, Prophecy, and Radical Religion* (New York: Doubleday, 1972), 79.

152 Ibid., 82.

152 William V. D'Antonio, James D. Davidson, Dean R. Hoge, and Mary L. Gautier, *American Catholics Today: New Realities of Their Faith and Their Church* (Lanham, MD: Rowman & Littlefield, 2007), 142, 144.

153 Encyclical of Pope Leo XIII, *Testem benevolentiae nostrae*, "Concerning New Opinions, Virtue, Nature and Grace, with Regard to Americanism," 22 Janu-ary 1899. Available at http://www.papalencyclicals.net/Leo13/l13teste.htm.

155 Pope Paul VI, "Declaration on Religious Freedom (Dignitatis Humanae): On the Right of the Person and the Communities to Social and Civil Freedom in Matters Religious," 7 December 1965. Available at http://www.vatican.va/archive/hist_councils/ii_vatican_council/documents/vat-ii_decl_19651207_dignitatis-humanae_en.html.

156 Father Greeley reflects on his earlier studies of Catholic attitudes and his more recent conclusions in Andrew Greeley, *The Catholic Revolution: New*

Wine, Old Wineskins, and the Second Vatican Council (Berkeley: University of California Press, 2004). On birth control, see especially pp. 34–40.

156 Associated Press, "Excerpts from Speech by Archbishop," *New York Times*, 30 September 1980.

156 Encyclical of Pope Leo XIII, *Rerum novarum*, "On Capital and Labor," St. Peter's, Rome, 15 May 1891.

157 John A. Ryan, *A Living Wage* (New York: Macmillan, 1906).

157 Lew Daly, "In Search of the Common Good: The Catholic Roots of American Liberalism," *Boston Review*, May/June 2007.

157 The Catholic Bishops' Program of Social Reconstruction is cited in Daly, "In Search of the Common Good."

159 See the Catholic Worker Movement's website: http://www.catholicworker .org.

160 David Leege, paper presented at "The Patterns of Catholic Civic Engagement: Change and Continuity," organized by American Catholics in the Public Square Project, Annapolis, MD, 2–4 June 2004.

161 Schoen and Gwirtzman wrote, respectively, an undergraduate paper and an undergraduate thesis on this subject. I draw here from their extensive conversations with me about their work.

162 Gerald H. Gamm, *Urban Exodus: Why the Jews Left Boston and the Catholics Stayed* (Cambridge: Harvard University Press, 1999).

163 Steve Wagner, "The Mind of the Catholic Voter," *Crisis Magazine*, November 1998.

163 David Leege, paper presented at "The Patterns of Catholic Civic Engagement."

163 "Faith-Based Funding Backed, but Church-State Doubts Abound," Pew Forum on Religion and Public Life, and Pew Research Center for the People and the Press, 10 April 2001.

164 William J. Bennett, *The Book of Virtues: A Treasury of Great Moral Stories* (New York: Simon & Schuster, 1993).

164 William Bennett quoted in Paul Starobin, "Rethinking Capitalism," *National Journal*, 18 January 1997.

165 Peter L. Berger and Richard John Neuhaus, *To Empower People: From State to Civil Society*, ed. Michael Novak (Washington, DC: American Enterprise Institute for Public Policy Research, 1977). Originally published in 1977, reissued in 1996.

167 Pope John Paul II, *Centesimus annus*, 1 May 1991.

167 Steven Wagner, paper presented at "The Patterns of Catholic Civic Engagement: Change and Continuity," organized by American Catholics in the Public Square Project, Annapolis, MD, 2–4 June 2004; and conversations with author.

168 See Frances Grandy Taylor, "Voter's Guide Sparks Controversy; Information distributed at some Catholic churches cites 5 'non-negotiable' issues," *Hartford Courant*, 30 October 2004.

168 David D. Kirkpatrick and Laurie Goodstein, "Group of Bishops Using Influence to Oppose Kerry, *New York Times*, 12 October 2004, A1.

169 Raymond Burke quoted in the Associated Press, "Bishop Would Deny Communion to Giuliani," 4 October 2007. For the entire transcript, see "All the News that's Fit to Print . . . Sort of" on the Archdiocese of Denver's website at http://www.archden.org.

169 Rev. Bernard W. Schmitt quoted by Vicki Smith, "Bishop's Abortion, Voting Message Sparks Some Backlash," Associated Press State & Local Wire, 25 October 2004.

169 Rev. John J. Myers, "Houses of Worship: A Voter's Guide," *Wall Street Journal*, 17 September 2004.

169 Julia Duin, "More Bishops Inject Faith into Catholic Political Life; Say follow tenets or forgo Communion," *Washington Times*, 15 May 2004.

169 Senator John F. Kennedy, address to the Greater Houston Ministerial Association, 12 September 1960, Houston, TX. Available at http://www.jfklibrary .org/Historical+Resources/Archives/Reference+Desk/Speeches/JFK/JFK+Pre -Pres / Address + of+Senator+John+F.+Kennedy+to+the+Greater+Houston+ Ministerial+Association.htm.

170 See Katharine Q. Seelye, "Kerry Dismisses Critics of Time That He Took Off Campaigning," *New York Times*, 6 April 2004.

171 George Weigel, "Cardinal Ratzinger and the Conscience of Catholic Voters," 29 September 2004. The Ethics and Public Policy Center runs Weigel's column, The Catholic Difference, on its website at http://www.eppc.org/ publications/pubID.2177/pub_detail.asp.

171 George Weigel, "Moral Clarity in a Time of War," *First Things*, January 2003.

172 Peter Steinfels, "Catholics Are Finding That Relating Religion and Politics Can Be a Complex Business," *New York Times*, 1 May 2004.

173 David R. Obey, "My Conscience, My Vote," *America*, 16 August 2004.

174 Fifty-Five Catholic Democrats in the U.S. House of Representatives released a "Statement of Principles" on 28 February 2006.

176 Pope John Paul II, Address to the Diplomatic Corps Accredited to the Holy See for the Traditional Exchange of New Year Greetings, 10 January 2005. Available at http://www.vatican.va/holy_father/john_paul_ii/speeches / 2005 / january / documents / hf_jp-ii_spe_20050110_diplomatic-corps_en .html.

177 Peter Berger, *The Heretical Imperative: Contemporary Possibilities of Religious Affirmation* (New York: Doubleday, 1980).

177 William Bole, "Communitarian Lite: American Catholics & their politics," *Commonweal,* 13 September 2002.

178 Pax Christi USA, "Life Does Not End at Birth: Catholics Called to Vote for the Common Good." Available at http://www.paxchristiusa.org/news_ events_more.asp?id=424.

180 Pope Benedict XVI, *Deus caritas est,* 25 December 2005. Available at http:// www.vatican.va/holy_father/benedict_xvi/encyclicals/documents/hf_ben-xvi _enc_20051225_deus-caritas-est_en.html.

180 Michael Lacey and William Shea, "Catholics and the Liberal Tradition," *Commonweal,* 11 October 2002.

7. Solidarity, Liberty, and Religion's True Calling

184 Jeffrey Stout, "The Spirit of Democracy in Dispiriting Times," lecture presented at Central Michigan University, 28 February 2006.

185 William Galston, "When in Doubt," *Democracy,* no. 5 (Summer 2007): 34.

185 Reinhold Niebuhr, *The Irony of American History* (New York: Charles Scribner's Sons, 1952), 63.

185 Reinhold Niebuhr, *The Children of Light and the Children of Darkness* (New York: Charles Scribner's Sons, 1944), 151.

186 Niebuhr, *The Irony of American History,* 143.

186 Galston, "When in Doubt," 37.

186 Jean Bethke Elshtain, *Augustine and the Limits of Politics* (Notre Dame: University of Notre Dame Press, 1995), 91.

186 Abraham Lincoln, Second Inaugural Address, 4 March 1865.

186 Niebuhr quoted in Price, "Faith in Public Office," in *One Electorate Under God?,* ed. Dionne, Elshtain, and Drogosz, 170.

187 Paul Starr, *Freedom's Power: The True Force of Liberalism* (New York: Basic Books, 2007), 65.

188 H. Richard Niebuhr, *Theology, History, and Culture*, ed. William Stacy Johnson (New Haven: Yale University Press, 1996), 144. Subsequent quotations are from pp. 149 and 151.

190 Fouad Ajami, "The Impossible Life of Muslim Liberalism," *New Republic*, 2 June 1986.

190 Mark Lilla, "The Politics of God," *New York Times*, 19 August 2007.

191 Will Herberg, *Protestant, Catholic, Jew: An Essay in American Religious Sociology* (Chicago: University of Chicago Press, 1955).

192 Abraham Joshua Heschel, *Moral Grandeur and Spiritual Audacity*, ed. Susannah Heschel (New York: Farrar, Strauss and Giroux, 1996), 270.

192 Hitchens, *god is Not Great*, 204.

193 Jonathan Sacks, *To Heal a Fractured World: The Ethics of Responsibility* (New York: Schocken Books, 2005), 9.

194 Karl Barth, *God Here and Now* (New York: Routledge Classics, 2003), 111, 113.

195 *CNN's Special Edition*: Sojourners Presidential Forum, 4 June 2007. Available at http://transcripts.cnn.com/TRANSCRIPTS/0706/04/sitroom.03.html.

196 Nancy Gibbs and Michael Duffy, "Leveling the Praying Field," *Time*, 23 July 2007.

196 Jose Casanova, "What Is Public Religion," in *Religion Returns to the Public Square: Faith and Policy in America*, ed. Hugh Heclo and Wilfred M. McClay (Washington, DC: Woodrow Wilson Center Press, 2003).

198 Michael J. Sandel makes the case in *The Case Against Perfection: Ethics in the Age of Genetic Engineering* (Cambridge: Belknap Press of Harvard University Press, 2007). The quotations in the text are from Sandel's address at the Pew Forum on Religion and Public Life's "The Pursuit of Perfection: A Conversation on the Ethics of Genetic Engineering," Washington, DC, 31 March 2004. The transcript is available at http://pewforum.org/events/?EventID=54.

199 Robert P. Jones and Rachel Laser, "Come Let Us Reason Together" (Washington, DC: Third Way, 2007).

199 Douglas B. Sosnik, Matthew J. Dowd, and Ron Fournier, *Applebee's America: How Successful Political, Business, and Religious Leaders Connect with the New American Community* (New York: Simon & Schuster, 2006).

199 John Kenneth White, *The New Politics of Old Values* (Hanover, NH: University Press of New England, 1990).

200 Frank Capra, *It's a Wonderful Life*, Liberty Films, 1946.

201 Chuck Collins and Mary Wright, *The Moral Measure of the Economy* (Maryknoll, NY: Orbis Books, 2007), 3–4.

202 Stout, "The Spirit of Democracy in Dispiriting Times."

203 Reinhold Niebuhr, *The Nature and Destiny of Man: A Christian Interpretation* (New York: Charles Scribner's Sons, 1964), 43.

Acknowledgments

I'll admit it: I enjoy writing acknowledgments because doing so provides a rare opportunity to say a public thank you to some of the people toward whom I feel genuine gratitude. So much of what I know that's of value is the fruit of conversations and arguments with others, the product of ideas and insights they have passed along to me, and readings they have urged upon me. In the case of this book, the debts are especially intricate to describe since they go back so far and involve so many different parts of my life. Having written acknowledgments for earlier books that friends have rightly mocked for chewing up an excessive amount of paper, I ask all mentioned in those volumes to consider themselves thanked again. Since the text itself—particularly the dedication, the introduction, and part of the conclusion—is reasonably clear about where this book comes from, I will confine myself to the particular debts connected to this book.

By sending me to Rome in 1984, the *New York Times* gave me an exceptional opportunity to cover the Vatican, to travel the world with Pope John Paul II, and to watch at close range as some of the most important issues confronting Catholicism were debated. My thanks in particular to the late Abe Rosenthal, then executive editor of the *Times,* for his enormous enthusiasm for this work; to Warren Hoge, my exceptional foreign editor; and to Annie Zusi, a brilliant editor with whom I worked almost every day. I draw on my Vatican reporting particularly in chapter 5, and I thank Jill Abramson, managing editor of the *Times,* for not only granting permission but also encouraging me to use some of that work here.

In Rome I learned from many colleagues and friends. My deep appreciation to John Tagliabue and Paula Butturini, Victor and Daniella Simpson, Clara Hemphill, Roberto Suro, Philip Pullella, Msgr. Steve Otellini, Cristina Fioravanti, Barbara Roffi, Claire Calcagno, Marco Politi, the late Don Schanche, and the late Luis Inturrisi. Many in the Vatican explained things, large and small, to me. Thanks to Joaquin Navarro-Valls, the Vatican spokesman, Archbishop Diarmuid Martin, the late Rev. Thomas Herron, Bishop William Murphy, and Archbishop John P. Foley—and to countless others who took the time to try to explain the Church's mysteries, both spiritual and temporal, to me. Needless to say, many of my friends and sources inside the Vatican will not agree with all of my conclusions, but I am very grateful for their help in understanding the Catholic Church, and two fascinating popes.

Some of the arguments advanced here were given a first airing in my op-ed column in the *Washington Post*. I am grateful for the opportunity to write the column and offer great thanks to editorial page editor Fred Hiatt for consistently encouraging me to write about topics related to religion, and to Autumn Brewington, the op-ed page editor, for her care, insight, and thoughtfulness. Thanks also to the smart and warmhearted editors who put out the page every day: Vince Rinehart, Michael Larabee, Gilbert Dunkley, Susan Wright, Tom Rowe, and Lauren Taylor. Thanks, as well, to Ken Ikenberry.

Alan Shearer, the talented maestro of the Washington Post Writers Group, offered me the chance in 1996 to syndicate my column and granted permission to use some material from the column here. I owe Alan my gratitude for this, for consistently intelligent advice, and for his loyal friendship. My week is not complete without at least two opportunities to engage with the astute and always perceptive James Hill in Socratic, Jesuitical, and Talmudic dialogues about my column, and so many other things more important. My thanks also to Richard Aldacushion, Karen Greene, Russell James, Kerrisue Wyson, Jennifer Ferrell, Sally Ragsdale, and Ann Himmelberg. And thanks to Anna Karavangelos, another fine editor who shares an interest in these subjects.

The *New Republic* encouraged me to write about Pope John Paul II at the time of his death and then sent me to Rome to cover the Conclave that elected Pope Benedict XVI. I offer deep thanks to Peter Scoblic, Franklin Foer, Peter Beinart, and Marty Peretz both for the assignments and for permission to draw on those two articles here.

Commonweal has been a kind of spiritual and political home for me over most of my life. I could go on, but I won't, except to express my deepest gratitude to Peter and Peggy Steinfels, two of the wisest people I know and two of the finest friends I will ever have, and the gifted Paul

Baumann. Thanks to Paul for permission to use some of the work I have done for *Commonweal* over many years.

Sojourners is another gift to our national dialogue, and Jim Wallis, its founder, is a friend and one of the truly transformative voices in our moral, political, and religious debate. My thanks to Jim for all he does, and to his committed colleagues at *Sojourners*. Thanks to the magazine, particularly Jim Rice, for allowing me to draw on material first published there.

The talented and generous Cullen Murphy at the *Atlantic* asked me to write an article about the culture wars that I draw upon here and was hugely helpful in clarifying my thoughts on some of these subjects. My thanks to Cullen, and also to the estimable John Fox Sullivan for allowing me to use parts of that essay here.

Over the years, I have had the opportunity to deliver lectures at a number of universities in which I could try out some of the themes reflected here. Particular appreciation goes to the American Studies Program at Columbia University, Yale Divinity School, Georgetown University, Harvard Divinity School, the Woodstock Center in Washington, DC, and St. John's University in Collegeville, Minnesota. Thanks also to the American Catholics in the Public Square project.

My debt to Georgetown University, where I teach, would also take many pages to describe. Particular thanks to the members of the committee that invited me to become a professor there, and especially to its chair, Prof. Cynthia Schneider. Preparing my lecture for that committee and writing my inaugural lecture were central to clarifying my thinking on many of the issues raised in this book. I have so many things for which I'd like to thank Jack DiGioia, president of Georgetown and an exceptional advocate of Catholic higher education, social justice, and intellectual freedom. I will confine myself here to thanking him for encouraging me to reengage with the thinking of Pope John XXIII. I thank my colleagues at the Georgetown Public Policy Institute and in the Government Department, and all of my students. I cannot list everyone here, but I must mention my remarkable, wise, warm, and infectiously energetic dean, Judy Feder; Clyde Wilcox, a brilliant scholar who has worked the fields of religion and politics with enormous insight; Father Ray Kemp, a great priest, citizen, and friend; and Sam Potolicchio, an early reader of this book who is insightful beyond his years.

The Brookings Institution, the Pew Forum on Religion & Public Life, and the Pew Charitable Trusts made it possible for me to engage the topic of religion and public life over an extended period and to work closely with many of the finest people in the field.

From the beginning of my time at Brookings, I have been encouraged to pursue this interest. My thanks to our former president, Mike Armacost, and our current president, Strobe Talbott, and to the directors of the Governance Studies Program during my time at Brookings—Tom Mann, Paul Light, Carol Graham, and Pietro Nivola. Strobe has a lively interest in this subject and is a champion of independent, out-of-the-box thinking. Tom has been with this book from before the beginning; his friendship is an enormous blessing. Paul was hugely generous with his time and skill in helping to get the Forum started.

None of my work would have been possible without John DiIulio, whose commitment drew me into an intensive engagement with the question of government's relationship to faith-based social action and charity. The collection of essays we edited together, *What's God Got to Do With the American Experiment?*, was a spark for further adventures in this area. I have written about John before, but I'll repeat one thing: he is a national treasure. As with all books produced by Brookings scholars and associates, the views expressed in this one are my own, not those of the Institution, a place that values free inquiry and a diversity of view.

The Brookings work was, in turn, made possible by the Pew Charitable Trusts and that energetic intellectual entrepreneur, Luis Lugo. As director of the Trusts' religion program, Luis approached Jean Bethke Elshtain and me in the late 1990s to establish what became the Pew Forum. Resolutely nonpartisan, transideological, and open to a broad range of religious (and nonreligious) points of view, the Forum has been exactly what its name implies: a meeting ground for debate, discussion, and research. Luis is now director of the Forum, with which I am still involved, and I cannot thank him enough for the opportunities he has afforded me. Thanks also to Rebecca Rimel, president of the Pew Charitable Trusts, who has cared passionately about the Forum's work and supported it generously. And special thanks to Andy Kohut, who now leads the Pew Research Center and has been a friend and wise counselor on matters related to public opinion (and other things, too) for nearly three decades. It should go without saying, but needs to be said, that this book is an expression of my own views, not those of the Trusts or the Pew Forum. Indeed, neither the Trusts nor the Forum is responsible for supporting this particular volume. I would not be surprised if Luis and other Pew colleagues disagree with some of my conclusions. But we have enjoyed both agreeing and disagreeing over many years now.

None of the Forum's work in its first years would have been possible without Melissa Rogers, who agreed to serve as its first executive director. Melissa is a marvel, a wise lawyer and an engaged intellectual who is capable of holding strong convictions while being utterly fair in considering the views of those with whom she disagrees. Thanks to Jean Elshtain, a brilliant public intellectual and a warm partner in these endeavors; to Sandra Stencel, the Forum's associate director; to Amy Sullivan, who continues to do brilliant work in the areas covered by this book; to Stacy S. Waldvogel, who was present at the Forum's creation; and to Michael Cromartie, with whom I now work on Forum matters and who, nearly two decades ago, introduced me to the work of Christian intellectuals who continue to enrich my understanding, flawed though it might be. (I know for certain that Mike will disagree with some of my conclusions.)

The Brookings Institution Press has published many works on religion and public life in which I've been involved, including the five volumes of the Pew Forum Dialogues on Religion & Public Life. My gratitude goes to all who contributed to those books. Special thanks to the editor of the press, Bob Faherty, who is learned on religious and theological matters and a loyal friend to all who write for him. Bob kindly granted me permission to draw on some of my work for the press, including an essay on religious polarization published in the volume *Red and Blue Nation*. (Thanks to Pietro Nivola for inviting me to contribute to that book.) Thanks as well to Kayla Meltzer Drogosz for her work on the dialogue series, which she coedited; to Ming Hsu Chen for her work on our book on faith-based charity; and to Christina Counselman and Andrea McDaniel for their work on that project and so many others. I owe very special gratitude to my friend and colleague William Galston, who combines an inspiring intellect with a moral compass that is always trustworthy.

Richard Wightman Fox was second only to Fred Appel, my editor, in making this book possible. Richard read an early version of the book and offered not only wise advice on particular points but also essential guidance on how to reorganize it. I joked with Richard that his comments on the book made me seem far more intelligent than I ever thought I was. Both Richard and Robert Wuthnow read a later draft of the book, and both offered so many excellent suggestions that made it much better. My thanks to Kenneth D. Wald, who also offered helpful ideas on the first draft.

Missy Daniel read the manuscript with the sympathy of an invaluable friend and the sharp eye of a gifted and experienced editor. I owe her a great debt. Claudia Deane, formerly of the *Washington Post* and now at the Kaiser Family Foundation, has my gratitude for immense help in analyzing data on religion from the 2004 national exit poll. I am also very grateful to Patricia Nelson, an excellent lawyer, not only for representing me on this book but also for her warm and lively interest in what's at stake in our politics. And there is not adequate space for all the thanks I owe to Korin Davis. She worked through several drafts and brought to them her love for the English language, attention to detail, great political savvy, and devotion to clarity. She organized the exacting task of creating the notes. She made sure that everything kept moving, and that the rest of our work got done. And she did all this with great humor, with her wonderfully ironic and irreverent sense of life, and without ever forgetting her friends or her colleagues. I was blessed with great interns as I was completing this book: Max Nacheman, Emily Goldman, and Dominique Melissinos. Max and Emily were essential not only to the production of the notes but also to the incorporation of many important changes in the closing stages. Dominique was especially generous with her time and skills at a moment when we were on a tight deadline.

Fred Appel of Princeton University Press is irreplaceable. He is like a pitcher with a curve, a changeup, a slider, a fastball, *and* a knuckleball. When I informally broached this idea with Fred, he responded instantly, enthusiastically, and creatively. He can fine-tune language and suggest big ideas. He is stunningly knowledgeable about religion and philosophy. He educated me throughout our time together, offering a steady flow of lectures I might read, scholars I might contact, research I might consult. He made writing this book a hugely enriching experience. Anita O'Brien was not only an excellent copy editor but provided stirring encouragement as she was reading the text. Debbie Tegarden is a production editor who makes things happen with both efficiency and sensitivity.

And how to thank a family that is loving, boisterous, opinionated, loyal, believing, questioning, strong-willed, sensitive, intelligent, and fun to hang out with? Mary Boyle and I have been talking about issues raised in this book for twenty years—from the very first day we met, an Easter Sunday as it happens. She is one of the wisest people I know on matters related to politics, justice, commitment, hope, and love. She understood before I did how this book would come to be. James, Julia, and Margot were not just along for the ride; they provoke discussions about the most important things, instruct me on matters about which I am thoroughly ignorant, and kept me focused by asking me over and over what the book was *really* about.

And speaking of rides, the title of this book is the product of a weekend car trip to Maryland's Eastern Shore. I had asked Mary, who came up with one of the best titles ever for an earlier book, *Why Americans Hate Politics*, to work her magic again. As she was riffing on some excellent titles involving the word "soul," James from the backseat shouted, "Soul*ed*!" In good call-and-response fashion, I yelled, "Out!" At that point, I realized that while I am formally responsible for this book and any of its errors, it really is a family creation.

Index

ABC Television, 99, 121–22

Aberdeen American News, 105–6

abortion, 8, 16–17, 20, 23, 29, 33, 123; Bush and, 64, 96; Catholics and, 102, 106, 151, 163–64, 168–74; criminalization of, 197; culture war and, 46, 48; election of 2004 and, 48; Giuliani and, 195; "God Gap" and, 62; incest and, 105; legal issues and, 104–6; partial-birth, 109–10; party lines and, 102–4; as political litmus test, 102–5; rape and, 105; reducing rate of, 106–11; religious Right and, 56–57; *Roe v. Wade* and, 36, 50, 101–3, 105, 163–64; Romney and, 51; South Dakota and, 104–5; teen pregnancy and, 107–9; values and, 55, 69, 71–72

Abrahamic tradition, 22

absolutism, 95–96

abstinence-only programs, 108

aesthetics, 14

Africa, 202

African Americans, 26, 32–33; American Catholics and, 161–62, 196–97; Bush and, 52–53; church-goers and, 52–53; class and, 160; culture war and, 49; voting gap and, 58; white hegemony and, 34–37

After Heaven: Spirituality in America since the 1950s (Wuthnow), 6

Age of Reason, 9, 43

AIDS, 115, 196–97

Ajami, Fouad, 190, 224n190

Alberigo, Giuseppe, 146

alcohol, 32, 35, 45, 75

Allen, Dan, 120, 217n120

Allen, George, 65–66

Allen, Mike, 217n118

Ambinder, Marc, 215n103

American Bishops, 20, 82–83, 85

American Catholics, 21; abortion and, 151, 163–64, 168–74; African Americans and, 161–62, 196–97; aggressive assertion of, 175–78; birth control and, 155–56; Bush and, 166–75; Carter and, 165; class and, 159–60; Clinton and, 164, 166; cloning and, 168; collegiality and, 155; Communion denial and, 172; communitarians and, 180–81; culture war and, 152–59; democracy and, 154–55; Democrats and, 156; Dionne and, 178–79; Eisenhower and, 160; election of 2004 and, 167–75, 179; ethnicity and, 159–62, 167; euthanasia and, 168; falling attendance of, 152, 156; family life and, 152; FBI and, 159; Ford and, 165; freedom of conscience and, 155; gay marriage and, 163, 168; gender gap and, 160; geographic differences and, 160–61; Giuliani and, 195; Gore and, 166; ideology and, 163–78; Kennedy and, 151–52, 160, 162, 165, 169–70, 173–74, 222n169; Kerry and, 168–72; labor movement and, 157–59; Latin American death squads and, 159; Latinos and, 196–97; leadership changes in, 164–65; liberty and, 155; minority rights and, 154–55; Nixon and, 162, 165; papal encyclicals and, 151, 154; parochial schools and, 153; politics and, 159–78; poor people and, 158–59; progressivism and, 152–59, 163–64, 167, 175–78; Reagan and, 159, 165; Rome and, 151; Rove and, 166; Second Vatican Council and, 151–55, 189; sex scandals and, 136, 152, 179; sexuality and, 152, 155–57; social justice and, 155–57, 167; solidarity and, 181–82; stem-cell research and, 163, 168;

American Catholics *(cont.)*
  subsidiarity and, 166–67, 181–82; Vietnam
  War and, 158–59; voting power of, 162–75;
  women's rights and, 155–57, 160
American Catholics Today (D'Antonio), 152
American Family Association, 124
American Life League, 105
American Mythos (Wuthnow), 5
American Spectator journal, 115
Americans United for Life, 105–6
Amherst, 161
Amos, Bible Book of, 16, 26
anarchists, 13
Anderson, David E., 219n133
angels, 126, 200
animists, 138
Annenberg Public Policy Center, 53, 210n53
anticlericalism, 27
anti-Semitism, 12, 32, 40, 129, 183
Applebee's America (Sosnik, Dowd, and
  Fournier), 199, 224n199
Archbishops Law and Order, 136
Armageddon, 30
Aronson, Ronald, 8, 206n8
Asefi, Hamid Reza, 40, 209n40
Associated Press, 40, 78, 105
atheists, 8, 30, 183; overreaction and, 10–11;
  pluralism and, 192–94; rationality and, 192–
  94; tolerance and, 9–10; white hegemony
  and, 35
Atheists for Niebuhr, 32
Attanasio, Salvator, 219n140
authority, 29, 136–37

Babington, Charles, 217nn118–19
Baha'i, 22, 191
Bane, Mary Jo, 76–77, 89, 213n76
Baptists, 71
Barber, Banjamin R., 69–70, 212n69
Bare Ruined Choirs (Wills), 152
Barnes, Robert, 216n105
Barone, Michael, 49, 210n49
Bartels, Larry, 57, 211n57
Barth, Karl, 4, 194, 224n194
Beats, 46
Belief and Unbelief (Novak), 8
Bell, Jeffrey, 90, 214n90
Bellah, Robert N., 69–70, 212n69

Benedictine monks, 11–13
Benedict XVI, 15, 22, 202; first encyclical of,
  180, 223n180; influence of, 127, 216n127;
  John Paul II and, 139–40, 143; Muslims
  and, 43–44, 210n44; relativism and,
  147–50, Vatican II and, 140. *See also*
  Ratzinger, Joseph
Bennett, William, 68, 79, 116, 163–64,
  212n68, 213n79, 221n164
Berger, Peter, 13, 18, 207n18; conservative/
  liberal issues and, 34, 37, 43, 165–66, 177,
  210n43, 221n165, 223n177; values issues
  and, 74–75, 213n75
Berkeley Divinity School, 188
Bernardin, Joseph, 163, 173
Bernini's altar, 139
Berrigan, Daniel, 14, 159
Berrigan, Philip, 14, 159
Bible: Amos, 16, 26; authority of, 29; Bush
  and, 96; Ephesians, 92; Exodus, 17; First
  Peter, 146; Gospels and, 124; Hebrews, 16,
  206n16; Isaiah and, 16, 26; justice and, 72–
  73; Lincoln on, 186; message of, 194; Micah,
  16, Old Testament prophets and, 27, 73;
  poor people and, 72–73, 76–77; prooftexting
  of, 27; schools and, 39; Social Gospel and,
  30, 74, 185–86; status quo and, 26; Ten
  Commandments, 46–47
Biden, Joe, 163
bigotry, 41, 69–70, 202; anti-Semitism and, 12,
  32, 40, 129, 183
birth control, 46, 124, 132, 154–56
Bishops' Synod, 143, 156
Blackwell, Ken, 64–65
Blackwell, Morton, 90
Blank, Rebecca, 90, 214n90
Bloom, Allan David, 212n68
Blumenthal, Sidney, 164
Boaz, David, 115, 216n115
Bobos in Paradise (Brooks), 5
Boff, Leonardo, 135, 219n135
Bole, William, 177, 223n177
Bologna's Institute for Religious Sciences, 146
Bono, 4
Bork, Robert H., 212n68
Boston College, 152, 161
Boston Review, 157
Branch, Taylor, 207n25

Brandeis, 161

Brazil, 135

Bromiley, Geoffrey W., 207n18

Brooks, David, 5, 113–15, 205n5, 216n113

Brown, David, 217n121

Brown, Judie, 105, 215n105

Brown, Sherrod, 64–65

Brownback, Sam, 163, 195

Bryan, William Jennings, 30, 33, 46, 194–95, 210n46

Buchanan, Pat, 163

Buckley, William F., Jr., 133, 161, 211n56

Buddhists, 11, 14, 22, 191

Burke, Edmund, 2, 179, 205n2

Burke, Raymond, 169, 173, 222n169

Buruma, Ian, 41, 209n41

Bush, George H. W., 75

Bush, George W., 4–5, 15, 20, 90–91, 195; abortion and, 20; African Americans and, 52–53; American Catholics and, 166–75; approval ratings of, 63; church-goers and, 5; compassion agenda of, 98–101, 166; conversion of, 96–97; corporations and, 60; departure of, 51; election of 2004 and, 48–61; end-of-life decisions and, 118–19, 217nn118–19; evangelical support of, 92; faith-based initiative and, 96–101; gay marriage and, 96, 117; as Methodist, 73; past of, 96; poverty and, 73–74, 213n73; religiosity of, 92–101, 214n93, 215n96; religious vote and, 49–52, 62, 64; Schiavo case and, 20, 117–23; school issues and, 40; small government and, 97–98; subsidiarity and, 166–67; terrorism and, 60–61

Bush, Jeb, 120

Buttiglione, Rocco, 155

Cahill, Lisa Sowle, 13, 152

California, 58, 162

Call to Action, 196

"Call to Renewal" conference, 77

Calvinism, 32

Canada, 45, 189

Canarsie: The Jews and Italians of Brooklyn against Liberalism (Rieder), 55, 162

capitalism, 137, 201; economic justice and, 82–88; John Paul II and, 31, 130

capital punishment, 25, 30, 163

Capra, Frank, 199–201, 224n199

Carter, Jimmy, 54, 90, 165

Carter, Stephen, 36, 209n36

Casanova, Jose, 196, 224n196

Casey, Robert, 62–65, 110, 163–64, 170, 172

Catholic Answers, 167–68

Catholic Bishops' 1919 Program of Social Reconstruction, 31

Catholic Campaign for Human Development, 196

Catholic Charities, 107

Catholic Ethic and the Spirit of Capitalism, The (Novak), 84

Catholicism and American Freedom (McGreevy), 39

Catholic Relief Services, 196

Catholics. *See* American Catholics; Roman Catholics

Catholics in Alliance for the Common Good, 173–74, 196

Catholic Theological Society of America, 145

Catholic University, 199

Catholic Worker movement, 14, 159, 221n159

Centesimus annus (John Paul), 81–86, 217n126

Central America, 159

Chain Reaction: The Impact of Race, Rights and Taxes on American Politics (Edsall and Edsall), 55

Changing American Mind, The: How and Why American Public Opinion Changes between 1960 and 1988 (Mayer), 116

Chaput, Charles J., 168–69

charism, 171

children, 69–70, 124; Clinton and, 74; gay marriage and, 115–16; health care and, 99

Chirac, Jacques, 40

Christian Coalition, 91, 94–95, 116

Christian Doctrine prize, 14

Christianity Today journal, 42

Christian Left, 14

Christian Right, 16, 22–23, 195, 197, 202

Christians, 2, 20; character of, 188; doubt and, 184–87; hope and, 16–17; Jewish persecution and, 10; Judaism and, 22; old divisions and, 72–73; poor people and, 4; reform and, 4–5; Religion and Diversity Survey and, 5–6; supply-side, 83–84; values issues and, 71–91; world wars and, 190–91

churches: black, 26; hypocrisy and, 12; megachurches and, 6–7, 199; money interests of,
6–7

church-goers: African Americans and, 52–53;
attendance rates of, 51–52; boring sermons
and, 6; Bush and, 5, 49–52, 62, 64; compromise and, 14–15; as interest group, 7; Latinos and, 52–53

civil rights, 11–12, 103, 165; African Americans and, 16, 35, 46, 52; American Catholics
and, 154–55; beloved community and, 31;
changing liberals and, 202; Clinton and, 39;
Falwell and, 26; King and, 16; Muslims and,
183; Niebuhr and, 33; white hegemony and,
34–37

Civilta Cattolica, La (Jesuit magazine), 144

Cizik, Richard, 4, 20l, 123–24

Clark, Matthew, 132–33

Clinton, Bill, 21, 76, 108; American Catholics
and, 164, 166; civil rights and, 39, 209n39;
culture war and, 47; God and, 92–93,
214n92

Clinton, Hillary, 20, 42, 195; abortion and,
107; capitalism and, 85; family life and, 74–
75; as Methodist, 73; poverty and, 73–75;
values issues and, 73–75, 77, 213nn74–75

cloning, 168

CNN, 195

Cold War, 26, 60

Coles, Robert, 13

College of Cardinals, 146

collegiality, 155

Collins, Chuck, 201, 225n201

Colombia, 134

Colorado, 162

Commentary magazine, 78–79, 144

Commonweal (Catholic magazine), 85, 177,
180–81

communion, 11, 128, 170, 172

communitarians, 180–81

compassion agenda, 98–101, 166

Confucianism, 191

Congregation for the Doctrine of the Faith,
135, 143, 146–47

Congregation of the Roman and Universal
Inquisition, 143

Connolly, Cici, 217n120

conscience, 27, 1155

conservatism, 1; abortion and, 101–11; African
Americans and, 53; American Catholics and,
153, 165–75; authority and, 29; Bush's religiosity and, 92–101; *Centesimus annus* and,
81–82; compassionate, 73–74, 98–101, 166;
culture war and, 45–70; defining, 19; election of 2008 and, 19; evangelicals and, 4–5;
gay marriage and, 111–17 (*see also* gay marriage); ideological, 4–5; Latinos and, 52–53;
prooftexting and, 27; Ratzinger and, 147–50;
religious Right and, 3–5 (*see also* religious
Right); rise of, 16; Schiavo case and, 117–23;
social justice and, 73–89; traditions and, 28–
29 (*see also* traditions); values and, 71–91;
white hegemony and, 34–37; world wars
and, 190–91

Conservative Mind, The (Kirk), 28–29

Consumed (Barber), 69–70

corporations, 55, 60, 86

Corrosion of Character, The (Sennett), 68

Cox, Harvey, 2, 5, 13, 15, 205n2, 205n5

Craig, Larry, 21

creationism, 96

Cromartie, Michael, 94, 211n56

Culture of Disbelief, The (Carter), 36

Culture War? The Myth of a Polarized Society
(Fiorina), 48–49

culture wars, 19, 203; abortion and, 46, 48;
African Americans and, 52–53; American
Catholics and, 152–59; birth control and,
46; civil rights and, 54–55; defeatism
and, 76; defining, 47–48; election of 2004
and, 48–61; election of 2006 and, 61–67;
family life and, 47, 50; gay marriage and, 45,
48; "God Gap" and, 61–62; historical perspective on, 45–47, 55–57; ideological harmony and, 67–70; journalist creation of,
48–49; Latinos and, 52–53, 58–59; lesbians
and, 48; Mexico and, 45–46; middle
America and, 56; Old Religion Gap and, 63–
66; Prohibition and, 45; sexuality and, 50;
Southern states and, 54–58; stereotypes and,
48; terrorism and, 60–61; U.S. Supreme
Court and, 46–47; values and, 71–91; vir-
tue/flaw of, 47–50; voting gap and, 57–58

Cuomo, Mario, 163

Curran, Charles, 132–33, 219n132

Daly, Lew, 157–58, 221n157
D'Antonio, William V., 152–53, 220n152
Darfur, 196
Darwin, Charles, 30
DaSilva, Percival, 179
Davis, Korin, 10–11
Davison, James D., 220n152
Dawkins, Richard, 8, 206n8
Day, Dorothy, 14, 159
death penalty, 25, 30, 163
DeLauro, Rosa, 109–11, 163, 175
DeLay, Tom, 122, 217n122
democracy, 32, 139; American Catholics and, 154–55; economic justice and, 87–88; Muslims and, 189–90; religion's public role and, 183–91; Second Vatican Council and, 189; white hegemony and, 35; world wars and, 190–91
Democratic Leadership Council, 166
Democrats, 1; American Catholics and, 156, 160–62; Andrew Jackson, 66; Book of Amos and, 26; culture war and, 45–70; election of 2004 and, 19, 48–61; election of 2006 and, 61–67; election of 2008 and, 195–96; "God Gap" and, 61–62; prooftexting and, 27; Reagan, 55; Senate control by, 66. See also liberalism
Deus caritas est (God Is Love) (Benedict XVI), 180
Dewey, John, 30
DeWine, Mike, 64
DiIulio, John, 79, 100, 213n79
Dionne, E. J., Jr., 207n26, 214n90; American Catholics and, 178–79; background of, 11–17; Catholicism and, 126–29; civil rights and, 113, 216n113; Kuo and, 100, 215n100; poor people and, 76, 213n76; Ratzinger election and, 149; traditions and, 126, 217n126
Djilas, Milovan, 56
Dobson, James, 4, 28, 124
Doing Well and Doing Good: The Challenge of the Christian Capitalist (Neuhaus), 82
door-to-door activity, 6
doubt, 15, 184–87
Douglass, R. Bruce, 206n9
Dowd, Matthew J., 199, 224n199
draft resisters, 55
Drogosz, Kayla, 207n26, 213n76, 214n90

drugs, 55, 99, 120
Duffy, Eamon, 145, 219n145
Duffy, Michael, 224n196
Duffy, Tom, 179
Duin, Julia, 222n169
Duke Divinity School, 71
Dulles, Avery, 13

Eagleson, John, 219n134
Easter, 14
Eastland, Terry, 36–37
economic issues, 20, 50; American Bishops and, 82–83; capitalism and, 31, 82–85, 130, 137; Catholic Church and, 81–85; class and, 159–60; Clinton and, 166; corporations and, 55, 60; election of 2004 and, 57; estate tax and, 77; GI Bill and, 78; government intervention and, 88; John Paul II and, 134; outsourcing and, 67; poverty and, 79 (see also poverty); sinful structures and, 137–38; trade agreements and, 164
economic justice: Catholic Church and, 81–86; Centesimus annus and, 81–86; defining, 81–82; poverty and, 73–89; Reagan and, 83; values issues and, 81–88
"Economic Justice for All" (American Bishops), 82
Ecuador, 137
Edgar, Bob, 4
Edsall, Mary D., 55, 211n55
Edsall, Thomas B., 55, 90, 211n55, 214n90
education, 20, 55, 195
Edwards, John, 42, 195–96
Eichenbaum, David, 25
Eisenhower, Dwight D., 160
elections: African Americans and, 52–53; American Catholics and, 167–75, 179; bishops' involvement in, 168–73; corporations and, 55; culture war and, 48–67; faith and, 37–38, 42; "God Gap" and, 61–62; Kennedy and, 37–38; Latinos and, 52–53; Lieberman and, 37–38; moral issues and, 63; Moral Majority and, 50, 90–91; Old Religion Gap and, 63–66; religious Right and, 54–57; Southern states and, 54–58; terrorism and, 60–61; 2000, 96; 2004, 19, 48–61, 167–75, 179, 195; 2006, 19, 61–67; 2008, 19–20,

elections *(cont.)*
194–95; values and, 72, 89; voting gap and, 57–58
Ellul, Jacques, 18, 207n18
El Salvador, 159
Elshtain, Jean Bethke, 13, 186, 207n26, 213n76, 214n90, 223n186
End of Faith, The (Harris), 9
end-of-life issues: Bush and, 117–23; euthanasia and, 119–20, 168; Schiavo case and, 20, 50, 117–23
End of Religion, The (Graham), 11
Enlightenment, The, 9, 43
environmental issues, 4, 95, 196
Enzler, John, 179
Ephesians, Bible Book of, 92
Episcopalians, 45
epistemology, 14–15
Espo, David, 213n78
estate tax, 77
ethics, 94, 194
Ethics and Public Policy Center, 94
ethnicity, 159–62, 167, 216n109
Eucharist, 11, 71, 128, 172
euthanasia, 119–20, 168
evangelicals, 5, 16, 21, 33, 42, 195; Bush and, 63, 92–101; election of 2006 and, 61–67; "God Gap" and, 61–62; moderation of, 123–25; Moral Majority and, 50, 90–91; National Association of Evangelicals and, 4, 123–24, 217n124; *Roe v. Wade* and, 36; self-assertion and, 183–84
evolution, 30
Exodus, Bible Book of, 17
Extraordinary Synod of Bishops, 139, 147

faith, 16; alienation from, 2–3; alternative, 41; angels and, 126; Bush's religiosity and, 92–101; Clinton and, 195–96; credulity and, 18; doubt and, 15, 184–87; Edwards and, 195–96; elections and, 37–38, 42; imposition of, 10; individual responsibility and, 7–8; Kennedy and, 37–38; Lieberman and, 37–38; as loyalty, 14; marginalization of, 36; New Deal and, 97; Obama and, 195; partisanship and, 174–75; poor people and, 4; predisposition and, 12–13; present life and, 193; purpose of life and, 194; rationalism and, 27;

self-interrogation and, 8; strain of, 192; tolerance and, 9–10; truth and, 9, 14–15; values and, 89–90
Faith Factor, The: How Religion Influences American Elections (Green), 63–64
Falwell, Jerry, 4, 25–26, 33, 56, 66, 90, 207n25
family life, 50, 95; American Catholics and, 152; Clinton and, 74–75; culture war and, 47; Romney and, 195; values and, 69–70
Family Research Council, 115
fanaticism, 15–18, 43
Far Glory, A (Berger), 18
Fascists, 13, 191
Federal Bureau of Investigation (FBI), 159
feminism, 46
Final Payments (Gordon), 144
Fiorina, Morris, 48–50, 210n48
First Amendment, 39
First Things magazine, 171
Fitzgerald, Thomas, 61–63, 65, 211n61
Fletcher, Michael A., 217n119
flexidoxy, 5–6
Florida, 162
focus groups, 25, 200–201
Focus on the Family, 95, 124
Foley, Mark, 21
Ford, Gerald, 165
foreign policy, 50
Fournier, Ron, 199, 224n199
Fox, Richard Wightman, 42–43, 210n43
Fox News, 97
France, 39–41
Francis, Diane, 93, 214n93
Frank, Barney, 118, 217n118
Frank, Thomas, 55, 211n55
Free Congress Foundation, 29
Freedom's Power (Starr), 187
French Canadians, 45, 159–60
Friedman, Milton, 86, 214n86
Frings, Joseph, 142
Frist, Bill, 121–22, 217n121
Fukuyama, Francis, 68–69, 212n68
Fundamentalism, 42; Bush's religiosity and, 92–101; Catholics and, 136; Nixon and, 54; tolerance and, 136

Galston, William, 49, 185, 210n49, 223nn185–86

Gamm, Gerald H., 162, 221n162
Gandhi, 138
gangs, 77
Ganley, Elaine, 209n40
Garrison, William Lloyd, 26, 207n26
Gautier, Mary L., 220n152
gay marriage, 8, 17, 20, 23, 123, 196; age and, 116; AIDS and, 115; American Catholics and, 163, 168; Brooks and, 113–15; Bush and, 96, 117; children and, 115–16; culture war and, 45; divorce and, 115–16; election of 2004 and, 48, 59; family values and, 95–96; "God Gap" and, 62; Hollywood and, 33; legal issues and, 116–17; Rauch and, 113–16; Romney and, 51; Sullivan and, 111–16; values and, 67, 69, 71–72
Gay Marriage: Why It Is Good for Gays, Good for Straights, and Good for America (Rauch), 113
Genevieve, Sister, 11–13
Genocide, 196
George, Robert, 164
Georgetown University, 144
Georgia, 58
Gephardt, Richard, 103
German Americans, 159–60
Germany, 43–44, 141
Gerson, Michael, 93, 166
Gibbs, Nancy, 224n196
GI Bill, 78
Giuliani, Rudy, 51, 103–4, 111, 195, 215n103, 216n111
Glazer, Nathan, 37, 56–57, 209n37, 211n56
global warming, 4, 124
God, 15, 23; Bush and, 92–93, 97; Declaration of Independence and, 93; discovery of, 7; existence of, 14; Kingdom of, 185, 188; knowing, 17–18; Lieberman campaign and, 38; love and, 14, 180; neo-atheists and, 8; Pledge of Allegiance and, 8; politicizing message of, 25–26; poverty and, 74, 76; Protestant view of, 28; purpose of life and, 194; reason and, 157; religion and, 192; will of, 186
Goldin, Murray, 12
Goldwater, Barry, 12, 54, 165
Good Morning America (TV show), 121–22
Goodnough, Abby, 217n119
Goodstein, Laurie, 168, 222n168
Gordon, Mary, 144, 219n144

Gore, Al, 60, 99, 103, 166
Graham, Aelred, 11, 206n11
Graham, Billy, 4
Great Britain, 189, 193
Great Commoner, 46
Great Disruption, The (Fukuyama), 68
Greater Houston Ministerial Association, 169, 222n169
Greeley, Andrew, 13, 53, 67, 151–52, 156, 210n53, 212n67, 220n152, 220n156
Green, John, 63–64, 71, 212n64
"Group of Bishops Using Influence to Oppose Kerry" (Kirkpatrick and Goodstein), 168
Gutierrez, Gustavo, 133–34, 219n134
Guttmacher Institute, 109, 216n109
Gwirtzman, Milton, 161, 221n161

Habits of the Heart (Bellah), 69
Hadley, Charles D., 56, 211n56
Hanford, John V., III, 40
Hannity & Colmes (TV show), 95
Harris, John F., 209n39
Harris, Sam, 8–10, 28, 206nn8–9
Harrison, Graham, 219n140
Harvard University, 161
Hatch, Nathan, 13
Haval, Vaclav, 75
Hayek, 86
Hayes, Patrick J., 221n157
health care, 20, 50, 195; AIDS and, 115, 196–97; children's, 99; ideology and, 100, 103; liberal Catholicism and, 170, 178; Medicaid, 120; Medicare, 79–80, 100, 170; universal, 89; values issues and, 79–80
Hebrews, Bible Book of, 16, 206n16
Hehir, J. Bryan, 85–86, 94, 179, 214n86
Hellwig, Monika, 13, 145
Helman, Scott, 216n115
Herberg, Will, 191, 224n191
Herron, Thomas, 153–54
Heschel, Abraham Joshua, 13, 24, 32–33, 192, 207n24, 208n32, 224n192
Himmelfarb, Gertrude, 68–69, 212n68
Hindus, 22, 191
hippies, 46
Hitchens, Christopher, 8, 192–93, 206n8, 224n192
Hitler, Adolph, 13

Hoge, Dean R., 220n152

Holden, Tim, 174

Hollenbach, David, 9, 44, 206n9, 210n44

Hollywood, 33–34, 37, 43, 67

Holmes, Stephen, 78–80, 213n78, 213n80

Holt Street Baptist Church, 25–26

Holy Cross, 161

Holy Office, 143

Holy Spirit, 148

homosexuals, 33, 70: election of 2004 and, 48; family values and, 95–96 (*see also* gay marriage); liberalism and, 116–17; Sullivan and, 111–12

hope, 16–17; democracy and, 32; poverty and, 78–79; rationality and, 192–94. *See also* faith

Hout, Michael, 53, 210n53

Huckabee, Mike, 19–20, 51, 110–11, 195

Hudson, Sun, 119

Human Events magazine, 105

Humphrey, Hubert, 28, 165

Hunter, James Davison, 49, 210n49

Hunter, Joel, 94–95, 197, 215n95

hypocrisy, 12, 45

ideology, 21, 67; abortion and, 101–11; absolutism and, 95–96; aggressive assertion of, 175–78; American Catholics and, 163–78; Bennett and, 68; Bush's religiosity and, 92–101; *Centesimus annus* and, 81–82; compassion agenda and, 98–101; conservatism and, 4–5; culture war and, 45–70; gay marriage and, 111–17; Himmelfarb and, 68; liberalism and, 7; overreaction and, 10–11; Schiavo case and, 117–23

immigration, 41

incest, 105

Inda, Caridad, 219n134

"In Defense of Religious America" (Eastland), 36

India, 132, 138

individualism: belief and, 11; Calvinism and, 32; culture war and, 45–70; doubt and, 184–87; freedom of conscience and, 27; Himmelfarb and, 69; liberty and, 155; personal freedom and, 43; segregationism and, 32–33; social responsibility and, 167; virtue and, 68–69

Industrial Revolution, 68

intellectual solidarity, 9, 44

intelligent designers, 46, 50

interest groups, 7

Internet, 67

Iranian Foreign Ministry, 40

Iraq War, 51, 60, 66, 89, 93, 169, 171

Irish Americans, 45, 159–60, 162

Isaiah, Bible Book of, 16, 26

Italian Americans, 45–46, 159–60, 162

Italy, 133

It's a Wonderful Life (film), 126, 199–201, 224n199

It Takes a Village (Clinton), 74

Jainists, 191

Jefferson, Thomas, 16, 93

Jesuits, 9, 144, 155

Jesus (Catholic magazine), 140

Jesus Christ, 1, 14, 22, 25; Bush's religiosity and, 93–95; caring for poor and, 26–27, 73, 197; conservatism and, 131; Eucharist belief and, 11, 71; John Paul II on, 134–35, 137; Sermon on the Mount and, 16

Jesusland, 15, 206n15

Jewish High Holidays, 39

Jews, 2, 22, 179; anti-Semitism and, 12, 32, 40, 129, 183; class and, 160; conservative/liberal issues and, 32–33; culture war and, 49; doubt and, 185; Heschel and, 24; John Paul II and, 129; old divisions and, 71–73; Old Religion Gap and, 63–64; persecution and, 10; religion's true calling and, 187, 190, 197; schools and, 39; social justice and, 158; traditions and, 189; values issues and, 63, 89–90; white hegemony and, 34–37; world wars and, 190–91

John Paul II, 4, 15, 20, 202; angels and, 126, 217n126; anti-Semitism and, 129; authority and, 136–37; Benedict XVI and, 139–40, 143; birth control and, 132; capitalism and, 31, 130, 137; *Centesimus annus* and, 81–86; Curran and, 132–33; economic issues and, 81–83, 134, 213n81; female priests and, 132; imperialistic monopolies and, 129; influence of, 128–40; John XXIII and, 131; liberalism and, 132–33, 136, 159, 164, 166, 169–70, 221n166; liberation theology and, 134–37, 219nn135–36; liberty and, 131–32;

luxurious egoism and, 129; Marxism and, 130, 137; modernity and, 128–32, 218nn130–31, 219n132; nature and, 138; New Age religion and, 138, 219n138; personality of, 139; poor people and, 176, 222n176; Ratzinger and, 146; reform and, 128; Second Vatican Council and, 129–31, 139; sexuality and, 132; sinful structures and, 137–38; technology and, 137; tolerance and, 131–32; values issues and, 81, 88

Johnson, Lyndon B., 165

Johnson, William Stacy, 224n188

John XXIII, 20–21, 31; Catholic future and, 130–31, 133, 135, 145; Kennedy and, 151–52; solidarity and, 189

Jones, Robert P., 199, 224n199

journalists, 48–49

Judis, John B., 211n56

Just Faith, 196

justice, 26, 31, 196–97, 202; Bible and, 72–73; Catholics and, 133, 135–36, 139; defining, 81–82; segregationism and, 32–33; values and, 81–88. *See also* economic justice; social justice

Kaine, Tim, 25, 207n25

Kamarck, Elaine, 49, 210n49

Kant, Immanuel, 194

Kazin, Michael, 27, 30, 207n27, 208n30

Keeter, Scott, 61–63, 212n61

Kelly, Michael, 74, 213n74

Kemp, Ray, 179

Kennedy, Eugene, 13

Kennedy, John F., 26, 34, 207n26; American Catholics and, 151–52, 160, 162, 165, 169–70, 173–74, 222n169; faith and, 37–38; God and, 43, 93, 210n43, 214n93; John XXIII and, 151–52; white hegemony and, 35

Kennedy, Ted, 103, 163

Kennedy Institute of Ethics, 144

Kerouac, Jack, 46, 210n46

Kerry, John, 59–60; abortion and, 151; American Catholics and, 168–72; church-goers and, 49–52; Communion denial and, 170, 172; Latinos and, 58; Old Religion Gap and, 64–66; religious vote and, 62

Kildee, Dale, 174

Kilgore, Jerry, 25

King, Martin Luther, Jr., 4, 11, 16, 25–26, 75, 207nn25–26

King, Peter, 163

Kingdom of God, 185, 188

Kirby, Doug, 108

Kirk, Russell, 28–29, 208n28

Kirkpatrick, David D., 168, 222n168

Kmiec, Douglas W., 122, 217n122

Komonchak, Joseph A., 131, 172, 218n131

Kondracke, Morton M., 215n94

Kristol, Irving, 56

Kung, Hans, 136, 144

Kuo, David, 100, 215nn100–101

labeling, 25

labor, 83, 85, 88, 103, 157–59

Laborem exercens, 85, 132, 217n126

Lacey, Michael, 180–81, 223n180

Ladd, Everett Carl, Jr., 56, 211n56

laïcité, 39–40

Lambert, Bruce, 216n107

Langevin, James, 174

Lasch, Christopher, 42

Laser, Rachel, 109–10, 199, 216n110, 224n199

Lash, Nicholas, 144, 219n144

Latin America, 159; liberation theology and, 129, 133–35; Medellin meeting and, 133–34, 219n133

Latinos, 37; Catholic, 53, 58–59, 161–62, 167, 196–97; conservatism and, 52–53; Kerry and, 58; Old Religion Gap and, 64; religious vote and, 58–59

Law, Bernard F., 136

Leege, David, 160, 163, 221n160, 221n163

Left. *See* liberalism

legal issues, 117–23

Leo, John, 216n116

Leo XIII, 154, 156–57, 220n154, 221n156

lesbians, 33, 70: election of 2004 and, 48; family values and, 95–96 (*see also* gay marriage); liberalism and, 116–17; Sullivan and, 111–12

Let the Oppressed Go Free (Garrison), 26

Letwin, Shirley Robin, 214n86

Lewis, C. S., 23, 207n23

liberalism, 1, 3, 17–18, 21; abortion and, 101–11; accepting change and, 42–44; American, 30–34; American Catholics and, 151–81

liberalism *(cont.)*
  (see also American Catholics); anticlericalism and, 27; change of, 202–3; culture war and, 45–70; election of 2008 and, 19; evangelicals and, 4–5; family and, 15–16; gay marriage and, 111–17 *(see also* gay marriage); intellectual solidarity and, 9; John Paul II and, 130–33, 136 *(see also* John Paul II); Kaine and, 25; Muslim, 190–91; progressivism and, 30–34; prooftexting by, 27; Ratzinger and, 148–50; realism and, 31–32; religious Right and, 4; secularism and, 25–27; as sin, 28, 31; social justice and, 73–89; traditions and, 28–29; values and, 15–16, 71–91; world wars and, 190–91

Liberalismo Es Pecado, El (Liberalism Is Sin) (Sarda y Salvany), 28

liberation theology: John Paul II and, 134–37; Marxism and, 129–30, 133–35; Medellin meeting and, 133–34

liberty, 30, 197; capitalism and, 82–85; Catholics and, 131–32, 140–41, 155; economic justice and, 81–88; First Amendment and, 39; John Paul II and, 131–32; white hegemony and, 34–37

Lieberman, Joseph, 37–38, 99, 209n38, 215n99

Lifting Up the Poor (Bane and Mead), 76

Lilla, Mark, 190–91, 224n190

L'Illusion liberal (Liberal Illusion) (Veuillot), 28

Limbaugh, Rush, 28

Lincoln, Abraham, 35, 157, 186, 223n186

Lindberg, Tod, 27, 188, 208n27

Liptak, Adam, 122, 217n119, 127n22

Living Wage, A (Ryan), 157

Lorschiter, Jose Ivo, 133

Louisiana, 58

love, 11, 14, 180

Lutherans, 45

McCain, John, 51

McCarrick, Theodore, 172

McCarthy, Joe, 13

McClay, Wilfred M., 41, 209n41

McConchie, Daniel, 105–6

McCormick, Richard A., 144, 219n144

McGovern, George, 54–56, 161–62, 211n55

McGreevy, John, 38–39, 209n39

McGurn, William, 214n90

McRoberts, Omra, 215n98

Madsen, Richard, 212n69

Malone, James W., 155

Marquis, Christopher, 209n40

Marsden, George, 13

Marxism, 2, 56, 147; as class struggle, 135; John Paul II and, 137; liberation theology and, 129–30, 133–35; Ratzinger and, 142–43

Massachusetts, 161–62

Massachusetts Institute of Technology (MIT), 161

Mater et magistra (Mother and Teacher) (John XXIII), 133, 217n126

materialists, 126

Maurin, Peter, 159

Mayer, William G., 116, 217n116

Mead, Lawrence M., 76–77, 89, 213n76

Medellin Conference, 133–34, 219n133

Medicaid, 120

Medicare, 79–80, 100, 170

megachurches, 6–7, 199

Menendez, Albert J., 54, 211n54

Merill, Walter M., 207n26

Messori, Vittorio, 140, 219n140

Methodists, 71, 73

Metz, Johannes B., 13, 133, 219n133

Mexican Americans, 58, 162

Mexico, 45–46

Micah, Bible Book of, 16

middle America, 56

Mill, John Stuart, 78

Miller, John, 212n68

Minnesota, 58

minority rights, 19, 154–55. *See also* African Americans; Latinos

Miroff, Bruce, 211n55

missionaries, 25

Missouri, 62

modernity, 128–32

Moltmann, Jurgen, 13, 17, 207n17

monopolies, 82

Moral Freedom (Wolfe), 5

moral issues: abortion, 101–11 *(see also* abortion); American Catholics and, 167; countercultural ideas and, 80; culture war and, 45–70; death penalty, 25, 30, 163; economic justice, 82–88; elections and, 19, 60, 63, 89; end-of-life decisions, 20, 50, 117–23; gay marriage, 111–17 (*see also* gay marriage); genetic manipulation, 198; Hollywood and, 34, 37, 43, 67; permissive ideas and, 80; persecution and, 10; poverty, 79–80 (*see also* poverty); puritanism and, 45; religious activism and, 26; science and, 197–99; secularism and, 29; stem-cell research, 17, 29, 33, 163, 168, 198; teen pregnancy, 20, 76–78, 107–9, 115, 216n109; values and, 71–91; virtue and, 68–69

Moral Majority, 50, 55, 90–91, 95

Moral Measure of the Economy, The (Collins and Wright), 201

Mormonism, 195

Mosaic covenant, 14

Moses, Robert, 75, 213n75

Mother Teresa, 15

Mount Holyoke, 161

Muhammad, 14

Muldoon, Peter J., 221n157

Murder in Amsterdam: The Death of Theo van Gogh and the Limits of Tolerance (Buruma), 41

Murnion, Philip, 80, 179, 213n80

Murphy, William, 107, 216n107

Murray, John Courtney, 4, 31, 155, 190

Murray, Shailagh, 217n121

Muslims, 22, 35, 148, 187, 191; Catholics and, 43–44; France and, 39–42; head scarves in schools and, 39–40; immigration and, 41; Pakistan and, 189–90; pluralism and, 197; traditions and, 189

Myers, John J., 169, 222n169

mystics, 13

NAACP, 12

Naked Public Square, The (Neuhaus), 36–37

Nation, 8

National Annenberg Election Survey, 53, 210n53

National Association of Evangelicals, 4, 123–24, 217n124

National Campaign to Prevent Teen and Unplanned Pregnancy, 107, 109

National Catholic War Council, 208n31

National Conference of Catholic Bishops, 155, 213n82

National Review journal, 56, 86, 115, 133

Navarro-Valls, Joaquin, 136–37, 143, 155

Nazis, 13, 31, 141

"Neither Pope nor King" slogan, 27

neo-atheists, 8, 30; as an overreaction, 10–11; pluralism and, 192–94

neoconservatism, 46, 56

Neuhaus, Richard John, 14, 211n56; conservative/liberal issues and, 36–37, 163–66, 209n37, 221n165; values issues and, 74–75, 82, 84, 213n82

Nevada, 162

New Age spirituality, 16, 138

New Blackfriars magazine, 144–45

New Deal, 31, 102; American Catholics and, 158, 160, 165; Faith-Based, 97; values issues and, 53, 55, 74, 88

New England Congregationalism, 30

New Hampshire, 45

New Reformation, 124

New Religion Gap, 64, 71

New Republic journal, 8, 217n126

New York, 45, 161

New York Times, 15, 40, 74, 113, 122, 126–27, 141–43, 146, 168, 172, 217n126

New York University, 76

Nicaragua, 159

Niebuhr, H. Richard, 13, 18, 28, 190, 207n18, 208n28

Niebuhr, Reinhold, 4, 21, 23, 190, 207n23, conservative/liberal issues and, 33–34, 42, 151, 220n151; pacifism and, 13; progressivism and, 31–32, 208nn31–32; religion's true calling and, 185–90, 203, 223nn185–86, 224n188, 225n203; sin and, 31

Nightline (TV show), 99

Nisbet, Robert A., 179

Nixon, Richard, 54–56, 150, 162, 165

Nolan, Simon, 148–49

Noll, Mark, 13

nonconformism, 145–46

Northland Church, 95

Novak, Michael, 8, 10, 14, 20, 206n10; Catholic future and, 164; values issues and, 82–89, 214n84, 214nn86–87

nuns, 132, 156, 159

Obama, Barack, 20, 42, 77–78, 85, 195, 213n78
O'Beirne, Kate, 115
Oberstar, James, 174
Obey, David R., 169, 173, 222n173
obscuratism, 27
O'Connor, John J., 136
Office of Faith-Based and Community Initiatives, 100
Ohio, 62, 64
Old Christian Right, 32
Old Religion Gap, 63–66, 71
One Nation, After All (Wolfe), 5
On the Road (Kerouac), 46
O'Reilly, Bill, 28
O'Reilly illustration, 1, 160
Orlando Sentinel, 95
outsourcing, 67
Overlooked Schism, 72

Pacem in terris (Peace on Earth) (John XIII), 133, 217n126
pacificism, 13–14, 158–59
Pakistan, 189–90
Pappu, Sridhar, 110, 216n110
parochialism, 38–39, 43, 47
Pasca, T. M., 219n133
paternalism, 76–77
Paul VI, 131, 164, 220n155
Pax Christi, 178, 196, 223n178
PBS news, 53
Pelikan, Jaroslav, 16, 29, 207n16, 208n29
Pennsylvania, 62, 64
Pepperdine University, 122
Peres, Judy, 216n106
persecution, 10
Peter, First Bible Book of, 146
Pew Forum on Religion and Public Life, 6, 54, 163, 211n54, 221n163
Pew Research Center, 61, 163
Philadelphia Inquirer, 61–63
Phillips, Kevin, 55–56, 211n55
Pinsky, Mark, 95, 215n95
Pius XII, 155
Pius XXIII, 170
Planned Parenthood, 107, 216n105
Pledge of Allegiance, 8, 40

pluralism, 18, 30, 173; Europe and, 40–42; Muslims and, 197; neo-atheists and, 192–94; religion's public role and, 183–91
Podhoretz, Norman, 46, 210n46
Poland, 133, 202
Polish Americans, 159–60, 162
Political Teachings of Jesus, The (Lindberg), 188
politics, 1; abortion and, 110–11 (see also abortion); American Catholics and, 151, 159–78; Communion denial and, 170, 172; compassion agenda and, 98–101, 166; consultant strategies and, 25; culture war and, 45–70; democracy, 32, 35, 87–88, 139, 154–55, 183–91; focus groups and, 25, 200–201; gay marriage and, 111–17 (see also gay marriage); interest groups and, 7; liberation theology and, 129, 133–37; Medellin meeting and, 133–34; minority coalitions and, 19; Moral Majority and, 50, 55, 90–91, 95; Muslims and, 22; New Deal and, 31, 53, 55, 74, 88, 97, 102, 158, 160, 165; public engagement and, 3–5; Schiavo case and, 117–23; separation of church and state, 27, 38–39, 169; Southern states and, 26, 54–58, 160; terrorism and, 60–61; turning point in, 196–97; values and, 71–91; Vatican and, 127–28; white hegemony and, 34–37
Politics of Polarization, The (Galston and Kamarck), 49
Popery, 39
Populist movement, 157
pornography, 67
Portsmouth Priory, 11
poverty, 4, 12, 20, 72, 163, 202; American Catholics and, 158–59; Bush and, 73–74; Centesimus annus and, 81–86; Christian Coalition and, 95; Clinton and, 73–75; compassion agenda and, 98–101; God and, 76; Gospel and, 76–77; hope and, 78–79; Jesus and, 26–27, 73, 197; paternalism and, 76–77; progressivism and, 74–75; reform and, 75–81; universal health care and, 89; values issues and, 73–75, 76–81, 89; White House disdain and, 100
"Poverty 101: What Liberals and Conservatives Can Learn From Each Other" (Kuo), 100
pragmatism, 14
prayer, 56–57

prejudices, 183–84

Price, David, 186

Princeton University, 164, 184

Procaccino, Mario, 56

progressivism, 32–34; accepting change and, 42–44; American Catholics and, 152–59, 163–64, 167, 175–78; culture war and, 49; poverty and, 74–75; Protestants and, 31; Ratzinger and, 142–43; Roosevelt and, 30; Social Gospel and, 185–86; social justice and, 80–81; values and, 74–75

Prohibition, 32, 35, 45, 75

prooftexting, 27

protectionism, 164

Protestants, 21, 25, 179, 191; culture war and, 45–70; gay marriage and, 196; "God Gap" and, 61–62; God without wrath and, 28; Latino, 58–59; old divisions and, 71; Old Religion Gap and, 63–64; progressivism and, 31; separation of church and state and, 38; social justice and, 158; white hegemony and, 34–37

puritanism, 45

Putnam, Robert D., 212n68

Quarterly Journal of Political Science, 57

Quinn, John R., 156

Radical Equations: Math Literacy and Civil Rights (Moses), 75

radicals, 14

rape, 105

rationalism, 17, 27, 49, 126

Ratzinger, Joseph, 129, 135, 155, 172, 219n135; background of, 141; as Benedict XVI, 15, 22, 43–44, 127, 139–40, 143, 147–50, 180, 202, 210n44, 216n127, 223n180; bishops' influence and, 141; as cardinal, 140; Congregation for the Doctrine of the Faith and, 143–47, 219n147; Congregation of the Roman and Universal Inquisition and, 143; existentialism and, 141; Herron and, 153; increased influence of, 146–48; John Paul II and, 146; liberalism and, 148–50; Marxism and, 142–43, 147; modernity and, 147; Nazi Germany and, 141; nonconformism and, 145–46; papal infallibility and, 144; progressivism and, 142–

43; relativism and, 147–48; Roman curia and, 140, 219n140; Vatican II and, 141, 143–45, 148; writing and, 142

Rauch, Jonathan, 113–16, 216n114

reactionism, 26

Reagan, Ronald, 83; abortion and, 102; American Catholics and, 159, 165; God and, 93; religious vote and, 54–55; values issues and, 90

realism, 31–32

Red Sox, 161

"Reducing the Need for Abortion and Supporting Parents Act," 109

Reed, Donna, 200

Reed, Ralph, 33, 37, 91, 209n37

reform, 4–5, 26; American Bishops and, 82–83; American Catholics and, 157–58; beloved community and, 31; compassion agenda and, 98–101; economic justice and, 82–88; John Paul II and, 128; labor movement and, 157–58; New Deal and, 31, 53, 55, 74, 88, 97, 102, 158, 160, 165; New Reformation and, 124; poverty and, 75–81; progressivism and, 30–34; social justice and, 73–89; values and, 75–81

Regensburg University, 43

relativism, 147–48

religion, 22; abortion and, 101–11; African Americans and, 52–53; belief choice and, 5–6; Bush and, 49–52, 62, 64, 92–101; corruption and, 23; culture war and, 45–70; doubt and, 184–87; European approach to, 187; God and, 192 (*see also* God); "God Gap" and, 61–62; gullibility and, 2; higher standards of, 2; intellectual structure and, 94; Kennedy campaign and, 37–38; Lieberman campaign and, 37–38; New Age, 16, 138; as opium of the people, 2; prejudices and, 183–84; public life and, 3–5, 183–91, 203; purpose of life and, 194; rationality and, 1–2, 192–94; relevancy and, 3; schools and, 38–40; separation of church and state, 27, 38–39, 169; true calling of, 183–203; U.S. apathy toward, 183; values and, 71–91; war and, 30; white hegemony and, 34–37

Religion and Diversity Survey, 5–6

"Religion and the Democratic Tradition" (Niebuhr), 188

religious Right, 3–5, 13, 197; compassion agenda and, 99; culture war and, 46; election influence and, 19–20, 54–57; Giuliani and, 195; Kerry and, 59; McCain and, 51; Old Christian, 32; progressivism and, 32–34; reactionism and, 10–11, 26; Schiavo case and, 117–23; Vatican and, 21; white hegemony and, 34–37

Religious Roundtable, 90

Republicans, 1, 3, 21; American Catholics and, 160–62; culture war and, 45–70; election of 2004 and, 19, 48–61; election of 2006 and, 61–67; election of 2008 and, 19; "God Gap" and, 61–62; prooftexting and, 27; Reagan, 66; Schiavo case and, 117–23. *See also* conservatism

Rerum novarum (Leo XIII), 156–57

revelation, 14, 43, 126

Ribuffo, Leo P., 32, 208n32

Riccardi, Nicholas, 215n95

Richburg, Keith B., 209n40

Rieder, Jonathan, 55, 162, 211n55

Right. *See* conservatism

Right Wing, Wrong Bird: Why the Tactics of the Religious Right Won't Fly with Most Conservative Christians (Hunter), 95

Robertson, Pat, 4, 21, 28, 56, 66, 91

Rockefeller, Nelson, 102

Roe v. Wade, 36, 50, 101–3, 105, 163–64

Roman Catholics, 8, 15, 17, 20–21, 125; abortion and, 102, 106; American Catholics and, 151 (*see also* American Catholics); authoritarian governments and, 131; authority and, 29, 136–37; Buddhists and, 11; Cajun, 58; capitalism and, 31, 82–85, 130; *Centesimus annus* and, 81–86; Communion and, 128; culture war and, 45–70; Dionne and, 126–29; economic justice and, 81–85; "God Gap" and, 61–62; intellectual elaboration and, 126; Irish, 38–39; John Paul II and, 126 (*see also* John Paul II); Kaine and, 25; Latino, 53, 58–59, 161–62, 167, 196–97; liberal fear of, 27–28; liberation theology and, 129, 133–37; liberty and, 131–32, 140–41; McCarthy and, 13; Marxism and, 133; Medellin meeting and, 133–34; modernity and, 128–32; Muslims and, 43–44; new unity for, 140–41; nonconformism and, 145–46; old divisions and, 71–73; Old Religion Gap and, 63–64;

papal infallibility and, 144; papal masses and, 128; progressivism and, 31–32; rationalism and, 27; Ratzinger and, 127 (*see also* Ratzinger, Joseph); Roman curia and, 140; schools and, 38–40; Second Vatican Council and, 31, 129–31, 139–41, 143, 146, 148; separation of church and state and, 38–39; sex-abuse scandals and, 136, 152, 179; South America and, 128–29; tolerance and, 136; white hegemony and, 34–37

Roman curia, 140

Romney, Mitt, 51, 103, 115, 195, 215n103

Roosevelt, Eleanor, 39

Roosevelt, Franklin, 158

Roosevelt, Theodore, 30, 208n30

"Roosevelt and Repeal" slogan, 75

Rosen, Jeffrey, 102, 215n102

Rossiter, Clinton, 207n19

Rounds, Mike, 105

Rove, Karl, 26, 33, 50, 60, 91, 117–18, 166

Rubenstein, Richard, 13

Russel, William T., 221n157

Russian Orthodox Church, 13

Ryan, John A., 110–11, 157–58, 164, 173, 221n157

Ryan, Tim, 109

Sacks, Jonathan, 13, 193–94, 224n193

Saddleback Valley Community Church, 6

St. Augustine, 185–86

"Saint Hillary" (Kelly), 74

St. Paul, 16, 92

St. Peter, 155, 192

St. Peter's Basilica, 147

Sandel, Michael J., 42–43, 198, 209n42, 224n198

Santorum, Rick, 62–65, 163, 172–73

Sarda y Salvany, Don Felix, 28

Satan, 28

Schiavo, Michael, 121

Schiavo, Terri, 20, 50, 117–23

Schmitt, Bernard W., 169, 222n169

Schoen, Douglas, 161, 221n161

schools, 137; culture war and, 47; intelligent designers and, 46, 50; parochial, 38–40, 153; prayer and, 56–57

Schrembs, Joseph, 221n157

Schultz, Debbie Wasserman, 119

science, 2, 11, 197–99

Scopes trial, 35

Scots-Irish, 45

Second Bill of Rights, 158

Second Vatican Council, 31; American Catholics and, 151–55, 189; democracy and, 189; John Paul II and, 129–31, 139; Ratzinger and, 139–41, 143, 146, 148

Secular City, The (Cox), 5

secularism, 3, 5, 27; culture war and, 46; modernity and, 128–29; moral issues and, 29; pluralism and, 40–42; religion's true calling and, 183–84

Seelye, Katharine Q., 169, 222n170

segregationists, 32–33

self-indulgence, 45

Sennett, Richard, 68–69, 212n68

separation of church and state, 27, 38–39, 169

Serenity of Prayer, The (Sifton), 33

Sermon on the Mount, 16

sexuality, 34; abortion and, 101–11 (see also abortion); abstinence-only programs and, 108; American Catholics and, 152, 155–57; Catholics and, 179; Catholic sex-abuse scandals and, 136, 152, 179; culture war and, 50; John Paul II and, 132; teen pregnancy and, 20, 76–78, 107–9, 115, 216n109; women and, 144

Shea, William, 180–81, 223n180

Shepard, Scott, 215n98

Shields, Mark, 170

Sifton, Elisabeth, 33, 209n33

Sikhs, 22, 35, 191

Simon, William, 83, 214n83

sin, 28, 31, 137–38

Sin, Jaime, 136

Skaggs, Calvin, 214n90

slavery, 26, 46, 104

Smith, Adam, 78

Smith, Al, 151, 162, 220n151

Smith, Chris, 103

Smith College, 161

Social Gospel, 30, 74, 185–86

social issues: abortion, 8, 17, 20 (see also abortion); birth control, 46, 124, 132, 154–56; Centesimus annus and, 81–86; church attendance and, 6–7; culture war and, 45–70; death penalty, 25, 30, 163; economic justice, 81–85; focus group study and, 200–201; gay marriage, 8, 17, 20 (see also gay marriage);

genetic manipulation, 198; Industrial Revolution and, 68; New Deal and, 74, 88; Pledge of Allegiance and, 8; progressivism and, 30–34; Religion and Diversity Survey and, 5–6; schools and, 38–40; segregationism and, 32–33; separation of church and state, 27, 38–39, 169; sinful structures and, 137–38; stem-cell research, 17, 29, 33, 163, 168, 198; teen pregnancy, 20, 76–78, 107–9, 115, 216n109; values issues and, 71–91; white hegemony and, 34–37

social justice, 103; American Catholics and, 155–57, 167; defining, 81–82; Jews and, 158; poverty and, 73–81, 89; progressivism and, 80–81; Protestants and, 158; values issues and, 73–89

Social Security, 169

Sojourners magazine, 195–96

solidarity, 181–82; doubt and, 184–87; religion's true calling and, 184–87, 197–99, 202–3; science and, 197–99

Sosnik, Douglas, 199, 224n199

South Dakota, 104–5

Southern Baptists, 38, 165

Southern states, 26, 54–58, 160

Soviet Union, 26, 60, 202

Spanish Civil War, 13

Specter, Arlen, 172–73

Spellman, Francis Joseph, 39

Spirit of Democratic Capitalism, The (Novak), 87

spiritual suburbanization, 5

Stalinists, 13, 31

Starr, Paul, 187, 223n187

"Statement of Principles by Fifty-Five Catholic Democrats in the U.S. House of Representatives," 174

Steinfels, Peggy, 13, 163, 179

Steinfels, Peter, 13, 163; Bush and, 75, Catholics and liberalism and, 27–32, 208n27, 208n32; Clinton and, 75, Pius IX and, 130, 218n130; political purity and, 172–73, 178–79, 222n172

stem-cell research, 17, 29, 33, 163, 168, 198

Stewart, Jimmy, 200

Stout, Jeffrey, 184, 202, 223n184, 225n202

Strength to Love (King), 11

Strickland, Ted, 64–65

Stuart, Laura, 215n98

Stupak, Bart, 174
subjectivism, 49
subsidiarity, 166–67, 181–82
suicide, 163
Sullivan, Amy, 4
Sullivan, Andrew, 111–12, 216n111
Sullivan, William M., 212n69
Suozzi, Thomas R., 106–7, 110, 216n107
Swidler, Ann, 212n69

talk shows, 46, 122, 163
taxes, 100, 169
Taylor, Frances Grandy, 222n168
teen pregnancy, 20, 115; abortion and, 107–9;
    rates of, 108–9, 216n109; values issues and,
    76–78
television, 34, 69, 122
*Tempting Faith: An Inside Story of Political Seduc-
    tion* (Kuo), 100
Ten Commandments, 46–47
Tennessee, 62
terrorism, 50, 60–61
*Testem benovolentiae nostrae (Witness to Our
    Good Will)* (Leo XIII), 154
Texas, 58, 97, 119, 162
Texas Advance Directives Act, 119
Texas Children's Hospital, 119
theocrats, 5, 92
Theology of Liberation (Gutierrez), 134
Third Way Culture Project, 109, 199
Thompson, Fred, 51
Tillich, Paul, 4
Time magazine, 195–96
Tinder, Glenn, 13, 178
Tipton, Steven M., 212n69
To Empower People (Berger and Neuhaus), 74–
    75, 165
To Heal a Fractured World (Sacks), 193
tolerance, 8, 12, 189; Catholics and, 136;
    Harris on, 9–10; John Paul II and, 131–32;
    schools and, 38–40; traditions and, 189
Toomey, Pat, 172
traditions, 4, 18, 44; abortion and, 8; Abra-
    hamic, 22; American Catholics and, 179–80;
    authority and, 29; Bush and, 20; Clinton
    and, 20, 73–75; common ground of, 28–29;
    doubt and, 184–87; gay marriage and, 8,
    116–17; liberal opposition to, 28–29;

prejudices and, 183–84; progressivism and,
    30–34; religion's public role and, 183–91;
    Romney and, 195; separation of church and
    state and, 27; tolerance and, 189; values and,
    71–91
Transformation of the American Party System
    (Ladd and Hadley), 56
Trenholm, Christopher, 216n108
Trinity, 71
Trujillo, Alfonso Lopez, 134
truth, 9, 14–15, 92, 136–37
Truth about Conservative Christians, The (Greely
    and Hout), 53
Turkey, 190

United Church of Christ, 43
United States: American liberalism and, 30–34;
    Bush's religiosity and, 92–101; capitalism
    and, 82–88; *Centesimus annus* and, 81–86; as
    Christian nation, 37; church attendance and,
    6–7; Cold War and, 26, 60; culture war and,
    45–70; democracy and, 154–55; distinctive
    approach of, 187; economic justice and, 81–
    88; fractious social history of, 45–47; Mexico
    and, 45–46; Muslims and, 22; pluralism and,
    30, 40–42; progressivism and, 30–34; Prohi-
    bition and, 32, 35, 45, 75; as Protestant na-
    tion, 154–55; Religion and Diversity Survey
    and, 5–6; religion's declining role in, 183;
    separation of church and state, 27; spiritual
    suburbanization and, 5; white hegemony
    and, 34–37
universalism, 43
*Urban Exodus: Why the Jews Left Boston and
    Catholics Stayed* (Gamm), 162
U.S. Civil War, 35, 46
U.S. Constitution, 38–39
U.S. Declaration of Independence, 16, 93
U.S. Supreme Court, 35; culture war and, 46–
    47; *Roe v. Wade* and, 36, 50, 101–3, 105,
    163–64; Schiavo case and, 119

Vaghi, Peter, 179
values, 200–201; abortion and, 71–72, 101–11;
    Bush's religiosity and, 92–101; capitalism
    and, 82–88; *Centesimus annus* and, 81–86;
    compassion agenda and, 98–101; corpora-
    tions and, 86; economic justice and, 81–88;

election of 2004 and, 89; end-of-life issues and, 20, 50, 117–23; Eucharist and, 71; gay marriage and, 71–72, 95–96; justice and, 81–88; Methodists and, 73; new division and, 75–81; New Religion Gap and, 64, 71; old divisions and, 71–73; Old Religion Gap and, 63–66, 71; paternalism and, 76–77; poverty and, 72–81, 89; progressivism and, 74–75; reform and, 75–81; Schiavo case and, 117–23; social justice and, 73–89; teen pregnancy and, 76–78; voters and, 89; Wolfe on, 71–72

Van Taylor, David, 214n90

Vatican, 15, 22, 29, 81; American Catholics and, 151–55, 159; capitalism and, 82; Congregation for the Doctrine of the Faith, 21, 135; John Paul II and, 126 (*see also* John Paul II); liberation theology and, 133, 136; as political organization, 127–28; religious Right and, 21; Second Vatican Council and, 31, 129–31, 139–41, 143, 146, 148, 151–55, 189; white hegemony and, 35

Vermont, 45

Veuillot, Louis, 28

video games, 70

Vietnam War, 158–59

Virgin Birth, 71

Virginia, 62–66

Virtually Normal: An Argument about Homosexuality (Sullivan), 111–12

Vitter, David, 21

Von Drehle, David, 90, 214n90

vouchers, 39

Wacker, Grant, 13, 71

Wagner, Steve, 163, 167, 221n163, 221n167

Wallace, George, 54, 165

Wallis, Jim, 4, 72–73, 99–100, 195, 212n72, 217n122, 217n124

Wall Street Journal, 82, 84, 169

Walzer, Michael, 17, 79, 207n17, 213n79

Warren, Earl, 35

Warren, Rick, 4, 6–7, 95, 187, 205n4, 206n7, 215n95

Washington Post, 90, 96, 110, 118, 120–21

Washington State, 58

WASPs (White Anglo-Saxon Protestants), 45

Webb, Jim, 65–66

Weber, Max, 85

Weekly Standard journal, 36, 90

Weigel, George, 82, 164, 169–71, 222n171

Weisman, Jonathan, 217n120

welfare, 55, 79

Wellstone, Paul, 28

Weyrich, Paul, 124

"What Good Is Government?" (Bennett and DiIulio), 79

What's the Matter with Kansas? (Frank), 55

White, John, 199

white hegemony, 34–37

Whitley, Tyler, 207n25

Why Can't They Be Like Us? (Greeley), 67

Wieseltier, Leon, 8–9, 206n9

Wildmon, Don, 124

Will, George F., 19, 207n19

William C. Velasquez Institute, 53, 210n53

Williams College, 161

Williamson, Chilton, Jr., 211n56

Wills, Garry, 13, 30, 152, 208n30

Wilson, James Q., 33

Wojtyla, Karol. *See* John Paul II

Wolfe, Alan, 5, 67, 71–72, 205n5, 212n67, 212n71

Wolpert, Julian, 79

women, 46; abortion and, 101–11 (*see also* abortion); American Catholics and, 155–57, 160; female priests and, 132; John Paul II and, 132; sexuality and, 144

World War I era, 191

World War II era, 13, 78, 191

Wright, Mary, 201

Wuthnow, Robert, 5–6, 206nn5–6

xenophobia, 40

X-rated movies, 67

Yankees, 161

yarmulkes, 39

Zen Catholicism (Graham), 11